REPRESENTING BLACK MEN

REPRESENTING BLACK MEN

EDITED BY

MARCELLUS BLOUNT

AND

GEORGE P. CUNNINGHAM

Routledge • New York and London

Published in 1996 by
Routledge
29 West 35th Street
New York, NY 10001

Published in Great Britain by
Routledge
11 New Fetter Lane
London EC4P 4EE

Printed in the United States of America on acid-free paper.

The editors gratefully acknowledge the permission of Alfred A. Knopf to reprint the following poem for this volume: "Minstrel Man" from the *Dream Keeper*, by Langston Hughes. Copyright © 1932 by Alfred A. Knopf, Inc. The editors also gratefully acknowledge the following journals for permission to reprint for this volume these essays: *Black American Literature Forum* (Summer 1991), for "But Compared to What?" by Wahneema Lubiano; *Wide Angel* (July-October 1991), for "The Absent One" by Manthia Diawara.

Library of Congress Cataloging-in-Publication Data

Representing Black men / Marcellus Blount and George P. Cunningham
p. cm.
Includes bibliographical references and index.
ISBN 0-415-97058-6 (cloth) — 0-415-90759-4 (paper)
1. Afro-American men. I. Blount, Marcellus. II. Cunningham, George Philbert
E185.86.R43 1995
305.31'08996071--dc20
94-31105
CIP

for Melvin and Markus

CONTENTS

INTRODUCTION

The "Real" Black Man?

MARCELLUS BLOUNT AND GEORGE P. CUNNINGHAM

> There are only two kinds of black men—the broken who fall and the true black men who have stumbled in the past but will rise again.
>
> . . .
>
> *Will the real black man please stand up?*
>
> —Nathan Hare[1]

> Behind the electric clippers, a muscular black man is trimming hedges with the intensity of a barber sculpting a fade; nearby, his wife empties groceries from the car. In most quarters, they might elicit barely a nod. But in this largely black, working-class community, the couple is one of the few intact families on the block. All too common are the five young women who suddenly turn into view, every one of them pushing a baby stroller, not one of them married. Resigned, Caballero says with a sigh, "Where are the men?"
>
> *Newsweek*, (August 30, 1993)[2]

As a site for exploring the intersections of race, gender, and sexualities, *Representing Black Men* is of necessity composed of a series of border crossings and engagements with the "multiple references that constitute different cultural codes, experiences, and languages" defining black men as discursive subjects or objects.[3] The irony, as well as the danger, in contemporary discussions of African American masculinities lies in the borders separating the critical discourses of race, gender, and sexuality from one another and often from black males as subjects. African American men as gendered, rather than racial, subject, rarely if ever provide a strategic site for interrogating constructions of gender and sexuality within contemporary theory. Conversely, the discursive domains that construct the most sustaining and cohesive vision of African American manhood—the social sciences, public policy debates, and racial(ist) discourses—are rarely informed by critical theory. In the absence of any true partnership between critical theory and the discourse of black manhood, representations of "the black man"—his sexuality, his relationships to black and white women, and his relationships to the abstract and ideological notion of manhood and family—have become an essential part of the elaboration of sometimes progressive, but more often conservative, public policy and cultural agendas.

A recent cover story in *Newsweek* illustrates the growing rapprochement between a conservative cultural agenda and representations of African American males. The cover features a photograph of a seven-year old black boy who is facing slightly away from us but who gazes (in)directly from the corners of his eyes. His portrait partially reinscribes the relationship between the reader as subject and Third World child as object in the mythos of advertisement for third world children dying of hunger, but this African American child speaks of an American cultural hunger that is embodied in the picture's bold white print logo: "A World Without Fathers: The Struggle to Save the Black Family." The eyes of the young black boy ask black and white readers to care rather than turn the page. But to care about what?

Where are the black men in the cultural work of this "cover story"?[4] The article's racial specificity veils another cultural drama—the nightmare of the collapse of patriarchy—in black face. Midway in the article, an African American minister puts the matter simply: "Dan Quayle was right," presumably referring to Quayle's criticism of the portrayal of single mothers on television.[5] More to the point, Daniel Patrick Moynihan was right. Indeed the world that shapes the *Newsweek* essay is the world of the social science consensus of the 1950s and early 1960s, the world of Moynihan's 1965 *The Negro Family: A Case Study for National Action* (the "Moynihan Report"). Moynihan's language of "family pathology—divorce, separation, desertion, female family head[s], children in broken homes, and illegitimacy" returns in this article with a normative vengeance.[6] The "World Without Fathers" is a world in which "fathers do things for the children that mothers often don't." It is a world where "it takes a man to raise a boy into a man. I mean a real man." Behind the racial veil, conventional gender and sexual norms are the saviors from the chaos of the "world without fathers." The collapsing of the time that separates the "Moynihan Report" and the *Newsweek* essay neatly elides, or rather squeezes out, all of the discussion of gender that has taken place in the last three decades. A world without fathers projects as its salvation for blacks (and, by implication, for all of American society) a world without feminism, without gays and lesbians. Most importantly, while the "Moynihan Report" was soundly condemned by African Americans in the 1960s, its normative premises and prescriptions have insinuated themselves in contemporary racial discourse, returning to us in the *Newsweek* article in a black voice.[7]

Representing Black Men is offered as an intervention and a call for sustained discussion of the complexity and diversity of African American men's agency in the production of ideology and culture. The essayists included in this anthology address in a variety of ways the breach between contemporary critical theory and the discourse of black manhood by examining and questioning the construction of the black male subject in American and African American literature, culture, and society. However different they may be, their analyses and enactments of the project of representing black men are held together by several common concerns. The essayists in this volume are committed to various modes of analyzing representation that originate in literary and cultural studies, and that foreground the agency of the subject. Their essays are shaped by, and at the same time in, dialogue with feminism(s), the discussion of men's relationship to feminism, the emergence of queer theory, and various discourses of race. The heterogeneity of their discourses, each with its own history, privileged subjects, and social agendas, forms the backdrop of this collection. As a result, the rhetoric of "antagonistic cooperation," not only *among* their essays but also *within* them, characterizes the tone of this volume as a whole. Steeped in dialogic relations with one or more of these modes of inquiry, these essayists begin the process of exploring the multiplicity of black male subjects that often alludes to the constructions of African American manhood in the social sciences, and they recontextualize the politics of black manhood as it is often constructed in racial discourses.

Yet no matter where feminism, gender studies, "male feminism," and queer theory have led us in the academy, any inquiry into the African American male must also take into account the strongly "engendered" contemporary racial discourse that is in dialogue with the increasingly bleak statistics on the black family and the status of African American men. Beginning in the 1960s, and certainly codified by the mid-1970s, gender became a specific and explicit site for discussions of the "state of the race." Under various generic topics—"black male-female relations," the "crisis of the black family," and the "conspiracy to destroy black men"—the stabilizing of the gendered male self and the reconstruction of the true black man are among the defining obsessions of contemporary racial discourse. Most often labeled as nationalist and recuperations of patriarchy, these racial discourses join, as in "The World Without Fathers," with a conservative cultural agenda to redefine the problem of race as a problem of skewed family structures and gender roles.

By eschewing the discourse of "the *real* black man," *Representing Black Men* attempts to explore from various vantage points the politics and ideologies at play in representing race and gender. Our contributors, all of whom are African Americanists, and some of whom are feminists or committed to gay and lesbian studies, bring their own stakes and sets of interests to the politics of African American masculinities. Cora Kaplan has the distinction of being the only contributor who is not African American, yet her essay on the sexual poetics of James Baldwin's early fiction is central to this larger theoretical project. Equally important to this anthology are the essays by black women and feminist perspectives. *Representing Black Men* also seeks to establish the place of black gay men as critics, artists, and agents of African American culture as central to understanding the complexities of the range of black male subjectivities. As these critics *construct* their identities as scholars and activists, it becomes difficult to know just who we are and impossible not to know why the complexity and diversity of African American men necessitates careful theoretical and political scrutiny.

Representing Black Men is divided into three parts. The authors in the first section write "Against Patriarchy" with vigor and nuance. In "A Black Man's Place(s) in Black Feminist Criticism," Michael Awkward re-envisions his individuality as a participant in the politics of the crucial project of engendering African American literary criticism. His essay issues a passionate call to community, as he seeks to elide the breach between black men and women who must somehow learn to continue to work together (and live together) in ways that are mutually sustaining and honest. Cora Kaplan offers "'A Cavern Opened in My Mind': The Poetics of Homosexuality and the Politics of Masculinity in James Baldwin" as a theoretical and textual analysis of the ways in which Baldwin's early work intersected with and contributed to a broader reworking of sexual and cultural politics in the early sixties. By demonstrating that Baldwin's attempts to clear a political space for himself as a black gay writer helped to de-territorialize the spaces available to white women as readers and activists, Kaplan enables us to reimagine the possibilities and pleasures of diverse "identifications" as we move from margin to center—however we would characterize our beginnings. In "'Ain't Nothin' Like the Real Thing': Black Masculinity, Gay Sexuality, and the Jargon of Authenticity," Kendall Thomas reminds us of the necessary connections between mourning and militancy as he compels us to theorize about the ritual silencing of black gay men in the African American community. Moving from Baldwin's funeral in the "cold, cavernous cathedral" of St. John the Divine to the bodies in danger rendered articulate in Marlon Riggs's video *Tongues Untied* (1989), Thomas does battle with heteronormative representations of racial identity.

The essayists presented in the second section of this volume are all acutely aware of the difficulties involved in "Negotiating 'Masculinity.'" In different ways, this section explores the complex relations between violence and violation. In "Violent Ambiguity: Martin Delany, Bourgeois Sadomasochism, and the Production of a Black National Masculinity," Robert Reid-Pharr rescues Martin Delany's *Blake* (1862) from critical obscurity and "tells it like it was," by providing an historical and theoretical basis for understanding the gender/sexual economies of racism. Donald Gibson's "Chapter One of Booker T. Washington's *Up from Slavery* and the Feminization of the African American Male" offers a revisionary reading of another important early black leader's writings about slavery and the political uses of the dominant culture's discourses about masculinity. In "'Stand By Your Man': Richard Wright, Lynch Pedagogy, and Rethinking Black Male Agency," Stephen Michael Best argues that the American historical practice of lynching black men betrays complex anxieties about black male sexuality and homoerotic desire, and Wright's literary treatment of lynching reveals the competing (and often contradictory) notions of black manhood that shaped his relations to the South and his image of himself as a writer. George Cunningham invites us to reconsider contemporary practices of violating black bodies, as his essay, "Body Politics: Race, Gender, and the Captive Body," connects the death of Emmett Till to the complex fates of Tawana Brawley, Yusef Hawkins, "Willie" Horton, and Charles Stuart.

In the final section of the volume, "Screening Men," we acknowledge the importance of mainstream and independent film and video to our larger cultural project of redefining black masculinities. Keenly sensitive to the ways in which representations of black men in mainstream film often betray a subtext of hostility and misappropriation, Elizabeth Alexander, in "'We're Gonna Deconstruct Your Life!': The Making and Un-Making of the Black Bourgeois Patriarch in *Ricochet*," shrewdly argues that Russell Malcahy's *Ricochet* (1991) is propelled by unacknowledged (and, therefore, potentially destructive) white male homoerotic desire, not to mention the anxieties of white male economic competition. In "'But Compared to What?': Reading Realism, Representation, and Essentialism in *School Daze*, *Do the Right Thing*, and the Spike Lee Discourse," Wahneema Lubiano focuses on Spike Lee's films as paradigms of African American cultural production and, as such, uses his work to discuss the problematics of speaking for the "community," representing the "community" to mainstream audiences, and remaining fully aware of the potentially conservative cultural project of media deification. "Screening Men" ends with Manthia Diawara's essay, "The Absent One: The Avant-Garde and the Black Imaginary in *Looking for Langston*," in which he places Issac Julien's controversial film *Looking for Langston* (1989) within the contexts of African American literary and cultural tradition, black gay aesthetics, and twentieth-century experimental cinema, thereby enabling us to understanding the film as a project of multiple recuperations. Like all of the scholars who contributed to this volume, Diawara resists easy interpretations and solutions to the problem of representing issues of race, gender, and sexualities as interdependent categories of analysis and identity.

In 1971 Nathan Hare called for "the real black man" to "stand up." Collectively, the essays in *Representing Black Men* issue a variation of that call by exploring the ways that feminism, critical theory, and gay and lesbian studies can impact on the politics and poetics of black manhood.

While fully cognizant of the urgency implied by the declining status of black men as it is measured in the social sciences and much of contemporary racial discourse, this volume looks to define the diverse postures that black men can take in "standing up" in all their "realness" within the humanities and critical theory.

Notes

1. Nathan Hare, "'Will the Real Black Man Please Stand Up?'" *Black Scholar* 2.10 (June, 1971), 35.
2. Farai Chideya, *et al.* "Endangered Family." *Newsweek* (August 30, 1993), 17.
3. Henry Giroux, *Border Crossings: Cultural Workers and the Politics of Education*, (New York: Routledge, 1992), 135.
4. We use the term "cover story" in the sense that Wahneema Lubiano gives it. "There are pictures that function as *cover stories* in and of themselves; they (both the pictures and the cover stories) simultaneously mask and reveal political power and its manipulations. Cover stories cover or mask what they make invisible with an alternative presence; a presence that redirects our attention, that covers or makes absent what has to remain unseen if the *seen* is to function as the *scene* for a different drama." ("Black Ladies, Welfare Queens, and State Minstrels: Ideological War by Narrative." *Race-ng Justice, En-gendering Power: Essays on Anita Hill, Clarence Thomas, and the Construction of Social Reality*. Ed. Toni Morrison [New York: Pantheon Books, 1992], 324.)
5. In that same issue of *Newsweek* the review of the new television season was called "Fractured Family Ties." The article reminded us that "nationwide, one in four families is headed by a single parent. But among television's new clans, nearly two thirds will be run by a single mom or dad" (50).
6. Daniel P. Moynihan, *The Negro Family: A Case for National Action* (Washington, D.C.: Office of Policy Planning and Research, United States Department of Labor, March, 1965), 19.
7. For insight in the controversy generated by the "Moynihan Report," see Lee Rainewater and William Yancy, eds. *The Moynihan Report and the Politics of Controversy*. (Cambridge: M.I.T. Press, 1967). For a contemporary African American feminist reading of the "*Moynihan Report*," see Hortense J. Spillers, "Mama's Baby, Papa's Maybe: An American Grammar Book," *Diacritics* 17.2 (1987), 65–81.

AGAINST PATRIARCHY

1

A BLACK MAN'S PLACE(S) IN BLACK FEMINIST CRITICISM

MICHAEL AWKWARD

> The main theoretical task for male feminists, then, is to develop an analysis of their own position, and a strategy for how their awareness of their difficult and contradictory position in relation to feminism can be made explicit in discourse and practice.[1]
> —Toril Moi

> She had been looking all along for a friend, and it took her a while to discover that a [male] lover was not a comrade and could never be—for a woman.[2]
> —Toni Morrison

> Critics eternally become and embody the generative myths of their culture by half-perceiving and half-inventing their culture, their myths, and themselves.[3]
> —Houston A. Baker, Jr.

> Nor is any theorizing of feminism adequate without some positioning of the person who is doing the theorizing.[4]
> —Cary Nelson

I

Many essays by male and female scholars devoted to exploring the subject of male critics' place(s) in feminism generally agree on the uses and usefulness of the autobiographical male "I." Such essays suggest that citing the male critical self reflects a response to (apparent) self-difference, an exploration of the disparities between the masculine's antagonistic position in feminist discourse, on the one hand, and, on the other, the desire of the individual male critic to represent his difference with and from the traditional androcentric perspectives of his gender and culture. Put another way, in male feminist acts, to identify the writing self as biologically male is to emphasize the desire not to be ideologically male, and to explore the process of rejecting the phallocentric perspectives by which men traditionally have justified the subjugation of women.[5]

In what strikes me as a particularly suggestive theoretical formulation, Joseph Boone articulates his sense of the goals of such male feminist autobiographical acts:

> In exposing the latent multiplicity and difference in the word "me(n)," we can perhaps open up a space within the discourse of feminism where a male feminist voice *can* have something to say beyond impossibilities and apologies and unresolved ire. Indeed, if the male feminist can discover a position *from which* to speak that neither elides the importance of feminism to his work nor ignores the specificity of his gender, his voice may also find that it no longer exists as an abstraction . . . but that it in fact inhabits a body: its own sexual/textual body.[6]

Because of an awareness that androcentric perspectives are learned, are transmitted by means of specific (and, at this point, well-identified) sociocultural practices in such effective ways that they come to appear natural, male feminists such as Boone believe that, through an informed investigation of androcentric and feminist ideologies, individual men can work to resist the lure of the normatively masculine. That resistance for the aspiring male feminist requires, in Boone's phrase, the exposure of "the latent multiplicity and difference in the word 'me(n),'" in other words, the (dis)rupturing of both ideologies' unproblematized perceptions of monolithic and/or normative maleness (as villainous, antagonistic "other" for feminism, and, for androcentricism, as powerful, domineering patriarch). At this early stage of male feminism's development, to speak self-consciously—autobiographically—is necessarily to explore, implicitly and/or explicitly, why and how the individual male experience (the "me" in men) has diverged from, has created possibilities for a rejection of, the androcentric norm.

While there is not yet agreement as to what constitutes an identifiably male feminist act of criticism or about the usefulness of such acts for the general advancement of the feminist project, at least one possible explanation for a male critic's self-referential discourse is that it is a response to palpable mistrust—emanating from some female participants in feminism, and perhaps from the writing male subject himself—about his motives. A skeptical strand of opinion with regard to male feminism is represented by Alice Jardine's "Men in Feminism: Odor di Uomo Or Campagnons de Route?"[7] Having determined that the most useful measure of an adequately feminist text is its "*inscription of struggle,* even of *pain*" (58)—an inscription of a struggle against patriarchy that Jardine finds absent from most male feminist acts, perhaps because "the historical fact that is the oppression of women [is] . . . one of their favorite blind spots" (58)—she admits to some confusion as to the motivations for males' willing participation: "Why . . . would men want to be in feminism if it's about struggle? What do men want to be in—in pain?"

In addition to seeking to cure its blindness (if such blindness still generally exists) where the history of female oppression is concerned, a male feminism must explore the motivations for its participation in what we might call, in keeping with Jardine's formulations, a discourse of (en)gendered pain. If one of the goals of male feminist self-referentiality is to demonstrate to females that individual males can indeed serve as allies in efforts to undermine androcentric power—and it seems invariably that this is the case—the necessary trust cannot be gained (if this type of trust is at all possible) by insisting that motivation as such does not represent a crucial area that must be carefully negotiated. For example, I accept as generally accurate and, indeed, reflective of my own situation Andrew Ross's assertion that "there are those [men] for whom the facticity of feminism, for the most part, goes without saying . . ., who are young enough for feminism to have been a primary component of their intellectual formation."[8] However, in discussions whose apparent function is a foregrounding of both obstacles to and possibilities of a male feminism, men's relation(s) to the discourse can never go "without saying"; for the foreseeable future at least, this relation needs necessarily to be rigorously and judiciously theorized, and grounded explicitly in, among other places, the experiential realm of the writing male subject.

Yet no matter how illuminating and exemplary one finds self-referential inscriptions of a male feminist critical self, if current views of the impossibility of a consistently truthful autobiographical act are correct, there are difficulties implicit in any such attempt to situate or inscribe that male self. Because, as recent theorizing of the subject of autobiography has demonstrated, acts of discursive self-rendering unavoidably involve the creation, for the duration of the writing process at least, of what is in some ways an idealized version of a unified or unifiable self. We can be certain only of the fact that the autobiographical impulse yields but part of the truth(s) of the male feminist critic's experiences. As is also the case for female participants, a male cannot—can never—always tell the whole truth and nothing but the truth about his relationship to feminist discourse and praxis.

But while autobiographical criticism, like the genre of autobiography itself, is poised tenuously between the poles of closure and disclosure, between one representation and another, between a lived life and an invented one, I believe that even in the recoverable half-truths of my life are some of the materials that have shaped my perceptions, my beliefs, the self and/or selves that I bring to the interpretive act. By examining discussions of the phenomenon of the male feminist—that is to say, by reading male and female explorations of men's place(s) in feminist criticism—and exploring responses of others to my own professional and personal relationships to feminism, I will identify autobiographically and textually grounded sources for my belief that while gendered difference might be said to complicate the prospect of a non-phallocentric black male feminism, it does not render such a project impossible.

At the outset, I acknowledge my own full awareness of the fact that, in this elaboration, mine is a necessary participation with regard to black feminist criticism in the half-invention, half-perception which, in Houston Baker's compelling formulation, represents every scholar's relationship to cultural criticism.[9] Such an acknowledgment is not intended to indicate that my (male) relationship to feminism is naturally that of an illegitimate child, as it were. Rather, it is meant to suggest, like Elizabeth Weed's insistence on "the impossibility" of both men's and women's "relationship to feminism," my belief that while feminism represents a complex, sometimes self-contradictory, "utopian vision" which no one can fully possess, a biological male can "develop political, theoretical [and, more generally, interpretive] strategies"[10] which, though at most perhaps half-true to all that feminist ideologies are, nevertheless can assist—in unison both with more voluminous and productive female myths and with other emerging antipatriarchal male acts—in a movement toward the actualization of the goals of feminism.

II

I have been forced to think in especially serious ways about my own relationship to feminist criticism since I completed the first drafts of *Inspiriting Influences,* my study of Afro-American women novelists.[11] I have questioned neither the explanatory power of feminism nor the essential importance of developing models adequate to the analysis of black female-authored texts, as my book attempts to provide on a limited scale—in harmony, I believe, with the black feminist project concerned with recovering and uncovering an Afro-American female literary tradition. Yet, I have been confronted with suspicion about my gendered suitability for the task of explicating AfroAmerican women's texts, suspicion which has been manifested in the forms of both specific responses to my project and general inquiries within literary studies into the phenomenon of the male feminist.

For example, a white female reader of the manuscript's first drafts asserted—with undisguised surpise—that my work was "so feminist," and asked how I'd managed to offer such ideologically informed readings. Another scholar, a black feminist literary critic, recorded with no discernible hesitation her unease with my "male readings" of the texts of Zora Neale Hurston, Toni Morrison, Gloria Naylor, and Alice Walker. I wondered about the possibility of my being simultaneously "so feminist" and not-so-feminist (i.e., so "male"), about the meanings of these terms both for these scholars and for the larger interpretive communities in which they participate. Consequently, in what was perhaps initially an act of psychic self-protection, I began to formulate questions for which I still have found no consistently satisfactory answers: Were the differences in the readers' perceptions of the ideological adequacy of my study a function of their own racially influenced views of feminist criticism, a product, in other words, of the differences not simply *within me* which could lead to the production of a discourse characterizable as both feminist and androcentric, but *within feminism itself*? And if the differences within feminism are so significant, could I possibly satisfy everybody with "legitimate" interests in the texts of Hurston, *et al.* by means of my own appropriated version(s) of black feminist discourse, my unavoidably half-true myth of what that discourse is, means, and does? Should my myth of feminism and its mobilization in critical texts be considered naturally less analytically compelling than that of a female scholar simply as a function of my biological maleness? And how could what I took to be a useful selfreflexivity avoid becoming a debilitating inquiry into a process which has come to seem for me, if not "natural," as Cary Nelson views his relationship to feminism,[12] then at least *necessary*?

Compelled and, to be frank, disturbed by such questions, I searched for answers in others' words, others' work. I purchased a copy of the then just-published *Men in Feminism,* a collection which examines the possibility of men's participation as "comrades" (to use Toni Morrison's term, which I will return to below) in feminist criticism and theory. Gratified by the appearance of such a volume, I became dismayed immediately upon reading the editors' introductory remarks which noted their difficulty in "locating intellectuals, who, having shown interest in the question, would offer, for instance, a gay or a black perspective on the problem."[13] While a self-consciously "gay . . . perspective" does find its way into the collection, the insights of nonwhite males and females are conspicuously absent.[14]

Even more troubling for me than the absence of black voices or, for that matter, general inquiries into the effects of racial, cultural, and class differences on males' relationships to feminism, is the sense shared by many contributors to *Men in Feminism* of male feminism's insurmountable obstacles. In fact, the collection's initiatory essay, Stephen Heath's "Male Feminism," begins by insisting that "[m]en's relation to feminism is an impossible one."[15] Heath's formulations are insightful and provocative, if not always, for me, persuasive, such as when he claims:

> This is, I believe, the most any man can do today: to learn and so to try to write or talk or act in response to feminism, and so to try not in any way to be anti-feminist, supportive of the old oppressive structures. Any more, any notion of writing a feminist book or being a feminist, is a myth, a male imaginary with the reality of appropriation and domination right behind.[16]

Is male participation in feminism restricted to being either appropriative and domineering or not "anti-feminist"? Must we necessarily agree with Heath and Robert Scholes, another contributor to *Men in Feminism*, that "a male critic . . . may work within the feminist paradigm but never be a full-fledged member of the class of feminists"?[17] To put the matter differently, is gender really an adequate determinant of "class" position?

Despite the poststructuralist tenor of Heath's work generally and of many of his perspectives here, his is an easily problematized essentialist claim—that, in effect, biology determines destiny and, therefore, one's relationship to feminist ideology; that womanhood allows one to become feminist at the same time that manhood necessarily denies that status to men. And while Heath embraces feminist notions of history as a narrative of male "appropriation and domination" of gendered Others, he appears resistant at this point in his discourse to evidence of a powerful feminist institutional *present* and *presence*. I believe that we must acknowledge that feminism represents, at least in areas of the American academy, an incomparably productive, influential, and resilient ideology and institution that men, no matter how cunning, duplicitous, or culturally powerful, will neither control nor overthrow in the foreseeable future; one whose perspectives have proven and might continue to prove convincing even to biological males. In other words, in surveying the potential implications of the participation of biological men in feminism, we must be honest about feminism's current persuasiveness and indominability, about its clarifying, transformative potential, and about the fact that the corruptive possibility of both the purposefully treacherous and the only half-convinced male is, for today at least, slight indeed. Surely it is neither naive, presumptuous, nor premature to suggest that feminism as ideology and reading strategy has assumed a position of exegetical and institutional strength capable of withstanding even the most energetically masculinistic acts of subversion.

Below, I want to focus specifically on the question—on the "problem," as the editors of *Men in Feminism*, among others, might put it—of a black male feminism. Rather than seeing black male feminism necessarily as an impossibility or as a subtle new manifestation of and attempt at androcentric domination, I want to show that certain instances of afrocentric feminism provide Afro-American men with an invaluable means of re-writing—of *re-vis(ion)ing*—our selves, our historical and literary traditions, and our future.

III

Few would deny that black feminist literary criticism is an oppositional discourse constituted in large part as a response against black male participation in the subjugation of Afro-American women. Treatments range from Barbara Smith's castigation of black male critics for their "virulently sexist . . . treatment"[18] of black women writers, and her insistence that they "are, of course, hampered by an inability to comprehend Black women's experience in sexual as well as racial terms"[19]; to, more recently, Michele Wallace's characterization of the "black male Afro-Americanists who make pivotal use of Hurston's work in their most recent critical speculations" as "a gang"—in such texts Afro-American men are generally perceived as nonallied Others of black feminist discourse.[20] Not only are Afro-American males often so regarded, but, as is evident in Wallace's figuration of male Hurston scholars as intraracial street warriors, they are also viewed at times as always already damned and unredeemable, even when they appear to take black women's writing seriously. We—I—must accept the fact that black male investigations informed by feminist principles—including this one—may never be good enough or ideologically correct enough for some black women who are feminists.

This sense of an unredeemable black male critic/reader is in stark contrast to perspectives offered in such texts as Sherley Anne Williams's "Some Implications of Womanist Theory." In her essay, she embraces Alice Walker's term "womanist"—which, according to Williams, connotes a "commit[ment] to the survival and wholeness of an entire people, female and male, as well as a valorization of women's works in all their varieties and multitudes"—because she considers the black feminist project to be separatist in "its tendency to see not only a distinct black female culture but to see that culture as a separate cultural form" from "the facticity of Afro-American life."[21]

I believe that a black male feminism, whatever its connections to critical theory or its specific areas of concern, can profit immensely from what female feminists have to say about male participation. For example, Valerie Smith's suggestion in "Gender and Afro-Americanist Literary Theory and Criticism" that "Black male critics and theorists might explore the nature of the contradictions that arise when they undertake black feminist projects"[22] seems to me quite useful, as does Alice Jardine's advice to male feminists. Speaking for white female feminists and to white males who consider themselves to be feminists, Jardine urges:

> we do not want you to *mimic* us, to become the same as us; we don't want your pathos or your guilt; and we don't even want your admiration (even if it's nice to get it once in a while). What we want, I would even say what we need, is your *work*. We need you to get down to serious work. And like all serious work, that involves struggle and pain.[23]

The womanist theoretical project that has been adopted by Williams, Smith, and others provides aspiring Afro-American male feminists with a useful model for the type of self-exploration that Smith and Jardine advocate. What Williams terms "womanist theory" is especially suggestive for Afro-American men because, while it calls for feminist discussions of black women's texts and for critiques of black androcentricism, womanism foregrounds a general black psychic health as a primary objective. For instance, Williams also argues that "what is needed is a thoroughgoing examination of male images in the works of black male writers." Her womanism, then, aims at "ending the separatist tendency in Afro-American criticism," at leading black feminism away from "the same hole The Brother has dug for himself—narcissism, isolation, inarticulation, obscurity," at the creation and/or continuation of black "community and dialogue."[24]

If a black man is to become a useful contributor to black feminism, he must, as Boone argues, "discover a position *from which* to speak that neither elides the importance of feminism to his work nor ignores the specificity of his gender."[25] However multiply split we perceive the subject to be, or deeply felt our sense of "maleness" and "femaleness" as social constructions, however heightened our sense of the historical consequences and current dangers of black androcentricism, a black male feminism cannot contribute to the continuation and expansion of the black feminist project by being so identified against or out of touch with itself as to fail to be both self-reflective and at least minimally self-interested. A black male feminist self-reflectivity of the type I have in mind necessarily would involve, among other things, examination of both the benefits and the dangers of a situatedness in feminist discourse. The self-interestedness of a black male feminist would be manifested in part by his concern with exploring "a man's place." Clearly if, as several feminists insist, convincing mimicry of female-authored concerns and interpretive strategies—or, in the words of a long-standing debate, speaking *like* a female feminist—is not in and of itself an appropriate goal for aspiring male participants (and I am not fully convinced that such mimicry is avoidable at present, at least as an initiatory moment of a male feminist's development), then a male feminism necessarily must explore, among other matters, males' various situations—in the (con)texts of history and the present—as one of its central concerns.

Perhaps the most difficult task for a black male feminism is striking a workable balance between male self-inquiry/interest and adequately feminist critiques of patriarchy. To this point, especially in response to the commercial and critical success of contemporary Afro-American women's literature, scores of black men have proven unsuccessful in this regard. As black feminist critics such as Valerie Smith and Deborah McDowell have argued, the contemporary moment of black feminist literature has been greeted by many Afro-American males with hostility, self-interested misrepresentation, and an apparent lack of honest intellectual introspection. McDowell's "Reading Family Matters" is a useful discussion for black male feminism, primarily as an exploration of what such a discourse ought not to do and be. She writes about widely circulated androcentric male analyses of Afro-American feminist texts by writers such as Toni Morrison and Alice Walker:

> [C]ritics leading the debate [about the representation of black men in black women's texts] have lumped all black women writers together and have focused on one tiny aspect of their immensely complex and diverse project—the image of black men—despite the fact that, if we can claim a center for these texts, it is located in the complexities of black female subjectivity and experience. In other words, though black women writers have made black women the subjects of their own family stories, these male readers/critics are attempting to usurp that place for themselves and place it at the center of critical inquiry.[26]

Although I do not believe that "the image of black men" is as microscopic an element in Afro-American women's texts as McDowell claims, I agree with her generally about the reprehensible nature of unabashed androcentricism found in formulations she cites by such figures as Robert Staples, Mel Watkins, and Darryl Pinckney. Nevertheless, where the potential development of a black male feminism is concerned, I am troubled by what appears to be a surprisingly explicit element of turf protection manifest in her perspectives. McDowell's formulations echo in unfortunate ways those of antifeminist male critics of the last two decades, white and black, who consider feminism to be an unredeemably myopic and unsupple interpretive strategy, incapable of offering subtle readings of canonical (largely male-authored) texts. Despite the existence and circulation of reprehensibly masculinist responses to Afro-American women's literature, black feminist literary critics do not best serve the discourses with which they are concerned by setting into motion homeostatic manuevers intended to devalue all forms of inquiry except for that which they hold to be most valuable (in this particular case, a female-authored scholarship that emphasizes Afro-American women's writings of black female subjectivity). If the Afro-American women's literary project is indeed as "immensely complex and diverse" as McDowell claims, bringing to bear other angles of vision, including antipatriarchal male ones, can assist in, among other things, the analysis of aspects of that complexity.

While the views of Staples, et al. are clearly problematic, those problems do not arise specifically from their efforts to place males "at the center of critical inquiry," any more than feminism is implicitly flawed because it insists, in some of its manifestations, on a gynocritical foregrounding of representations of women. Rather, these problems appear to result from the fact that the particular readers who produce these perspectives do not seem sufficiently to be, in Toril Moi's titular phrase, "men against patriarchy."[27] Certainly, in an age where both gender studies and Afro-American women's literature have achieved a degree of legitimacy within and outside of the academy, it is unreasonable for black women either to demand that black men not be concerned at all—or even centrally, if this is their wish—with the ways in which they are depicted by Afro-American women writers or necessarily to see that concern as intrinsically troubling in feminist terms. If female feminist calls for a nonmimicking male feminism are indeed persuasive, then black men will have very little of substance to say about contemporary Afro-American women's literature if we are also to consider as transgressive any attention to figurations of black manhood. It seems to me that the most black females in feminism can insist upon in this regard is that examinations that focus on male characters treat the "complexity" of contemporary Afro-American women novelists' delineations of black manhood with an antipatriarchal seriousness, somethingthe essays McDowell cites clearly lack.

From my perspective, what is potentially most valuable about the development of a black male feminism is not its capacity to reproduce black feminism as it has been established and is being practiced by black females who focus primarily on "the complexities of black female subjectivity and experience."[28] Rather, its potential value lies in the possibility that, in being antipatriarchal and as self-inquiring about their relationship(s) to feminism as Afro-American women have been, black men can expand feminist inquiry's range and utilization, that they will be able to explore other fruitful applications for feminist perspectives, including such topics as obstacles to a black male feminist project itself and new figurations of "family matters" and black male sexuality.

For my purposes here—for the purpose of theorizing about a black male feminism—perhaps the most provocative, enlightening, and inviting moment in womanist scholarship occurs in Hortense Spillers's "Mama's Baby, Papa's Maybe: An American Grammar Book." Indeed, Spillers's essay represents a fruitful starting point for new, potentially nonpatriarchal figurations of family and of the black male's relationship to the female. Toward the end of this illuminating theoretical text, which concerns itself with, among other matters, slavery's debilitating effects on the Afro-American family's constitution, Spillers envisions black male identity formation as a process whose movement toward successful resolution seems necessarily to require a serious engagement of black feminist principles and perspectives. Spillers asserts that as a result of the specific familial patterns that functioned during American slavery and beyond, which "removed the African-American male not so much from sight as from *mimetic* view as a partner in the prevailing social fiction of the Father's name, the Father's law," "[t]he African-American male has been touched . . . by the *mother*, *handed* by her in ways that he cannot escape."[29] Because of separation from traditional American paternal name and law,

> the black American male embodies the *only* American community of males which has had the specific occasion to learn *who* the female is within itself. . . . It is the heritage of the *mother* that the African-American male must regain as an aspect of his own personhood—the power of "yes" to the "female" within.[30]

Rather than seeing the "female" strictly as Other for the Afro-American male, Spillers's afrocentric re-visioning of psychoanalytic theory insists that we consider the "female" as an important aspect of the repressed in the black male self.[31] Employing Spillers's analyses as a starting point, we might regard Afro-American males' potential "in-ness" vis-à-vis feminism not, as Paul Smith insists in *Men in Feminism*, as a representation of male heterosexual desires to penetrate and violate female spaces,[32] but, rather, as an acknowledgement of what Spillers considers the distinctive nature of the Afro-American male's connection to the "female." If Afro-American males are ever to have anything to say about or to black feminism beyond the types of reflex-action devaluations and diatribes about divisiveness that critics such as McDowell and Valerie Smith rightly decry—diatribes that have too often marked our discourse and patently ignore the extent to which the practice of patriarchy has already divided us—the investigative process of which womanist acts by Spillers and Williams speak is indispensible. Such a process, if pursued in an intellectually rigorous manner, offers a means by which black men can participate usefully in and contribute productively to the black feminist project. Black womanism demands neither the erasure of the black gendered other's subjectivity (as have male movements to reacquire a putatively lost Afro-American manhood) nor the relegation of males to prone, domestic, or other limiting or objectifiable positions. What it does require, if it is indeed to become an ideology—a world view—with widespread cultural impact, is a recognition on the part of both black females and males of the nature of the gendered inequities that have marked our past and present and a commitment to working for change. In that sense, black feminist criticism has not only created a space for an informed Afro-American male participation, but it also heartily welcomes—in fact, it insists upon—the joint participation of black males and females as *comrades*, to invoke, with a difference, this paper's epigraphic reference to *Sula*.

IV

Reading "Mama's Baby, Papa's Maybe" was of special importance to me, in part because, as nothing I had read previously or since, it helped me to clarify and articulate my belief that my relationship to feminism need not mark me necessarily as a debilitatingly split subject.[33] The source of that relationship can only be traced autobiographically, if at all. Having been raised by a mother who, like too many women of too many generations, was the victim of male physical and psychological brutality—a brutality that, according to my mother, resulted in large part from my father's frustrations about his inability to partake in what Spillers calls masculinity's "prevailing social fiction"—my earliest stories, my familial narratives, as it were, figured "maleness" in quite troubling terms. My mother told me horrific stories, one of which I was, in a sense, immediately involved in: my father, who left us before I was one year old and whom I never knew, kicked her in the stomach when my fetal presence swelled her body because he believed she'd been unfaithful to him and that I was only "maybe" his baby.

As a youth, I pondered this and other such stories often and deeply, in part because of the pain I knew these incidents caused my mother, in part because, as someone largely without a consistent male familial role model, I sought actively a means by which to achieve a gendered self-definition. As one for whom maleness as manifested in the surrounding inner city culture seemed to be represented only by violence, familial abandonment, and the certainty of imprisonment, I found that I was able to define myself with regard to my gender primarily in oppositional ways. I had internalized the cautionary intent of my mother's narratives, which also served as her dearest wish for me: that I not grow up to be like my father, that I not adopt the definitions of "maleness" represented by his example and in the culture generally. Because the scars of male brutality were visibly etched—literally marked, as it were—on my mother's flesh and on her psyche, "maleness," as figured both in my mother's stories and in my environment, seemed to me not to be a viable "mimetic" option. I grew up, then, not always sure of what—or who—I was with respect to prevailing social definitions of gender, but generally quite painfully aware of what I could not become.

In order to begin to understand who my mother was, perhaps also who my father was, what "maleness" was, and what extrabiological relationship I could hope to have to it, I needed answers that, for a variety of reasons, my mother was unable to provide. I found little of value in the black masculinist discourse of the time, which spoke ceaselessly of Afro-American male dehumanization and castration by white men and black women (our central social narrative for too long). This rhetoric seemed, perhaps because of my particular familial context and maturational dilemma, simplistic and unself-consciously concerned with justifying domestic violence and other forms of black male brutality.

Afro-American women's literature, to which I was introduced in 1977 as a sophomore at Brandeis University, along with black feminism, helped me to move toward a comprehension of the world, of aspects of my mother's life, and of what a man against patriarchy could be and do. These discourses provided me with answers nowhere else available to what had been largely unresolvable mysteries. I work within the paradigm of black feminist literary criticism because it explains elements of the world about which—for strictly autobiographical reasons—I care most deeply. I write and read what and as I do because I am incapable of escaping the meanings of my mother's narratives for my own life; in their enunciation to the next generation, the pain and the sense of hope for better days that characterize these familial texts are illuminatingly explored in many narratives by black women. Afro-American women's literature has given me parts of myself that, incapable of a (biological) "fatherly reprieve," I would not otherwise have had.

I have decided that it is ultimately irrelevant whether these autobiographical facts—facts that, of course, are not, and can never be, the whole story—are deemed by others sufficient to permit me to call myself "feminist." Like Toril Moi, I have come to believe that "the important thing for men is not to spend their time worrying about definitions and essences ('am I *really* a feminist?'), but to take up a recognizable anti-patriarchal position."[34] What is most important to me is that my work contribute, in however small a way, to the project whose goal is the dismantling of phallocentric rule by which black females—and, I am sure, countless other Afro-American sons—have been injuriously "touched."

V

My indebtedness to Spillers's and other womanist perspectives is, then, great indeed, as is my sense of their potential as illuminating, originary moments for a newborn—or not-yet-born—black male feminist discourse. However, utilizing these perspectives requires that we be more inquiring than Spillers is in her formulations: not in envisioning liberating possibilities of an acknowledgment of "the 'female' within" the black community and the male subject, but in noting potential dangers inherent in such an attempted embrasure by traditional and/or historically brutalized Afro-American men whose relationship to a repressed "female" is not painstakingly (re)defined.

Clearly, more thinking is necessary not only about what "the 'female' within" is, but also about what it can be said to represent for black males; there also needs to be serious analysis of useful means and methods of interacting with a repressed female interiority and subject. Spillers's theorizing does not perform this task, in part because it has other, more compelling interests and emphases—among them the righting/(re)writing of definitions of "woman" so that they will reflect Afro-American women's particular, historically conditioned "female social subject" status. But a black male feminism must be especially focused on exploring such issues if it is to mobilize Spillers's suggestive remarks as a means of developing a fuller understanding of the complex formulations of black manhood found in many (con)texts, including Afro-American women's narratives.

Below, I want to discuss these matters a bit more fully, to build on Spillers's provocative theorizing about the Afro-American male's maturational process and situation on American shores. To this end, I will briefly look at an illuminating moment in Toni Morrison's *Sula*, a text that is, to my mind, not only an unparalleled Afro-American woman's writing of what McDowell calls "the complexities of black female subjectivity and experience," but also of black males' relationship to "the 'female' within" as a consequence of their limited access to "the prevailing social fiction" of masculinity. In this novel, the difficulty—the near impossibility—of negotiating the spaces between black male lack and black female presence is plainly manifested in such figures as the undifferentiatable deweys; BoyBoy, whose name, in contrast to most of the authorial designations in *Sula*, speaks unambiguously for him; and Jude, whose difficulty in assuming the mantle of male provider leads him to view his union with Nel as that which "would make one Jude."[35]

The response of Plum, the most tragic of *Sula*'s unsuccessful negotiators of the so-called white man's world, vividly represents for me some of the contemporary dangers of black male "in-ness" vis-à-vis the "female." Despite (because of?) a childhood characterized by "float[ing] in a constant swaddle of love and affection" (unlike Hannah, who is uncertain whether her mother ever loved her, Eva's son did experience traditional manifestations of maternal love, reflecting a gender-determined disparity in treatment) and his mother's intention to follow the Father's law by "bequeath[ing] everything" (38) to him, Plum appears incapable of embracing hegemonic notions of masculinity. Instead, he returns from World War I spiritually fractured, but, unlike a similarly devastated Shadrack, lacks the imaginative wherewithal to begin to theorize or ritualize a new relationship to his world. Consequently, he turns to drugs as a method of anesthetizing himself from the horrors of his devastation and, in his mother's view, seeks to compel her resumption of familiar/familial patterns of caretaking. In the following passage, Eva explains to Hannah her perception of Plum's desires as well as the motivation for her participation in what amounts to an act of infanticide:

> When he came back from that war he wanted to git back in. After all that carryin' on, just gettin' him out and keepin' him alive, he wanted to crawl back in my womb and well . . . I ain't got the room no more even if he could do it. There wasn't space for him in my womb. And he was crawlin' back. Being helpless and thinking baby thoughts and dreaming baby dreams and messing up his pants again and smiling all the time. I had room enough in my heart, but not in my womb, got no more. I birthed him once. I couldn't do it again. He was growed, a big old thing. Godhavemercy, I couldn't birth him twice. . . . [A] big man can't be a baby all wrapped up inside his mamma no more; he suffocate. I done everything I could to make him leave me and go on and live and be a man but he wouldn't and I had to keep him out so I just thought of a way he could die like a man not all scrunched up inside my womb, but like a man. (62)[36]

What is significant about this passage for a theorizing of the possibilities of a nonoppressive black male relationship to feminism—to female experience characterized by a refusal to be subjugated to androcentric desire(s)—is its suggestiveness for our understanding the obstacles to a revised male view of the repressed "female" that result in large part from black males' relative social powerlessness. If black feminism is persuasive in its analysis of the limitations of Afro-American masculinist ideology, which has emphasized the achievement of black manhood at the expense of black female subjectivity, if, as a growing body of social analyses indicates, we can best describe an overwhelming number of Africa's American male descendants as males-in-crisis, then the question a black male feminism must ask itself is: On what basis, according to what ideological perspective, can an Afro-American heterosexual male ground his notions of the female? Beyond its (hetero)sexual dimension, can the "female" truly come to represent for a traditional black male-in-crisis more than a protective maternal womb from which he seeks to be "birthed" again and a site upon which to find relief from or, as in the case of Jude's relationship to Nel, locate frustrations caused by an inability to achieve putatively normative American male socioeconomic status? If embracing normative masculinity requires a movement beyond, indeed an escape from, the protection and life-sustaining aspects symbolized by maternal umbilical cords and apron strings, and an achievement of an economic situation wherein the male provides domestic space and material sustenance for his dependents (including "his woman"), black manhood generally is, like Plum, in desperate trouble. And if, as has often been the case, a black female can be seen by an Afro-American male-in-crisis only if she has been emptied of subjectivity and selfhood, if she becomes visible for the male only when she is subsumed by male desire(s), then the types of refiguration and redefinition of black male subjectivity and embrasure of the "female" central to Spillers's formulations are highly unlikely. This question of seeing and not seeing, of the male gaze's erasure and re-creation of the "female," is central to *Sula*'s general thematics. It seems to me that Morrison's figuration of black female subjectivity in all of her novels is largely incomprehensible without some serious attention both to her representation of black manhood and to her exploration of the relationships between socially constructed gendered (and racial) positions. To return explicitly to the case of Eva: what Eva fears, what appears to be a self-interested motivation for her killing of her intended male heir, is that Plum's pitiful, infantile state has the potential to reduce *her* to a static female function—to a self-sacrificing mother—that, according to Bottom legend, had already provoked her decision to lose a leg in order to collect insurance money with which to provide for her children. Having sacrificed so much of herself already, Eva chooses instead to take the life of her self-described male heir. And if Plum dies "like a man," in Eva's estimation, his achievement of manhood has nothing to do with an assumption of traditional masculine traits, nothing to do with strength, courage, and a refusal to cry in the face of death. Instead, that achievement results from Eva's creation of conditions that have become essential components of her definition of manhood: death forces him to "leave" her and to "keep . . . out" of her womb. It would appear that manhood is defined here not as presence, as it is represented typically in Western thought, but rather—by and for Eva at least—as liberating (domestic and uterine) absence.

VI

One of the intentions of this essay is to suggest that feminism represents a fruitful, potentially nonoppressive means of reconceptualizing, of figuratively birthing twice the black male subject. But, as a close reading of the above passage from *Sula* suggests, interactions between men and women motivated by male self-interest (such as necessarily characterizes an aspect of male participation in feminism) are fraught with possible dangers of an enactment of or a capitulation to hegemonic male power for the biological/ideological female body. Indeed if it is the case that, as Spillers has argued in another context, "the woman who stays in man's company keeps alive the possibility of having, one day, an unwanted guest, or the guest, deciding 'to hump the hostess,' whose intentions turn homicidal,"[37] then male proximity to feminism generally creates the threat of a specifically masculinist violation. If, as I noted earlier, the dangers of a hegemonic, heterosexual, Euro-American male's "in-ness" vis-à-vis feminism include (sexualized) penetration and domination, then those associated with a heterosexual black male's interactions with the ideological female body are at least doubled and potentially involve an envisioning of the black female body as self-sacrificingly maternal and/or self-sacrificingly sexual. Because of a general lack of access to the full force of hegemonic male power, Afro-American men could see in increasingly influential black female texts not only serious challenges to black male fictions of the self but also an appropriate location for masculine desires for control of the types of valuable resources that the discourse(s) of black womanhood currently represents.

But a rigorous, conscientious black male feminism need not give in to traditional patriarchal desires for control and erasure of the "female." To be of any sustained value to the feminist project, what such a discourse must provide are illuminating and persuasive readings of gender as it is constituted for blacks in America—sophisticated, informed, and contentious critiques of phallocentric practices—in an effort to redefine our notions of black male (and female) textuality and subjectivity. And in its differences with black feminist texts that are produced by individual Afro-American women—and surely there will be differences, for such is the nature of intellectual and political life—a black male feminism must be both rigorous in its engagement of these texts and self-reflective enough to avoid, at all costs, the types of patronizing, marginalizing gestures that have traditionally characterized Afro-American male intellectuals' response to black womanhood. What a black male feminism must strive for, above all else, is the envisioning and enactment of the possibilities signaled by the differences feminism has exposed and created. Being an Afro-American male in black feminist criticism does not mean attempting to invade an/other political body like a lascivious soul snatcher or striving to erase its essence in order to replace it with one's own myth of what the discourse should be. Such a position for black men means, above all else, an acknowledgment and celebration of the incontrovertible fact that "the Father's law" is no longer the only law of the land.

Notes

1. Toril Moi, "Men Against Patriarchy," in *Gender and Theory: Dialogues on Feminist Criticism,* ed. Linda Kauffman (New York: Basil Blackwell, 1989), 184.
2. Toni Morrison, *Sula* (New York: Plume, 1973), 71.
3. Houston A. Baker, Jr., *Afro-American Poetics: Revisions of Harlem and the Black Aesthetic* (Madison: Univ. of Wisconsin Press, 1988), 8.
4. Cary Nelson, "Men, Feminism: The Materiality of Discourse," in *Men in Feminism,* eds. Alice Jardine and Paul Smith (New York: Methuen, 1987), 156.
5. For example, Joseph Boone's and Gerald MacLean's essays "Of Me(n) and Feminism: Who(se) Is the Sex That Writes" and "Citing the Subject," in *Gender and Theory: Dialogues on Feminist Criticism*, ed. Linda Kauffman (New York: Basil Blackwell, 1989), assume that the foregrounding of gendered subjectivity is essential to the production of a male feminist critical practice. Consequently, in an effort to articulate his perspectives on the possibilities of a male feminist discourse, Boone shares with us professional secrets: he writes of his disagreement with the male-authored essays that begin Alice Jardine's and Paul Smith's *Men and Feminism* (New York: Methuen, 1987), and of being excluded, because of his gender, from a Harvard feminist group discussion of Elaine Showalter's "Critical Cross-Dressing: Male Feminists and the Woman of the Year." And MacLean's essay (composed in the form of letters to Jane Tompkins that, as a response to Tompkins's response to Ellen Messer-Davidow's "The Philosophical Bases of Feminist Literary Criticisms," assumes an at least doubly supplemental position vis-à-vis female-authored feminist discourse) discloses painfully personal information about his difficult relationship with his mother, his unsatisfying experience with psychoanalysis, and an incident of marital violence.

6. Joseph Boone, "Of Me(n) and Feminism: Who(se) is the Sex that Writes," in *Gender and Theory*, 159. For my purposes here, Boone's remarks are suggestive despite their employment of language that might seem to mark them as a (hetero)sexualization of men's participation in feminism ("open up a space," "discover a position"). I believe that Boone's passage implies less about any desire for domination on his part than it does about the pervasiveness in our language of terms that have acquired sexual connotations and, consequently, demonstrate the virtual unavoidability—the seeming naturalness, if you will—of the employment of a discourse of penetration to describe interactions between males and females. But it also appears to reflect a sense of frustration motivated by Boone's knowledge that while feminism has had a tremendous impact on his thinking about the world he inhabits, many of the discourse's practitioners do not see a place in it for him or other like-minded males. In order to make a place for himself in the face of female opposition to his involvement in feminism, violation and transgression seem to Boone to be unavoidable. Also, Boone's self-consciousness about the implications of using a discourse of penetration to describe male participation in feminism is further evidence that we should not read his statement as possessing a (hetero)sexualized subtext. For example, toward the end of his essay, he argues that "a recognition of the presence and influence of gay men working in and around feminism has the potential of rewriting feminist fears about 'men in feminism' as a strictly heterosexual gesture of appropriation" (174).
7. Alice Jardine, "Men in Feminism: Odor di Uomo or Compagnons de Route," in *Men in Feminism*, eds. Alice Jardine and Paule Smith (New York: Methuen, 1987), 58. Subsequent page references are included parenthetically in the text.
8. Andrew Ross, "No Question of Silence," in *Men and Feminism,* 86.
9. Houston A. Baker, Jr., *Afro-American Poetics: Revisions of Harlem and the Black Aesthetic* (Madison: Univ. of Wisconsin Press, 1988), 8.
10. Elizabeth Weed, "A Man's Place," in *Men in Feminism,* 75.
11. Michael Awkward, *Inspiriting Influences: Tradition, Revision, and Afro-American Women's Novels* (New York: Columbia Univ. Press, 1989).
12. About his own relationships to feminism, Nelson writes: "Feminism is part of my social and intellectual life, has been so for many years, and so, to the extent that writing is ever 'natural,' it is natural that I write about feminism" (153). Nelson's "Men, Feminism: The Materiality of Discourse" (*Men in Feminism,* 153–72.) is, in my estimation, a model for self-referential male feminist inquiries which assume—or, at the very least, seek to demonstrate—a useful place for males in the discourse of feminism.
13. Jardine and Smith, "Introduction," *Men in Feminism*, vii–viii.
14. See Craig Owens, "Outlaws: Gay Men in Feminism," in *Men in Feminism* 219–32. It is hard for me to believe that Jardine and Smith's difficulty

reflected a lack of interest among Afro-Americans in exploring the relationship(s) of men to black feminism. Texts such as the 1979 *Black Scholar* March/April special issue devoted to investigating black feminism as manifested primarily in Ntozake Shange's *for colored girls who have considered suicide when the rainbow is enuf* and Michele Wallace's *Black Macho and the Myth of the Superwoman* (see Robert Staples, "The Myth of Black Macho: A Response to Angry Black Feminists," *Black Scholar*, March/April 1979); the Mel Watkins and Darryl Pinckney essays published in the *New York Times Book Review* and the *New York Review of Books,* respectively (Watkins, "Sexism, Racism, and Black Women Writers," *New York Times Book Review*, June 15, 1986, 1, 35–36; and Pinckney, "Black Victims, Black Villains," *New York Review of Books* 34 [January 29, 1987]: 17–20); and others that critique such black male investigations of feminism, offer clear evidence of Afro-American interest in "the problem." Jardine's and Smith's difficulties, it would appear, at least where inclusion of Afro-American male perspectives was concerned, might have stemmed from the fact that (1) most of the men who had spoken publicly on the subject were open about their hostility to black feminism, and (2) they generally did not speak the language of contemporary theory, a high academic idiom that demonstrates that the contributors to *Men in Feminism* are, despite significant differences between them, members of the same speech community.

15. Stephen Heath, "Male Feminism," in *Men in Feminism*, 1.
16. Ibid., 9.
17. Robert Scholes, "Reading as a Man," in *Men in Feminism*, 207.
18. Barbara Smith, "Toward a Black Feminist Criticism," *Village Voice Literary Supplement,* April 1988, 173.
19. Ibid., 720.
20. Michele Wallace, "Who Dat Say Dat When I Say Dat?: Zora Neale Hurston Then and Now," *Village Voice Literary Supplement,* April 1988, 18.
21. Sherley Anne Williams, "Some Implications of Womanist Theory," *Callaloo* 9 (1986): 304.
22. Valerie Smith, "Gender and Afro-Americanist Literary Theory and Criticism," in *Speaking of Gender*, ed. Elaine Showalter (New York: Routledge, 1989), 68.
23. Jardine, "Men in Feminism," 60.
24. Williams, "Some Implications," 307.
25. Boone, "Of Me(n) and Feminism," 159.
26. Deborah McDowell, "Reading Family Matters," in *Changing Our Own Words: Essays on Criticism, Theory, and the Writing by Black Women*, ed. Cheryl Wall (New Brunswick: Rutgers Univ. Press, 1989), 84.

27. Toril Moi, "Men Against Patriarchy," in *Gender and Theory*, 181–88.
28. It seems to me that a full reading of the figurations of gender in the writings of Hurston, Marshall, Morrison, Walker, et al. is impossible without some attention to these novelists' diverse and complex figurations of black male subjectivity. McDowell's views notwithstanding, constructions of black male and black female subjectivity are too obviously interrelated in black women's narratives for feminist criticism to profit in the long run from ignoring—or urging that others ignore—the important function delineations of black male subjectivity possess for these narratives' thematics. Certainly the threat of antifeminist male critical bias—especially when that bias is as transparent and easily deconstructed as in the examples that McDowell cites—is not cause to erase or minimize the significance of black male characters in these writers' work.
29. Hortense J. Spillers, "Mama's Baby, Papa's Maybe: An American Grammar Book," *Diacritics* (1987): 80.
30. Ibid.
31. In this sense, Spillers's perspectives complement those of Sherley Anne Williams. Williams demands, in effect, that we consider the extent to which black male repression of the "female" results from an attempt to follow the letter of the white Father's law.
32. Paul Smith, "Men in Feminism: Men and Feminist Theory," in *Men in Feminism*, 33.
33. Henry Louis Gates Jr. "Whose Canon Is It, Anyway?" *New York Times Book Review,* February 26, 1989, 1, 44–45. Because it introduced me to Spillers's formulations and because of its (apparently controversial) discussion of connections between black mothers and sons, expressed by a self-consciously male critical voice employing elements of black feminist methodology, Henry Louis Gates, Jr.'s essay served as an enabling pretext to this essay. Gates states that his initial encounter with Spillers's essay was a crucial, illuminating moment—the point at which he began to understand that "much of my scholarly and critical work has been an attempt to learn how to speak in the strong, compelling cadences of my mother's voice" (45). However, the autobiographical elements of my essay were inspired not only by what Gates might call his own "autocritographical" moment, but as importantly by the recent call for an Afro-American autobiographical criticism by Houston Baker and by the self-referential dimension in much feminist criticism and theory (especially, because of my own positionality, that which appears in the work of male feminists). These acts convinced me of the crucial nature of self-referentiality in this initial effort on my part to theorize about a black man's place(s)—or, perhaps more accurately, *my* place—in black feminist criticism.
34. Moi, "Men Against Patriarchy," 184.

35. Toni Morrison, *Sula* (New York: Plume, 1973), 71. Subsequent references to this novel appear in the text in parentheses.

36. At least one other reading of Eva's murder of her son is possible: as protection against the threat of incest. In a section of her explanation to Hannah—very little of which is contained in my textual citation of *Sula*—Eva discusses a dream she has had concerning Plum:

> I'd be laying here at night and he be downstairs in that room, but when I closed my eyes I'd see him . . . six feet tall smilin' and crawlin' up the stairs quietlike so I wouldn't hear and opening the door soft so I wouldn't hear and he'd be creepin' to the bed trying to spread my legs trying to get back up in my womb. He was a man, girl, a big old growed-up man. I didn't have that much room. I kept on dreaming it. Dreaming it and I knowed it was true. One night it wouldn't be no dream. It'd be true and I would have done it, would have let him if I'd've had the room but a big man can't be a baby all wrapped up inside his mamma no more; he suffocate. (72–73)

In this construction, Morrison reverses to some extent the traditional dynamics of the most prevalent form of intergenerational incest. Instead of the physically and psychologically irresistible male parent creeping to the bed and spreading the legs of his defenseless female child, in Eva's dream, her large man-child Plum is the active agent of violation. Eva's emphasis on Plum's physical immensity and her own uterus's size—and, clearly, the obvious intent of this is to suggest the impossibility of a literal return of even the regressive male body to the womb—makes connections to incestuous creeping and spreading possible. It is not difficult to imagine, given Plum's constantly drugged state, that frustrations caused by an inability to reinsert his whole body into his mother's womb during what Eva views as an inevitable encounter might lead to a forced insertion of a part that "naturally" fits, his penis. At any rate, a reading of this scene that notes its use of language consistent with parent-child incest serves to ground what appear to be otherwise (at least in literal terms) senseless fears on Eva's part concerning both the possible effects of Plum's desire for reentry into her uterine space and her own inability to deny her son access to that space ("I would have done it, would have let him").

37. Hortense Spillers, "Black, White, and in Color, or Learning How to Paint: Toward an Intramural Protocol of Reading." Paper presented at the "Sites of Colonialism" retreat, Center for the Study of Black Literature and Culture, Univ. of Pennsylvania, March 15, 1990.

2

"A CAVERN OPENED IN MY MIND"

The Poetics of Homosexuality and the Politics of Masculinity in James Baldwin

CORA KAPLAN

In an essay on Harlem, "Fifth Avenue, Uptown," first published in the July 1960 issue of *Esquire*, James Baldwin eloquently interpreted the demands he believed to be at the heart of the new black consciousness and the civil rights movement for the magazine's largely white male readership:

> *Negroes want to be treated like men*: a perfectly straightforward statement, containing only seven words. People who have mastered Kant, Hegel, Shakespeare, Marx, Freud, and the Bible find this statement utterly impenetrable. The idea seems to threaten profound, barely conscious assumptions. A kind of panic paralyzes their features, as though they found themselves trapped at the edge of a steep place. (211–212)[1]

Read some six years after Baldwin's death, from the partially refigured ground of the politics of race and sexuality, this passage reminds us of the genealogical changes—uneven, discontinuous, but profound—that have taken place since the publication of "Fifth Avenue, Uptown." Thirty years on, the political and cultural contexts have been transformed by, among other things, the rise of black feminism and the gay and lesbian movements. Little in Baldwin's seven-word slogan now seems "straightforward": neither its historically routine slippage in which "Negro" metonymically means black male (virtually including but actually suppressing what black women might or might not "want"), nor the conscious common sense that both black writer and *Esquire* reader know what kind of treatment or subjectivity are being evoked by the phrase "treated like men."

Inevitably, reading "Fifth Avenue, Uptown" through the narrowed lens of present consciousness highlights the difference history makes to discourse, in this case its ruthless defamiliarization of the normative categories of gender, race, and culture that Baldwin seemed to take for granted. Yet this retroactive focus needs to be joined with another kind of historicizing perspective, lest, by itself, the focus misleadingly anchors Baldwin too firmly in the more conservative assumptions of the ideological moment that he did so much to resist and disturb, blurring his radical differences with 1960s sexual and racial discourses. In this essay, I explore both the dynamism and the limits of Baldwin's complex negotiation of masculinity in the fifties and early sixties.[2]

Like so much of Baldwin's writing in these years, the quoted passage at once referred its readers to the "straightforward" codes of a masculine humanism that it seemed to affirm, while fundamentally questioning, the definition and stability of the male subject position constructed through them. The unambiguous demand for a parity of treatment with the most privileged of gendered subjects induced, Baldwin argued, an extreme psychic crisis in those groups who must share such privilege. Not the Negro who "wants" but the white "master" of masculine Western discourse is figured as abject in this vignette. It is these "people" whose panic and paralysis in the face of the "Negroes'" desire for masculine equity is equated with a fear of falling from a height suddenly dangerously steep rather than safely superior. This racial scenario of threatened masculinity (for Baldwin's "people" here seem imaginatively, if not sexually, to inhabit the gendered category they are being asked to expand) embedded racial distinction in the very meaning of the dominant masculine.

Nor is the sexuality of this masculinity left intact. Those members of his *Esquire* audience who had also read Baldwin's second novel, *Giovanni's Room* (1956),[3] might draw a parallel between his vision of the ethical vertigo of the educated white westerner faced with a demand for an ethnically inclusive homosociality and the terror he ascribed to the white male who acknowledges and repudiates his same-sex desire. In the morning after the adolescent David, the white protagonist of *Giovanni's Room,* has his first sexual encounter with the "quick and dark" Joey, his pleasure turns to acute fear: Joey's brown "body suddenly seemed the black opening of a cavern in which I would be tortured till madness came, in which I would lose my manhood" (12). Like the male subject of "Fifth Avenue, Uptown," David is tormented by a set of "barely conscious assumptions" (12): "A cavern opened in my mind, black, full of rumor, suggestion, of half-heard, half-forgotten, half-understood stories, full of dirty words. I thought I saw my future in that cavern" (12). Far from being a natural or secure subjectivity, white heterosexual masculinity is imagined in Baldwin as the effect of a series of denials and exclusions, a position constantly threatened by the knowledges negated—in the Freudian sense of a simultaneous expression and disavowal—in its own construction.[4] At the same time, the Shakespearean and classical images of precipice and cavern join Baldwin's critique to another androcentric theme in the western episteme, the tragic fall or fatal retreat of a male heroism.[5] An ideal of masculinity discursively presented as both philosophy and action deliberately links Baldwin's revisions of the masculine to western history and culture, invoking, perhaps even supporting, as well as undermining, certain dominant values.

In what follows, I want to explore the playing out of these tensions around race, masculinity, homosexuality, and culture in Baldwin's early work as it intersected with and contributed to the broader reworking of sexual and cultural politics in the early sixties. In the tributes, memoirs, and appraisals that followed Baldwin's death, many speakers testified to the powerful influence of his work—and his life—on his women readers in the fifties and sixties: today's middle-aged feminist writers, scholars, and activists. The testimonials of black women formed the core of this acknowledgement. Toni Morrison, for example, said that Baldwin gave her "a language to dwell in. . . . No one possessed or inhabited language for me the way you did. You made American English honest . . . ungated it for black people so that in your wake we could enter it, occupy it, restructure it in order to accommodate our complicated passion."[6] Another kind of access to passion marked black lesbian feminist poet Cheryl Clarke's tribute:

> The first serious work of fiction I read by a black writer was Baldwin's *Another Country* in 1963, and it was the first novel I read that treated homosexuality, albeit male. *Another Country* made me imagine freedom from traditional monogamous heterosexuality and set me to thinking about the possibility of a "variant" life. . . . *Another Country* unsettled me forever and made me see the complexity of living as a sexual person.[7]

Cheryl Clarke's response to *Another Country* was, I want to argue, echoed and shared by many of Baldwin's women readers in the early sixties. A few years older than Clarke, I too was a Jewish red-diaper baby living in New York, involved in the civil rights movement, and powerfully drawn to Baldwin's interracial, sexually polymorphous fiction, hearing in it a kind of sexually and racially postlapsarian utopianism in which one could acknowledge the exquisite pain and betrayals of both heterosexual and homosexual relationships that crossed the hierarchies and divides of class, race and culture. I saw in these intimate alliances a hope that was more than merely personal, if still something less than fully political. Just as Baldwin's essay style—his remarkable syncretism of the sermon, of autobiography, and of the composite elements of an anglophone tradition of political polemic extending forward from Thomas Paine and Frederick Douglass—transformed for me the idea and possibilities of engaged writing, so his "unsettling" fiction freed up and opened out the complexity of a lived and imagined sexuality. This response, however, was not an obvious or straightforward one. For women to read Baldwin as Clarke and I did was to engage us not only in an empathetic, even desiring, identification with the figures of masculinity in his texts, but also (if only subliminally) in a repudiation of the feminine, if not exactly of women. Modern femininity, as I suggest in this essay, was as problematic a category for Baldwin in this period as it was for his contemporaries of both sexes, and its masculinization in the image of the mannish "dyke" even more so. As Cheryl Clarke wryly notes, there was nothing in *Another Country* "to recommend lesbianism"; its poetics of homosexuality, its utopian erotics are quintessentially "between men," between Rufus and

Eric, Eric and Yves, Vivaldo and Eric. And it is Eric, the thirty-something white actor, the least compromised figure in the novel, who becomes, in his homoerotic relations, which are the strong bias of his bisexuality, the vanguard bearer of the novel's sexual ethics. In contrast, the two central black characters—the jazz musician Rufus, who commits suicide before the main action of the book, and his younger sister Ida, a singer—are figures whose "tragic, insistent knowledge" and "lived reality" (to borrow from Morrison again) strip the Americans in the text of not just their English but "of ease and false comfort and fake innocence and evasion and hypocrisy" (76). The politics of race, with its grim psychic and social implications, emerge through the emotional and sexual histories of Rufus and Ida, who each enact a flawed heterosexual politics, betraying their naively liberal white lovers. Their lives and choices form the ground of the novel as well as constituting its pedagogy. Their respective death and survival mark out the postedenic racialized terrain on which modern metropolitan subjects must, of necessity, conduct both their public and affective lives.

I want to pursue a bit further my exploration of the significance of Baldwin's early fiction for women readers in the fifties and early sixties. Any exploration of this kind must, of course, recognize a spectrum of such meanings. To raise the question of "women's" response suggests at once the incommensurabilities and connections between the responses of women of different classes and races, between women who would opt for "variant" lives or remain within a dominant heterosexuality. From my own location in left-wing politics, Baldwin's critique and revision of black and white masculinities in *Go Tell It On the Mountain*, *Giovanni's Room*, and *Another Country* seemed to put into discourse, set up as an urgent question, something profoundly repressed in the left cultures of my own and my parents' generation. More than that, however, the celebratory expression of the male homoerotic, the productive rather than punitive notion of multiple relationships and varieties of transgressive coupling, and the utopian elements so often criticized in Baldwin's work as being insufficiently political sketched out a landscape of sexual liberation joined at the groin to a wider politics that no other writing of that time quite addressed. It acted, in my consciousness at least, as a countervailing force to the hopelessness that other contemporary androcentric American narratives induced in me—I am thinking here of the beat writers in particular, but also of Miller, Mailer, Roth, or Bellow. In these authors, the subjection and abjection of women are the premise and occasion of the masculine. It is not that these novels do not trigger forms of female identification with versions of their masculinity; on the contrary, I would argue that they often do. But this identification is not only unstable in the way that all psychic identifications are, but particularly volatile in its negative response to its own process, inducing a reactive revulsion to the vulgarly expressive, although often semiparodic, sadomasochism of the texts. Baldwin's novels also offer the pains and pleasures of modern sexuality, but, for the most part, his sexual scripts stage the sadomasochism at the heart of sexuality very differently.

Another Country is a bold novel for its time. It explicitly challenges both the spectacle of degradation as a radical, transgressive erotic and the notion that women or men invite or enjoy violence, framing the brutality Rufus displays toward his southern white girlfriend Leona as sexist and abusive, a bleakly tragic failure both of heterosexual love and interracial alliance. In Baldwin's work, pleasure and pain appear in their most utopian guise, mediated by and processed through the mutual desires of the sexual imaginary, as a consenting and experimental erotic.

How, then, might a woman reader be engaged by the erotic in Baldwin's fiction at its most freshly imagined and most emotionally and libidinally moving; that is, when described between men? In "On Becoming a Lesbian Reader," Alison Hennigan, exploring her sexual odyssey through literature in the fifties and sixties, concludes that the fact that "so many of the books I came to value most were the product of gay male love" was, in retrospect, both "an indication of my difficulties" and a political and emotional advantage in that she "was instead compelled to explore the teasing bonds and barriers which separate and unite homosexual women and men."[8] The psychic nature of that exploration is itself of interest. We might speculate that at least part of what was compelling about Baldwin's work for women readers, whatever their sexual bias, was the lowered threshold he provided for fantasies that were not about the fixing of gender or sexual orientation but about their mobility and fluidity. Women could take up shifting and multiple fantasy positions within his fictional narratives: that possibility, itself wonderfully, if terrifyingly, liberating, allowed an identification not just with specific characters but with the scenarios of desire themselves. And, as one of my colleagues commented about reading Baldwin in high school, the appeal of these scenarios was enhanced by the artfulness and high seriousness of Baldwin's lyric prose, including its classical resonances that for her placed him in favorable competition with the cultural ambitions—and pretensions—of the canonical white male prosodists from early modernism through the postwar cultural formation. "He was right up there with those guys."[9]

Through an engagement with Baldwin's fiction and essays, with their ethical and transgressive elements focused in narratives of revised masculinity and rewritten relations between blacks and whites, a wide range of women readers of the fifties and sixties could reach beyond their own subaltern inscriptions in dominant sexuality and culture, acknowledging both directly and through analogy other scenes of social and sexual desire—"variant" lives of all kinds. There is, however, a distinctly dystopian side to this productive effect that emerges when I bring my thoughts about women's response to Baldwin together with new work on feminism and popular culture today. In a thoughtful exploration of women fanzine rewritings of *Star Trek* as homoerotic romances between Captain Kirk and Spock, Constance Penley asks why the bodies seized on by the mainly heterosexual women fans must be male. Partly, she argues, their choice is a positive project to "retool masculinity by making it sensitive and nurturant without being wimpy, decisive and intelligent without being macho . . . able to combine love and work without jealousy or rivalry." Its negative valence, however, is the "fan's rejection of the female body . . . as a terrain of fantasy or utopian thinking . . . the body of the woman as it has been constituted in this culture."[10] This rejection of the female body—of the modes of the feminine available to women in the fifties and early sixties—was, certainly, a motivation in my strong female identification with Baldwin's scenes of male sexuality and desire, but that identification itself implies an abjection, a repudiation of something that lay not just "outside" women's psychic subjectivity but also deeply "within" being, a reflex that, always incomplete, must be constantly repeated.

Some sense of this paradox is articulated in the way in which Baldwin at his most protofeminist depicts modern women. The female body worked over and overworked by ideology, what Penley terms "a legal, moral and ideological battleground"[11] (but also in Baldwin the female body as sinner), is represented with great sympathy and poignancy in *Another Country* by Ida, who thinks all white men see her as a whore; by Leona, abused by husband, lover, and brothers; by Cass, who panders to her husband's febrile vanities. And while at least two of these characters, Ida and Cass, may live to change as well as challenge these inscriptions,

Baldwin's central project is not to "retool" femininity. His texts taken as a whole are not punitively or lubriciously littered with broken female bodies, yet neither is their repair his central concern. Women are, like Eve, the bearers of important but bitter knowledge for men, not the agents or vehicles of hope.

Baldwin's urban figures build their enclaves of hope within the walls of a "fallen" city, post-Christian as well as post-Eden, but images of Eden erupt there, selectively illuminating their fates. *Another Country* has two contrasting final scenes, one postlapsarian, its referent distinctly Old Testament, the other a reincarnation of the edenic as a modern, homoerotic metropolis. In the first, a night scene with rain, Ida and Vivaldo, exhausted in their struggle to preserve their love, cling together like "weary children," "nothing erotic" in Ida's caress that strokes Vivaldo's "innocence out of him" (431). In the second, a morning scene in which sunshine strikes the skyscrapers, Yves arrives in New York full of hope and desire to a city "which the people from heaven had made their home" to meet his lover, Eric, the city's emmisary, "with his short hair spinning and flaming about his head" (435–36). The generic and symbolic alterities of these incommensurable finales indicate the libidinal weighting toward the ethical erotics of male bodies in *Another Country* and suggest why these moments may be so discursively seductive for women. In their "desubjectivized" relation to Baldwin's utopian scenarios, women readers could have an out-of-body experience of the body, one that freed them from the sad, gendered historical body, freighted, weighted down with tragic messages.

In Baldwin's first two novels, *Giovanni's Room* and *Another Country*, which explicitly textualize homosexual relations as potentially redemptive as well as potentially tragic, the adult male couples in which redemption and tragedy are most centrally located are all what their culture designates as white. In the foreground of these two novels, cross-class, ethnic, and national differences, rather than black-and-white racial difference, represent the vital heterogeneity as well as the less positive divisions within same-sex male relations.[12] However, initiation into the homoerotic for Baldwin's white American males is often imagined through black lovers, although this difference may, as in the case of Joey, be only suggested; or, in the case of Vivaldo, be part of a dream in which desire for and identification with Rufus are conflated, a dream that precedes and enables his encounter with Eric.[13] For the Alabama-born Eric, recognition of his desire comes through Henry (the family's hired man) and experience through his older black friend LeRoy. In racial *and* sexual terms, African Americans come to symbolize "experience" and self-understanding set against the dangerous, self-imposed, and self-deluding "innocence" of whites. In a racially coded Eden, it is African American men and women who take up the structural position of Eve; it may be, then, that in terms of one (but only one) of Baldwin's interracial scriptings of homoerotic desire that the Adamic male figure is white.

The reasons for this and other related divisions of labor and figuration in his work may be at once elusive and overdetermined, part of Baldwin's careful negotiation of what got said about race and sexuality in the different genres of his writing. He rarely wrote about homosexuality in his nonfiction; those explored in this essay represent the few occasions when he did so. Yet this reticence represented complex and delicate tactical decisions made in the context of his overexposed image in these years of constant political advocacy and high public visibility. But they may be, as well, an ironic effect of the remarkable insights of his early proto-feminism, which he articulates without collapsing the ways in which abject subject positions are constructed in western culture: linking the hatred and subordination of women with the racism that ascribes inferiority to people of Africa and its diaspora, as well as to the homophobia that leads men to invent, abuse, and desire "faggots." Baldwin's most illuminating and uneasy early essay on homosexuality, first published in 1954 in *The New Leader* as "Gide as Husband and Homosexual" and suggestively retitled "The Male Prison," draws these themes together but in no way resolves them.[14] Late essays and interviews from the eighties, especially "Here Be Dragons" (1985) and "Go the Way Your Blood Beats" (1984), open out much more fully Baldwin's retrospective sense of his own history, but they too provoke as many questions as they answer. In his poignant memories of his "season in hell"—his teens and early twenties in Greenwich Village as seen from the vantage point of the mid-eighties—it is much clearer that Baldwin's wish "not to seem or sound like a woman" and his fear "that I already seemed and sounded too much like a woman" was at war both with his basic respect and liking for women and his ambivalent sexual interactions with white women in which "the fear of the world" unbearably "entered the bedroom" in the guise of their colonizing, vengeful or subordinating "motives"—"more than one white girl had already made me know that her color was more powerful than my dick."[15] In "Here Be Dragons," he says ironically of this period, "I don't think I felt absolutely, irredeemably grotesque—nothing that a friendly wave of the wand couldn't alter" (685). What, we might ask, would the wand have altered, and who, given its conscious or unconscious metonymic reference, would wield it? In this same essay, Baldwin strategically poses psychic androgyny as a radical alternative to American masculinity. Rephrasing an analysis embedded in his work from the fifties onward, he attacks America's "paralytically infantile . . . ideal of sexuality . . . rooted in the American ideal of masculinity," constructed as a series of regressive binaries within dominant masculinity "cowboys and Indians, good guys and bad guys, punks and studs, tough guys and softies, butch and faggot, black and white" (678). Yet this essay, like "The Male Prison" some thirty years earlier, largely accepts as fundamental another binary—that of sexual difference itself. The "grotesque," even the "absolutely, irredeemably grotesque," haunts Baldwin's work across three decades as the terrifying failure of that difference: its concatenation in a space where there are no "men." The fall into that category of the grotesque is "hell," and in "Here Be Dragons" this hell is narratively, syntagmatically linked with the painful inversions of power relations between two incommensurably subordinated groups, black men and white women, inversions that, like the blurring of boundaries and binaries in the grotesque, threaten masculinity.

Talking about sexuality, in his tense but revealing interview with Richard Goldstein in 1984,[16] Baldwin reiterated his discomfort with the word "gay," which "has always rubbed me the wrong way . . . 'homosexual' . . . didn't quite cover what it was I was beginning to feel." "Even when I began to realize things about myself, began to suspect who I was and what I was likely to become, it was still very personal, absolutely personal . . . a matter between me and my God." In his "early years in the Village . . . what I saw of that world absolutely frightened me" (174). Acknowledging a responsibility to stand as "witness" for the "phenomenon" we call "gay," he insisted that his contribution is "a public announcement that we're private, if you see what I mean" (175). What can be less private than the textualization of homosexuality in his fiction? The "homosexuality" of *Giovanni's Room*, Baldwin tells Goldstein, is "the vehicle through which the book moves," functioning in the same way as the church does in *Go Tell It On the Mountain*. "*Giovanni* is not really about homosexuality. It's about what happens to you if you're afraid to love anybody" (176).

Although he says he had to take what Goldstein terms the initial "risk" of writing about homosexuality in *Giovanni's Room,* "to clarify something for myself . . . [w]here I was in the world. I mean, what I'm made of" (176), the "risk" taken to make sense of a specific fear is quickly moved to the more general humanist plain of a fear of loving. In this interview too, Baldwin states very clearly the priority of race in the construction of difference and subordination. While he argues that "the sexual question and the racial question have always been entwined," (178) he goes on to say that a "black gay person who is a sexual conundrum to society is already, long before the question of sexuality comes into it, menaced and marked because he's black or she's black. The sexual question comes after the question of color" (180). This priority denotes a developmental temporality in the case of gay black men and women, a sequential staging of the experience of forms of degradation; for white gay men (and perhaps, for Baldwin, white women too) sexual degradation is the first and sometimes only such experience, preceded by an unacknowledged understanding of race as privilege. For while Baldwin thought it "very important for the male homosexual to recognize that he is a sexual target for other men, and that is why he is despised, and why he is called a faggot" (179), the level and quality of "complaint" that white gay men express contains, for Baldwin, an element of feeling cheated of the advantages that accrue to "white people" (180). His ongoing distaste for the homosexual subculture—"It's a hermetically sealed world with very unattractive features including racism"(180)—is given a rather tight-lipped, formal expression in the interview, but his sense of it as reproducing white privilege through its special pleading and its defensive enclosure underpins, at least in part, his reluctance to endorse a coalition politics of "blacks and gays," which he argues is "less than a firm foundation" for social movements that must be based on the "grounds of human dignity" and not on the inversion of the language of the oppressor (181). "Homosexual is not a noun. Not in my book. . . . Perhaps a verb" (181). The particularist and identitarian claims of the gay rights movement are, for Baldwin, almost a way of undermining its universal and transhistorical character—"Men will be sleeping with men when the trumpet sounds" (182).

"Men . . . sleeping with men" returns me to my opening quotation, "Negroes want to be treated like men," as each reinvokes its romantic shadow-text, Wordsworth's definition in the introduction to *Lyrical Ballads* of a modern democratic poetics as "a man speaking to men," and reproducing, if with a difference, the anxieties and hierarchical binaries hidden in its excluding equivalence. In Baldwin's argument with Goldstein, it is not really made clear why homosexuality must remain a poetics while race demands a politics, but it is clear that while men sleeping with men must be part of a revised masculinity, "a man is a man, a woman is a woman . . ."(183). This binary, as I have suggested, has a defining priority in Baldwin's work; it is, in a sense, what secures his more radical, psychological argument about construction.[17] In "The Male Prison," he refuses the debate about whether homosexuality is "natural" on two grounds. The first, an intellectual one, is that it explains very little: "I really do not see what difference the answer makes" (102). The other is ironic, strategic, and explains exactly what difference the answer makes: the answer "never can be Yes" for "it would rob the normal—who are simply the many—of their sense, perhaps, that the race is and should be devoted to outwitting oblivion" (102). A page or so later he tries and fails at a more a lyrical restatement of this bottom line: "It is one of the facts of life that there are two sexes, which fact has given the world most of its beauty, cost it not a little of its anguish, and contains the hope and glory of the world" (104). The first of these oblique formulations denaturalizes heterosexual relations; the second carefully naturalizes and celebrates difference without exactly celebrating relation. The "fact" of two sexes, then, not the primacy of their sexual relation, is what needs to be secured.

This "fact" is never fully interrogated by the kind of question that Baldwin insistently posed about the making of certain forms of subordinated, marginal, or outcast identities; "People invent categories in order to feel safe," he says in his 1973 dialogue with Nikki Giovanni. "White people invented black people to give white people identity. . . . Straight cats invent faggots so they can sleep with them without becoming faggots themselves."[18] But while he eloquently details the modes through which dominant American male culture exploits women by inventing for itself a crude hypermasculinity, and accepts with sorrow that black men are rarely all they could be to their women, Baldwin never argues that a projective paranoia quite leads men to invent women. To do so would be to follow a logic in which gender becomes as mutable as it is fictional, a logic that might point toward a route he early found a "horrible phenomenon of today's homosexuality," where the deviate must "save himself by the most tremendous exertion of all his forces from falling in to an underworld in which he never meets either men or women, where it is impossible to have a lover or a friend, where the possibility of genuine human involvement has altogether ceased."[19] This bleak passage spells out some of the "terror" of his early life in the Village, adumbrating the elaboration of the homosexual "underworld" in *Giovanni's Room*, the novel whose textualization of so many of the key terms I have been exploring helps to unlock the antitheses and contradictions in Baldwin's revision of what he somewhere calls that "kaleidescopic word, men."

It is the great strength of Baldwin's writing that he identifies and theorizes the palimpsestic relationship of racial and psychosexual narratives. Across his essays and fiction he develops an analysis in which dominant masculinity depends on the dramatic enactment and the repression of scenes of racial violence and transgressive desire. This double move, as he represents it, produces an oedipalizing narrative, at once a screen for and an expression of the way in which sexual identity is constructed through the defiles of cultural as well as gendered signification and fantasy.[20] More powerfully than any of his other fiction, *Giovanni's Room* attempts to make sense of the cultural and psychic fear at the heart of homophobia, a panic that Baldwin most productively situates within homosexual desire and, more problematically, in relation to an idealized homoerotic masculinity. The effect of this fear is implosive, shattering such masculinity at worst, "impeding its growth" at best. It cannot be wholly or accurately framed through the simpler paradigm that Baldwin also deploys of psychic projection or ideological invention—the cultural construction of "dragons." The more complex model of a "revolt within being" is something Baldwin does not have a name for but that Julia Kristeva has developed through the concept of "abjection" and that Judith Butler, Elizabeth Gross, Jacqueline Rose, and Iris Marion Young have appropriated and elaborated to interpret the making of sexed subjects.[21] The abject describes the necessary condition of an embodied subject, the incorporating and expelling activity of apertures defined by rims, and the dangers to that subject posed by this active corporeality, dangers made concrete as food, waste, and the signs of sexual difference. Gross's evocative reading of the abject suggests how closely allied Baldwin's discussions of its most vertiginous moment are. Her images are of the subject teetering "on the brink of this gaping abyss, which attracts (and also repulses) it. . . . This abyss is the locus of the subject's generation and the place of its potential obliteration, . . . it is the space inhabited by the death drive or its Hegelian equivalent, negativity."[22]

In *Giovanni's Room,* the phantasm of the "abyss" or the "cavern" (12) threatens David first when he glimpses the "power and the promise and the mystery" of that "beautiful creation," Joey's body (11). It is that brown body that is terrifyingly transformed into the "black opening of the cavern" (in this context evoking the anus and the racialized body) in which mind and manhood could be lost (12). Precisely at the moment where "cohesion and integration" of the self as homoerotic subject are revealed as a phantasmatic possibility, the fear of abjection acts as interdiction. Just when the male body seems most beautiful and complete and masculinity most sexually self-sufficient, it suddenly becomes most vulnerable to obliteration, the space of its apotheosis, also the space of death. The incident with Joey, superfically forgotten, lay "at the bottom of . . . [David's] . . . mind, still and awful as a decomposing corpse" (23). David comes by his murderous instincts genetically; tall and "blond haired," he tells us at the beginning that his "ancestors conquered a continent, pushing across death-laden plains, until they came to an ocean which faced away from Europe into a darker past" (3). The interracial component of his desire for a "boy" who is small and brown, and the subliminal racism and imperialism of his subsequent revulsion and abandonment of him, emphasize the boundaries and taboos crossed by homosexual desire by doubling its logistics.

The repudiation of Joey and all he represented is even more strongly governed by the strength and ambivalence of David's filial feelings, grounded in his recognition of his origins in the heterosexual couple. Just before his moment of terror, David remembers his father "who had no one in the world but me, my mother having died when I was little" (12). His possible guilt toward or fear of his living father is much less resonant here than the more archaic threat posed by an identification with the feminine. The dead mother and the "forgotten" incident with Joey are dreadfully merged as abject terrors of decomposition and helpless incorporation:

> I scarcely remember her at all, yet she figured in my nightmares, blind with worms, her hair as dry as metal and brittle as a twig, straining to press me against her body; that body so putrescent, so sickening soft, that it opened, as I clawed and cried, into a breach so enormous as to swallow me alive. (12–13)

If dead women represent an engulfing maternal femininity in which birth, played backward, swallows men alive, living females in *Giovanni's Room* are doubly threatening, equipped with a lethal orality and phallic props.[23] David's unmarried aunt Ellen is a thoroughly modern women, a relentless consumer who reads "all the new books" and goes to the "movies a great deal" (16–17). "Over-dressed, over made-up, with a face and figure beginning to harden, and with too much jewelry everywhere . . . she was always carrying a great bag full of dangerous looking knitting needles" (16–17). At parties

> she was, dressed, as they say, to kill, with her mouth redder than any blood . . . the cocktail glass in her hand threatening, at any instant, to be reduced to shards, to splinters, and that voice going on and on like a razor blade on glass. (17–18)

Too soft or too hard, women are morbidly or murderously excessive, their mouths their most effective weapons. By turns prurient and avid, too conservative and too modern, Ellen's "over-dressed," contradictory performance of the feminine is marked both by its violent ambitions and its lack of authenticity even as performance. Yet the rotting engulfing mother, all orifice, and the all-too-lively aunt, armed to the teeth, are themselves both aspects of a murderous maternality that represents a law that can, through its simulacra, operate from the grave. David's mother's "photograph, which stood all by itself on the mantelpiece, seemed to rule the room . . . her photograph proved how her spirit dominated that air and controlled us all" (18).[24]

A third female character, David's fiancée Hella, completes a ghastly trinity of women in *Giovanni's Room*.[25] Hella is, as her name suggests, a demonic reincarnation of Ellen, a desperate, possessive figure of feminine modernity. Like Ellen, only younger and prettier, Hella drinks and "watches men," simultaneously usurping male prerogatives and stifling their polymorphous sexuality with her neediness. It is not so much David per se that Hella needs as an unambiguous heterosexual masculinity that will let her "be a woman"—an idealized identity here represented from the woman's perspective, not as a sturdy and immutable "fact" of difference (as in "The Male Prison") but as an elusive, imaginary relationship.[26] In the absence of such confirmation, womanliness becomes an ugly masquerade, an embittered attitudinizing performance, all dress and make-up that convinces no one, least of all the performer. Before Hella leaves David, she first applies her lipstick then taunts him with an infantilizing and feminizing inversion of Freud's question to—and about—women:

> "Little girls want little boys. But little boys—!" She snapped her compact shut. "I'll never again as long as I live, know *what* they want." . . . [W]ith the lipstick, and in the heavy, black coat, she looked, again cold, brilliant, and bitterly helpless, a terrifying woman. (243)

Women *are* terrifying in *Giovanni's Room*. They are rendered vulnerable and vicious by a combination of unanswered need and their inscription as "modern" types: feminine parodies of privileged western masculinity: vocal, aggressive, and, in Hella's case, global adventurers. There are at least two curious things to be said about them. First, their appropriation of male prerogatives is coded as hyperfeminine—their orientation is always officially heterosexual; they may stand "in" for that "out" figure of female modernity that Baldwin cannot, for whatever reason, represent in his writing, the mannish lesbian.[27] Second, there is something both belated and secondhand about their vices and their representation, which evoke an earlier, interwar staging of modernist misogyny.[28] The most purely misogynist images in Baldwin's entire oeuvre, they constitute an attack that, in spite of its textual waivers which ascribe the hatred and fear of women to David's and even Giovanni's consciousness, is unrepeated in its cruelty and intensity in Baldwin's earlier and later fiction.[29] It is, however, only too congruent with the pervasive sexism of masculinist narrative in the postwar period. These women are, it should be remembered, almost exclusively white and bourgeois; their class status makes them easier targets. In *Giovanni's Room,* ethnic differences are present but soft-pedaled, incorporated into national distinctions.[30] The whiteness, privilege, and Americanness of Ellen, Hella, and Sue become conflated negative attributes of their gender.[31]

However, the terrifying spectrum of the feminine as the homosexual male's dystopian "future" extends well beyond David's nightmare about his dead mother and these crudely caricatured portraits of his aunt and fiancée. Both Giovanni and David use feminine homosexuality, encoded as "fairy," as a term of abuse for each other.[32] David's description of the men in the homosexual "underworld" of the Paris bar scene where he meets Giovanni evokes precisely the images of vulnerability, hardness, and danger associated with Ellen and Hella:

> The usual paunchy, bespectacled gentlemen with avid, sometimes despairing, eyes, the usual, knife-blade lean, tight-trousered boys . . . after money or blood or love . . . cadging cigarettes and drinks, with something behind their eyes at once terribly vulnerable and terribly hard.(38–39)[33]

Like the women whose desperation they share, these figures remain just within the terrain of the human, even within a flawed masculinity, a "redeemable" grotesque. They are only one rank above a much more frightening category, in Baldwin's declension of homosexualities, in which degraded elements of the feminine and animal are combined:

> There were of course, *les folles,* always dressed in the most improbable combinations, screaming like parrots the details of their latest love-affairs. . . . I always found it difficult to believe that they ever went to bed with anybody, for a man who wanted a woman would certainly have rather had a real one and a man who wanted a man would certainly not want one of *them*. (39)

In the repudiation of *"les folles"* as "barnyard" (39) figures so horribly hybrid as to be unidentifiable in David's native tongue, Baldwin's reversion to natural and conventionally cultural sexual difference as a basis for object choices (either hetero- or homosexual), together with his denial of the erotics of the grotesque or perverse, surfaces strongly. This rejection delivers, as an horrific final vignette, an image—one might think quite an ordinary and unfrightening image within the spectrum of perverse sexualities—of a transvestite boy who "came out at night wearing makeup and earrings and with his heavy blond hair piled high. Sometimes he actually wore a skirt and high heels" (39–40). Yet the "utter grotesqueness" of this figure produces a violent unease in David, "perhaps in the same way that the sight of monkeys eating their own excrement turns some people's stomachs. They might not mind so much if monkeys did not—so grotesquely—resemble human beings" (40). This analogy to a revulsion triggered by the disturbing indeterminacy of the binary between human and animal rests on the confusion between the anal and the oral functions as well as the grotesque resemblance between monkeys and humans. It calls up a tradition of racial tropes that mine this same psychic vein, especially those almost hallucinatory images conjured by the nineteenth-century liberal imagination. Compare, for example, Charles Kingsley's similar response to the degradation of the Irish, seen on a visit in 1860:

> But I am haunted by the human chimpanzees I saw along that hundred miles of horrible country. . . . [T]o see white chimpanzees is dreadful; if they were black, one would not feel it so much, but their skins, except where tanned by exposure, are as white as ours."[34]

It seems impossible that David's "instinctive" response to the young transvestite, is not, however obliquely, to be marked down to his imperial American imagination, one sign among many of his ethical unreliability as a narrator. In fact, neither his colonizing gaze nor his visceral response is ever disavowed. Read intertextually with Baldwin's essays, it is striking how close David's reflex of disgust, if divested of its racialized undertones, is to Baldwin's expressive distase for homosexual cultures. But the novel provides its own legible valorization of David's gut-level reaction to the subculture, for it is shared by the novel's eponymous hero and victim, Giovanni, whose final desperate act to escape his abject incorporation into it is to kill the bar owner, the "silly old queen" Guillaume (227). Guillaume's effeminacy is metonymically expressed by his love of silks, colors, and perfume; his "flabby" and "moist" body (227) that seems to "surround" Giovanni "like the sea itself" (228) reactivates the earlier nightmare image of the dead mother. Although David abandons and betrays Giovanni, giving him up to the inhumanities of the "underworld" that then provoke his murder of the feminized grotesque, in that assault David and Giovanni act as one, the peasant male performing the violence that the metropolitan subject can only voice.

How might we understand the function of the grotesque in *Giovanni's Room* as it condenses those culturally degraded figures—the feminine, the homosexual, the racial other—linked through their threatened abjection, their common failure to achieve physical, moral, or emotional integrity? Throughout the novel, the grotesque is associated with women's repeated performance of their own femininity as well as with men who deliberately or involuntarily enact the feminine or are placed in positions of powerlessness and humiliation.[35] On the other hand, the specular figure of the male transvestite who deliberately embraces the ascription "woman" represents the most abject and degraded category in the novel's spectrum of homosexualities, much more disturbing than the parodic "parroting" of the queens. Perhaps this is because Baldwin's representation of the male in drag who seriously attempts to impersonate femininity, whose performance, however pathetic, is generically intended as "real," is at best a stumbling block and at worst a graphic challenge to his theory that "faggots" are just an invention of straight men's fears and desires. Crystallizing a whole nexus of "half understood" fears and prejudices within, not just outside, the homoerotic imagination he/she disturbs the primordial order of men and women; a distinction—biological, social, and psychic—that, for Baldwin, secures the very fact of difference underwriting the possibility of an ideal, masculine, homosexual subject. These men, like David, Giovanni, and Eric, are all bisexual in practice. Their ability to desire and even love—as well as hate—women secures their identities as men and allows them to insist, as Baldwin does autobiographically, that their feeling about themselves and for men had "nothing to do with women." Within this psychic economy, the lesbian is rendered invisible, too terrible perhaps because, as the phallic mother, she is too intimately related to that archaic space where the child is captive to the engrossing body of the mother that has neither boundaries nor sexual distinction, and where generation and death are confused. The male transvestite evokes disgust rather than terror and is punished by being syntagmatically connected with monkeys, racial Others, and "real" women, who all become the sites of a cultural atavism.

Yet even within this passage the effort of the text to abject the feminine by punitively excluding it from the human as grotesque animal and excrement fails. The comparison between the distress induced by a man dressed as women and a monkey eating its shit is meant to bracket the grotesque but instead serves to link it to more generally prevalent sexual practices—here, perhaps, the taboo oral and anal preoccupations of male homoerotics. Placed as a strategic warning the moment before David meets Giovanni, the bar scene in general and the transvestite in particular attempt, nevertheless, to structure a binary between an idealized masculine and abject feminine homosexuality. This divide occurs within the male gay subculture—the setting, the occasion, after all, of David and Giovanni's romantic encounter—and, through their expressive, if doomed, refusal of it, is an attempt to cordon it off.

The final pages of the novel invoke, only in part ironically, fragments of biblical narrative. David, naked before his mirror that reflects his "lean, hard, and cold" (247) body, imagines in grim, gritty detail Giovanni's execution and death as, nevertheless, his long-sought gateway "out of this dirty world, this dirty body" (247)—Christ's martyrdom reworked. For David, the troubling question of becoming a man, a process impeded and accelerated by his "troubling sex" (247) for which he suffers Adam's expulsion and Cain's mark, is revealed and resolved as an act of faith, a determination thereafter to hold the "vile" flesh (and presumably its desires) sacred (248). But the elevation of the discourse and the simultaneous reassertion of the specular integrity of the fallen but redeemable male body and soul sublates, without resolving, the deeper, dirtier questions the novel has posed. For these, the grotesque serves as *leitmotif*, as the site of knowledge, as the source of terror, and as the limit point of Baldwin's courageous inquiry. Its troubling presence in this, his bleakest novel, makes *Giovanni's Room*, finally, a more resonant exploration of sexuality than those of his texts in which the utopian themes and scenarios are more prominent.

At the beginning of this essay I suggested the complexity of the appeal of Baldwin's writing on race and sexuality for women in the fifties and sixties—its opening out of the possibilities of pleasure, politics, and identifications; its collusion with a female terror and rejection of the feminine. Baldwin's multiple contexts and legacies cannot here be spelled out—though the gathering international body of work in many genres on race and sexuality, much of it by gay men and lesbians of color, continues the exploration of questions he made legible and thinkable.[36] I want to end, however, by placing Baldwin in apposition to, if not quite in dialogue with, philosopher and theorist Judith Butler, whose provocative work on sexuality touches at many points the issues that concerned Baldwin, not least the vexed question of the politics of homosexuality "identity." In "Phantasmatic Identification and the Assumption of Sex," Butler explores the "irrecoverable sense of *constitutedness and constraint*" (93) that marks our lived sexual identities, at once a political and psychic constraint (1).[37] She asks that constructivism begin to "take account of the domain of constraints" which includes along with "the radical unendurability of desiring otherwise, the absence of certain desires, the repetitive compulsion of others, the abiding repudiation of some sexual possibilities, panic, obsessional pull, repetition compulsion, and the nexus of sexuality and pain" (94). The relationship between such deep constraints, overdetermined at the social and psychic levels and the radical possibility of what Butler calls "resignification" is at the heart too of Baldwin's theoretical work on the axes of masculinity—and femininity—as they are crossed and recrossed by categories of race and of desire. *Giovanni's Room* gives certain of those constraints an agonistic narrative, disclaiming and unpacking some, enacting and confirming others, in a contradictory story of punishment and productivity, making what Butler describes as constitutive moves in the process of all identifications. More provocatively, she appropriates Lacan to suggest that

> Implicit in the figure of castration, which operates differentially to constitute the constraining force of gendered punishment, are at least two inarticulate figures of abject homosexuality, the feminized fag and the phallicized dyke . . . the terror over occupying either of these positions is what compels the assumption of a sexed position within language, a sexed position that is sexed by virtue of its heterosexual positioning, and that is assumed through a move that excludes and abjects gay and lesbian possibilities. (96)

Yet, asks Butler, complicating Lacan's too heterosexist paradigm, what happens when these sites of prohibition and taboo are themselves eroticized, when "primary prohibitions against incest produce displacements and substitutions which do not conform to the models" of heterosexual desire (98)? She answers this question in terms of the possibilities of refiguration, speculating hopefully about the multiple and cross-gendered possibilities of identification and desire, but registering at both the theoretical and pragmatic levels the exclusions, prohibitions, and taboos that structure the variety of transgressive as well as normative subjects.[38]

Baldwin's article "Here Be Dragons," cited earlier, which was first published as "Freaks and the American Ideal of Manhood" in *Playboy*, January 1985, was one of his last attempts to formulate his views on the intersections of sexuality, race, masculinity, and nationality; and, in doing so, to speak honestly to some of the issues raised by gay consciousness and activism. As in his *Esquire* article a quarter of a century earlier, he again sought to address that broad audience of presumed heterosexual male readers who most needed to hear his stinging critique of the "American ideal of masculinity." Toggling between contemporary reference and memoir, the article is full of good stuff—and stuffed with contradictions. Baldwin's rather static mobilization of androgyny, is, for example, at odds with the dynamism of his assertion that "all of the American categories of male and female, straight or not, black or white, were shattered, thank heaven very early in my life" (681). It begins boldly, however, with the question of the grotesque or the "freak," visually concretized as the "hermaphrodite" who represents in "intimidating exaggeration, the truth concerning every human being" (677). It ends with an observation that provides a gloss, a commentary, and a move beyond the unresolved questions adumbrated in his earlier writing on manhood and race, manhood and homosexuality, and that still linger in certain passages and corners of this late essay. Although the essay shifts gears a little clumsily, it nevertheless makes a definitive turn toward a new paradigm, one still formulated along the axes of the binary and set in the style of Baldwin's defiant, heroic notion of inclusive humanism. Yet in its decisive inclusion of the grotesque as the ineluctable condition of the normal (presented with Baldwin's characteristic insistence on historical and national mediation), it approaches from another route, and perhaps even arrives in advance at that mined field on which is staged our present debates on sexuality, debates in which his voice still echoes:

> Freaks are called freaks and are treated as they are treated—in the main, abominably—because they are human beings who cause to echo, deep within us, our most profound terrors and desires.
>
> Most of us, however, do not appear to be freaks—though we are rarely what we appear to be. We are, for the most part, visibly male or female, our social roles defined by our sexual equipment.
>
> But we are all androgynous, not only because we are all born of a woman impregnated by the seed of a man but because each of us, helplessly and forever, contains the other—male in female, female in male, white in black and black in white. We are a part of each other. Many of my countrymen appear to find this fact exceedingly inconvenient and even unfair, and so very often, do I. But none of us can do anything about it. (689–690)

Yet, the continuing project of trying to change that sense of unfairness in ourselves and in our culture remains an unfinished legacy of what was, for Baldwin, unfinishable business.

Notes

This essay grew out of a talk given in a panel on James Baldwin at the Gay and Lesbian Studies Conference held at Rutgers University in November 1991. I learned much from the other papers and the discussion that followed. Some of the essay's ideas were generated in a senior seminar I taught on James Baldwin in Spring 1991. I am grateful to all the students in that class for engaging with me on these complex and sometimes painful questions of race and sexuality. The essay has been strengthened in the course of its development by discussions with and suggestions from Marcellus Blount, Wesley Brown, Judith Butler, Cheryl Clarke, Ed Cohen, Marianne DeKoven, David Glover, Jaime Hovey, Bianca Nebab, and Jacqueline Rose. Thanks to these helpful interlocuters, and to Judith Butler and Cheryl Clarke for letting me use their unpublished chapters and articles, which are so central to my argument.

1. "Fifth Avenue, Uptown," in *The Price of the Ticket: Collected Nonfiction, 1948–1985* (New York: St. Martin's, 1985), 205–213. All references to this and other Baldwin essays are from this edition. Page numbers are included parenthetically in the text.
2. For a riveting discussion of Baldwin in the context of white and black representations of racialized masculinity, see Lynne Segal, "Competing Masculinities (III): Black Masculinity and the White Man's Black Man," in her excellent *Slow Motion: Changing Masculinities, Changing Men* (London: Virago, 1990), ch. 7. Segal calls Baldwin "one of the most powerful and persuasive male commentators on white American masculinity over the past three decades" (177).
3. James Baldwin, *Giovanni's Room* (New York: Dial, 1956). All subsequent page citations refer to this edition and are included parenthetically in the text.
4. A comparison, which would require another essay, needs to be made between Baldwin's and Frantz Fanon's crucial work on race, imperialism, and masculinity in both *The Wretched of the Earth* (New York: Grove, 1963) and *Black Skin, White Masks* (London: Pluto, 1986). More current work on this topic cites Fanon rather than Baldwin, perhaps because the question of sexual orientation can be elided. Fanon's arguments, however, form an interlocutary substructure to my own thinking, as does the work on colonialism and subjectivity by Homi Bhabha, who has, among other things, reinterpreted Fanon for this present conjuncture.
5. In a more upbeat scene of sexuality in *Another Country* (New York: Dial, 1962) between Vivaldo and Eric, Vivaldo as the passive partner "felt that he had stepped off a precipice into an air which held him inexorably up, as the salt sea holds the swimmer" (307). All subsequent page citations refer to this edition, and are included parenthetically in the text.
6. Toni Morrison, "Life in His Language," in *James Baldwin: the Legacy*, ed. Quincy Troupe (New York: Simon and Schuster, 1989), 76. Among those passions, Morrison includes "our sleek classical imagination" (76).

7. Cheryl Clarke, "Living the Texts Out: Lesbians and the Uses of Black Women's Traditions," in *Theorizing Black Feminisms: the visionary pragmatism of Black women*, ed. Stanlie James and Abena Busia (New York: Routledge, 1993).
8. Alison Hennigan, in "On Becoming a Lesbian Reader," in *Sweet Dreams: Sexuality, Gender and Popular Fiction*, ed. Susannah Radstone (London: Lawrence and Wishart, 1988), 189.
9. 1993 Conversation with Professor Marianne deKoven, my colleague in the Rutgers University English Department.
10. Constance Penley, "Feminism, Psychoanalysis and the Study of Popular Culture," in *Cultural Studies,* ed. Lawrence Grossberg, Cary Nelson, and Paula Treichler (New York: Routledge, 1991), 498. My citations are in fact from the "Discussion," 494–500, which appear (edited by the authors) after each article. Within Penley's essay itself, I would refer readers to her discussion of whether the "slash" versions of Star Trek intentionally portray Kirk and Spock as homosexuals. Her analysis of the socio-political reasons why this program, rather than other homosocial popular texts, were chosen for rewriting is also particularly relevant to my discussion of both Baldwin's work and women's identification with his writing.
11. Ibid., 498.
12. Baldwin often emphasizes the constructed and conjunctural nature of racial categories: "White people are not really white," from "Color," *Esquire*, December 1962; see also *The Price of the Ticket*, 319; and "Negroes do not strictly, or legally exist in any other [country]," from *The Fire Next Time*, (New York: Dial, 1963); Ibid., 342.
13. "Book Three: Towards Bethlehem," ch. 1, *Another Country,* 381–383.
14. This essay first appeared in *The New Leader*, December 13, 1954. Its title is changed when it is republished in *Nobody Knows My Name: More Notes of a Native Son* (New York: Dial, 1961), 155–162. Cited here from *The Price of the Ticket*, 101–105.
15. "Here Be Dragons," *The Price of the Ticket*, 685–86.
16. "'Go the Way Your Blood Beats': An Interview with James Baldwin," by Richard Goldstein, in *James Baldwin: The Legacy,* 173–85.
17. "For, no matter what demons drive them, men cannot live without women and women cannot live without men"; (see"The Male Prison," 104). At the very end of "The Male Prison," Baldwin points out that Gide's "prison" "is not very different from the prison inhabited by, say, the heroes of Micky Spillane. Neither can get through to women . . . [W]hen men can no longer love women they also cease to love or respect or trust each other, which makes their isolation complete" (105). Even in this last resonant observa-

tion, men's love of women is instrumentally figured as a route to their love of each other.

18. *James Baldwin/Nikki Giovanni: A Dialogue* (Philadelphia: Lipincott, 1973), 88–89.
19. "The Male Prison," 104.
20. Perhaps his most powerful narrative statement of this theme occurs in his extraordinary short story, "Going to Meet the Man," about the effects of watching a lynching, in James Baldwin, *Going to Meet the Man* (New York: Dial, 1965). For a very different but suggestive interpretation of the black male spectator's relation to racialized oedipal narrative, see Manthia Diawara, "Black Spectatorship: Problems of Identification and Resistance," *Screen* 29 (1) (Autumn 1988): 66–76. An important "collage" of "articles, images and arguments" by Kobena Mercer and Isaac Julien from the mid- to late eighties is gathered together in "Race, Sexual Politics and Black Masculinity: A Dossier," *Male Order: Unwrapping Masculinity*, ed. Rowena Chapman and Jonathan Rutherford (London: Lawrence and Wishart, 1988), 97–164.
21. See Julia Kristeva, *Powers of Horror: An Essay on Abjection*, trans. Leon S. Roudiez (New York: Columbia Univ. Press, 1982); Elizabeth Gross, "The Body of Signification," in *Abjection, Melancholia and Love: The Work of Julia Kristeva*, eds. John Fletcher and Andrew Benjamin (New York: Routledge, 1990), 80–103; Judith Butler, *Gender Trouble: Feminism and the Subversion of Identity* (New York: Routledge, 1990), especially ch. 4, "Subversive Bodily Acts"; Jacqueline Rose, *The Haunting of Sylvia Plath* (London: Virago, 1991); Iris Marion Young, *Justice and the Politics of Difference* (Princeton, NJ: Princeton Univ. Press, 1990).
22. Gross, "The Body of Signification," 89.
23. For an immensely suggestive discussion of the figure of the dead mother in men's writing and its relationship to race and sexuality, see Part 2, "Conrad and Others," in Marianne DeKoven, *Rich and Strange: Gender, History, Modernism* (Princeton, NJ: Princeton Univ. Press, 1991).
24. There are other important moments in Baldwin's work where women assume the patriarchal function. In *Go Tell It On the Mountain* (New York: Alfred A. Knopf, 1953), John comes under the sway of the woman minister; *The Amen Corner* (New York: Dial, 1968) focuses this theme, and *Just Above My Head* (New York: Dial, 1979) replays it through the figure of Julia. In each of these texts, female control is a site of ambiguity and ambivalence.
25. There is a fourth woman character in the novel, a rich blonde American, Sue, who David—in self-described cruelty and shame—uses to shore up his fears about his heterosexual adequacy. David describes her as "puffy," despairing, and desperate, "with the quality" if not the looks "of the girls who are selected each year to be Miss Rheingold" (139), who acts "like a broken down movie

queen facing the cruel cameras again after a long eclipse" (145). David finds her "disquietingly fluid" (144) as well as hard and constricted; his final image of her is as a ghastly, grotesque cameo of abjection: "She wore the strangest smile I had ever seen. It was pained and vindictive and humiliated but she inexpertly smeared across this grimace a bright girlish gaiety—as rigid as the skeleton beneath her flabby body" (149). Sue combines the softness and hardness, abjection and violence, to be feared in femininity.

26. In their final bitter exchange, Hella reiterates her view expressed throughout *Giovanni's Room* that the identity of women is entirely conditional on their relation to men. Without a man, Hella is "terrified that I'm *not* one" (185). She leaves David before she forgets "what its like to be a woman" (239).

27. Although we may recognize in them an adumbration of the construction of lesbian hyperfemininity in recent film texts like *Basic Instinct*, it is striking that even in the bar scene in *Giovanni's Room* the females are typed as heterosexual lookers-on, as "chic Parisian ladies" with "gigolos," "lovers," or their male "country cousins."

28. We might want to read Hella intertextually with figures like Brett Ashley in Hemingway's *The Sun Also Rises*.

29. Giovanni says of women, "Women are like water. They are tempting like that, and they can be that treacherous, and they can seem to be that bottomless, you know? and they can be that shallow. And that dirty. . . . I perhaps don't like women very much, that's true. That hasn't stopped me from making love to many and loving one or two. But most of the time—most of the time I made love only with the body" (116). Giovanni leaves his Italian "girl" "screaming in my mother's house" because they had made a baby "born dead . . . grey and twisted" (204).

30. A North/South, as well as an East/West, Europe/America divide operates in the novel, with David as a nordic type in contrast to Giovanni's peasant southerner. Giovanni is a poor southerner in relation to the Parisians, too. As well as rewriting in a different key the Jamesian texts of cultural/national alterity, Baldwin's contrasts evoke a shadow text of American North/South, black/white relations.

31. Trudier Harris in *Black Women in the Fiction of James Baldwin* (Knoxville: Univ. of Tennessee Press, 1985) argues persuasively for the conservatism and limitation in Baldwin's depiction of black women, while recognizing that his treatment of women is considerably less misogynist than that of many other African American male writers. This comparison also holds true for his white female characters; both Leona and Cass in *Another Country*, for example, are sympathetic figures.

32. When David meets Giovanni with Jacques after their final separation, he comments: "I could not endure something at once abject and vicious which I

began to see in his eyes, nor the way he giggled at Jacques' jokes, nor the mannerisms, a fairy's mannerisms, which he was beginning, sometimes, to affect" (216).

33. The novel with which *Giovanni's Room* seems most closely in dialogue in its address to masculinity, homosexuality, and subcultures is Radclyffe Hall's lesbian classic, *The Well of Lonliness* (New York: Covici, Friede, 1928). Both novels share an idealization of the masculine and distaste for homosexual subcultures, although Baldwin's text resists a biological paradigm of inversion. Hall introduces two African American figures in her novel in a brief and disturbing cameo in chapter 45 that sets the "animal" and "primitive force" (417) of "all slowly evolving races" (416) against the superior claims of the third sex. The bar scene in *Giovanni's Room* under discussion here needs to be read against and alongside chapter 48 of Hall's novel. See also Jonathan Dollimore's evocative discussion of these two scenes and their normative, essentialist assumptions in *Sexual Dissidence: Augustine to Wilde, Freud to Foucault* (Oxford: Oxford Univ. Press, 1991), 55–58.

34. *Charles Kingsley: His Letters and Memories of his Life*, edited by his Wife, Vol. 2 (London: 1891), 111–112. This often cited passage in which Kingsley denies that the impoverishment of the Irish is "our fault" is preceded by his exuberant masculine boast that he has "killed a real actual live salmon, over five pounds in weight" (111).

35. In David's final recoil from Hella he finds her underclothes "unaesthetic and unclean. A body which had to be covered with such crazy catty-cornered bits of stuff began to seem grotesque." This image immediately invokes engulfment and the mother. "I was fantastically intimidated by her breasts, and when I entered her I began to feel that I would never get out alive" (232). Giovanni is described by David as being "grotesquely playful" at one point in their final scene together, a reference that recalls Sue's behavior in a similar scene earlier in the novel.

36. A very truncated list of critics, writers, and filmmakers who have been crucial to the making of this analysis and debate would include Audre Lorde, Cheryl Clarke, Barbara Smith, Cherie Moraga, and Marlon Riggs in the United States; Isaac Julien, Kobena Mercer, Pratibha Parmar, Gail Lewis, and Carmen Williams from the black British diaspora; as well as the contributors to this present volume.

37. Judith Butler, "Phantasmatic Identification and the Assumption of Sex," in *Bodies That Matter: On the Discursive Limits of "Sex"* (New York: Routledge, 1993), 93–119.

38. In this essay, Butler makes two further points especially relevant to my argument. The first pertains to the question of priority in the marking of the body as sexed, in which she argues that "we can . . . never tell a story about how it

is that a body comes to be marked by the category of sex, for the body before the mark is constituted as signifiable only *through* the mark . . . any story we might tell about such a body making its way toward the marker of sex will be a fictional one, even if, perhaps, a necessary fiction" (98). I would argue that *Giovanni's Room* is Baldwin's "necessary fiction," borne out by his comment to Goldstein that "if I hadn't written that book I would probably have had to stop writing altogether"; ("'Go the Way Your Blood Beats'," 176). Butler's second point is that "it may be that we desire most strongly those individuals who reflect in a dense or saturated way the possibilities of multiple and simultaneous substitutions. . . . Insofar as a number of such fantasies can come to constitute and saturate a site of desire, it follows that we are not in the position of *either* identifying with a given sex *or* desiring somone else of that sex; indeed, we are not, more generally, in a position of finding identification and desire to be mutually exclusive phenomena." (99)

3

"AIN'T NOTHIN' LIKE THE REAL THING"

Black Masculinity, Gay Sexuality, and the Jargon of Authenticity

KENDALL THOMAS

Some years ago, I found myself sitting with hundreds of other people in the sanctuary of the Cathedral of St. John the Divine in New York City, just a few blocks away from where I live and work in Morningside Heights, on the other side of Harlem. We had gathered to remember and celebrate the life of James Baldwin, a writer whose novels, plays, and essays are a powerful record of his historical moment.

During the ceremony, a number of prominent African Americans from the literary world paid tribute to this man whose prophetic pen had given us such pain and pleasure. They all praised Baldwin as a son of Harlem who had faithfully borne witness to the suffering and struggle of his people. This, of course, was Jimmy the "bug-eyed griot" (in Amiri Baraka's words), the Baldwin of *Go Tell It on the Mountain*, *The Amen Corner,* and *The Fire Next Time*. Not one of these speakers mentioned the "other" Jimmy, the Baldwin of *Giovanni's Room*, *Another Country,* and *Just Above My Head*, whose stories I had read as a confused teenager in Oroville, California. As I sat in that cold, cavernous cathedral, the silence about this

Baldwin cut me to the core, because I knew that while Baldwin may have left America because he was black, he left Harlem, the place he called "home," because he was gay. It was this "other" Jimmy whose stories I had devoured by flashlight under the bedsheets, late at night when I was supposed to be asleep. This Jimmy knew that many held him in contempt as a "sexually dubious . . . unspeakably erratic freak."[1] It was in the words of this Jimmy and in "the heavy grace of God"[2] that I, like so many other confused teenagers, began to understand that those who called me "homo," "punk," or "sissy" did not really know my name. Reading Baldwin, I began to understand that I had another name. Somebody who lived somewhere in the south of France knew that name and had written with deep insight and beauty about the experience that this name so imperfectly expressed. As Baldwin put it in a late interview, he had felt a "special responsibility" to serve as "a kind of witness" to "that phenomenon we call gay."[3]

In the years since his death in 1987, Baldwin's testimony as a witness to gay experience has become the object of a certain revisionist impeachment. One (but by no means the only) representative instance of this tendency is a recent review by Ekwueme Michael Thelwell of James Campbell's *Talking at the Gates: A Life of James Baldwin*.[4] Thelwell launches a scathing attack on the Campbell biography by asserting that "certain writers—these days, mostly men and mostly white"—find James Baldwin "a source of unending mystery and provocation."[5] Thelwell contrasts the "challenge" that Baldwin poses for white readers with his reception among "most of us in the black world," for whom "Baldwin's life and career, though admittedly complex, are neither so ambigous nor so troubling. . ." (90). On Thelwell's account, *Talking at the Gates* belongs to a disturbing "new dispensation" in which "'major,' 'corrective' new biographies by white men" of figures like Frederick Douglass, Paul Robeson, Martin Luther King, Jr., and Malcolm X seek to "supplant the accounts of their lives left by the men themselves" (90). For Thelwell, the chief characteristic Campbell's life of Baldwin shares with other recent biographical work on these "luminaries of the Afro-American experience" is its "spirit" of "intellectual appropriation, an assertion of literary and conceptual proprietorship" (90–91).

Now, there is more than a little irony in all this, since Thelwell betrays the very spirit of appropriation and proprietorship that he finds so objectionable in *Talking at the Gates*. I refer here to Thelwell's treatment of

Baldwin's sexuality, to which the review first alludes in discussing the "virtues" of the Campbell biography. It is odd (to say the least) that the sole example Thelwell offers of the "thoughtful clarifications" for which *Talking at the Gates* should be commended is Campbell's observation that "Baldwin was essentially *androgynous* rather than homosexual" (my emphasis) (92). As one progresses through the essay, Thelwell's favorable assessment of this purported "clarification" of Baldwin's biography seems all the more curious. On the very next page of the review, Thelwell mentions the discomfort that Baldwin's "openly admitted sexual orientation" provoked among some of "the more 'established' Negro leaders" (93). The image of Baldwin as androgyne becomes even more perplexing when one comes to Thelwell's assertion (in the final paragraphs of his essay) that "slender, gay James Baldwin taught a generation of us how to be black men in this country, and he gave us a language in which to engage the struggle" (113). Needless to say, these two last remarks about Baldwin's sexuality sit uneasily with the earlier insistence on the writer's essential androgyny.

What is at stake here? One could argue that Thelwell has simply failed to say what he means. Perhaps he intends to argue that Baldwin was "essentially bisexual" rather than "essentially androgynous," and unwittingly confuses an expression for gender identity (androgyny) with a reference to sexual orientation (bisexuality). Indeed, this reading would comport with the known facts, at least of Baldwin's early erotic life. Unhappily, Thelwell's utter silence about the body of work Baldwin produced on homoerotic themes (about which Campbell himself has a great deal to say) leads the mind to a less comfortable conclusion. Taken together, Thelwell's equivocations about Baldwin's sexuality and his evident indifference to Baldwin's writings on the subject suggest that something more is involved here than linguistic mistake or conceptual confusion. Stated bluntly, Thelwell's vision of a "neutered" Baldwin betrays a deep and disturbing ideological investment regarding the connections among masculinity, sexuality, and "authentic" black identity.

How is this claim to be understood? The beginnings of an answer to this question will take us to the dictionary. "Androgyne" is a compound noun that consists of the Greek words (respectively) for man and woman. In its "positive" meaning, the word refers to an individual who embodies "a mixing of secondary masculine and feminine sexual characteristics";[6] in its "negative" sense, the word refers to someone who is neither a man *nor* a woman. Moreover, the term "androgyny" has historically been the semantic site of a vertiginous slippage. As Francette Pacteau has noted, the "sexually ambiguous" figure of the androgyne simultaneously possesses a "dual sexual identity" *and* a "non-sexual identity."[7]

Both of these "impossible referents"[8] appear to be at work in the Thelwell review, and they suggest two different, but equally disturbing, understandings of the "androgyny" thesis. To interpret Thelwell's remark as a claim that Baldwin possessed a "dual sexual identity" is to view it as making an underlying, unstated argument about masculinity and male homosexuality. One might infer from Thelwell's remarks that he takes gay identity to be at odds with the very idea of masculinity. In this conception, which has a long pedigree, the male homosexual may be said to possess "a woman's soul confined by a man's body."[9] Ascribing an ambiguous "dual" sexual identity to Baldwin allows Thelwell to confer a degree of masculinity on the writer to which a homosexual (read "enfeminized") man cannot, by definition, lay claim. Needless to say, this understanding of the relationship between masculine identity and gay male sexuality betrays a very narrow vision of both.

A second possible reading of the "androgyny" thesis would take Thelwell's remark as a claim that Baldwin was not "bisexual" but "asexual" in personality and practice. The implicit assumption here appears to be that sexual identity can be read off from sexual activity. According to this logic, if we want to know who Baldwin was (sexually speaking), we need only to know what (sexually speaking) he did or did not do. Presumably, we are to conclude that because Baldwin did not lead an active sexual life (a fantastication that does not square with the known facts), he could not have been homosexual.[10]

This latter interpretation is even more distressing than the first, since it does not merely introduce an element of ambiguity regarding Baldwin's erotic affinities, it excludes them altogether. For better or worse, we live in a world in which individual identities are forged in and through constructs of gendered sexual difference. The very notion of human subjectivity has come to rest on the fictional foundation of a stable, unified sexuality in which we are all inserted at birth. To say in such a world that someone is androgynous in this second, neutered sense is in effect to deny that s/he exists: the androgyne has no sexual identity, which means that s/he has no identity at all. Nobody can know the androgyne's name, because there is no name by which s/he can be called.

In any event, I am less interested here in what the "androgyny" thesis *means* than in what it *does*. As I have already noted, Thelwell begins his essay by arguing that "most of us in the black world" do not find Baldwin's "admittedly complex" life and literary legacy "ambiguous" or "troubling." Nevertheless, it is clear that Thelwell's review may be read as a brief defending Baldwin's place in the patriarchal pantheon of "luminaries of the Afro-American experience" (the names of black women are tellingly absent from this list). While "most of us in the black world" may not doubt the significance of James Baldwin's contributions to the struggle against white racism in America (indeed, the world), some of "us" do: one can point to any number of African Americans for whom Baldwin's sexuality raises an irrebuttable presumption against his inclusion in the annals of black American freedom fighters. Seen in this light, Thelwell's characterization of Baldwin's sexuality serves as a preemptive identificatory strike. Thelwell is surely aware of the ugly homophobic history of Baldwin's reception in certain quarters of black America. Sadly, his defensive insistence that Baldwin was "essentially androgynous" betrays the degree to which the writer's sexuality poses an evidentiary embarrassment for Thelwell himself. In making the case that Baldwin "almost single-handedly elevated the terms of our discourse on race" (113), Thelwell cannot resist the felt but false necessity to discount, indeed to deny, the sexual dimensions of Baldwin's life. In doing so, Thelwell's essay reveals the depths of its dependence on the homophobic rule of racial recognition, to which his defense of the "androgynous" Baldwin is meant to provide a response. I refer here to the heteronormative logic that conditions the ascription of "authentic" black identity on the repudiation of gay or lesbian identity. The jargon of racial authenticity insists, as the gangsta-rapper Ice Cube has put it, that "true niggers ain't gay."[11]

Whatever its motivation, Thelwell's awkward answer to those who would "deracinate" Baldwin and reduce the writer to his sexuality is to "desexualize" Baldwin and reduce him to his race. To be sure, these two equally misguided moves are impelled by very different purposes: where Baldwin's detractors magnify his sexuality in order to renounce him, Thelwell minimizes Baldwin's sexuality in order to redeem him. Ultimately, however, this is a distinction without a difference. For in the final instance, the Thelwell essay stands as yet another example of the symbolic violence that has been inflicted on the name of James Baldwin even by black intellectuals who count themselves among the writer's most passionate proponents. The disingenuous disavowal of Baldwin's sexuality implicit in the contention that he was "essentially androgynous" not only deforms the facts of Baldwin's life but dismembers the man himself. Thelwell manages to maneuver his way around the question of Baldwin's sexuality, but only to engage in the very "mythmaking, denial and distortion" (93) of which he accuses others. To paraphrase Thelwell, there is a "spirit" of "appropriation" and "proprietorship" behind the confident claim that, sexually speaking, James Baldwin was "essentially" not who and what he himself said he was: a man who slept with other men. Baldwin once remarked of his early years, "I did not have any human identity."[12] In divesting the writer's biography of its homoerotic substance, Thelwell dishonors the memory of Baldwin's struggle to resolve what for a time was "the most tormenting thing"[13] in his life: the recognition, as Baldwin put it in his diary, that "I am a homosexual."[14] Seen in this light, Thelwell's "redemption" of Baldwin's name exacts too brutally high a price.

I do not wish my own interest in the case of James Baldwin to be misunderstood. Despite his willingness to talk and write publicly about his sexuality, Baldwin held that, for him, "one's sexual preference is a private matter."[15] Indeed, reading Baldwin's public pronouncements on the subject of sexuality, one cannot help but be struck by their ambivalence. In this respect, Baldwin falls short of the achievement of his fellow writer Audre Lorde, whose contemporaneous reflections on gay and lesbian sexualities not only reveal an intellectual rigor but an uncompromising existential self-assurance regarding the "right and responsibility" of black women "to love where we choose."[16] In the one interview in which he treated the question of gay and lesbian sexualities at some length, Baldwin insisted that his own erotic life "had nothing to do with these labels."[17] For Baldwin, the difficulty with the term "gay" was that it "answers a false argument, a false accusation" "Which is that you have no right to be here, that you have to prove your right to be here. I'm saying I have nothing to prove. The world also belongs to me."[18] Moreover, Baldwin's own experience persuaded him that "homosexual" was not a "noun" but a "verb": "I loved a few people and they loved me."[19]

Finally, Baldwin once stated that for black gay men and lesbians, "the sexual question comes *after* the question of color: it's simply one more aspect of the danger in which all black people live."[20] "A black person who is a sexual conundrum to society is already, long before the question of sexuality comes into it, menaced and marked because he's black or she's black."[21] At the same time, however, Baldwin remained emphatic about the indivisibility in his life and work of race, on the one hand, and of sexuality, on the other: "The sexual question and the racial question have always been entwined, you know."[22] Baldwin refused to say that his sexuality had been "the most important part" of what he was about. "But," he added, "it's indispensable."[23]

My point is this. While I agree with Thelwell that James Baldwin "taught a generation of us how to be black men in this country, and he gave us a language in which to engage the struggle" (113), that was not Baldwin's only lesson. For all its ambivalence, the example of "slender, gay" (113) James Baldwin taught some of "us" one way to be *gay* men in, and of, black America. The life and work of James Baldwin give the lie to the notion that black and gay identity are hostile to one another at all points. They show, too, that while "it is difficult to be despised,"[24] black gay men and lesbians must resist the demand (heard in some quarters) that we choose between these two sources of the self and commit a kind of psychic suicide. Baldwin provides us with an exemplary instance of a gay black man who refused to make this forced, false, and ultimately fatal choice. We find in James Baldwin an often equivocal, but always articulate, response to the call that gay and lesbian African Americans who want to prove that they are "really" black must renounce their sexuality: "I'm saying I have nothing to prove."

The jargon of racial authenticity is alive and well in African American sexual politics. Indeed, recent events suggest that this jargon has gained new force. My project here is to challenge the terms of this jargon and to indicate the direction a critical account of the jargon might take. I believe that the jargon of racial authenticity has had debilitating consequences for black American sexual politics. My hypothesis, in brief, is that the homophobia and virulent masculinism that underwrite the politics of racial authenticity in the current conjuncture are best understood as the displaced expression of internalized racism, which is in turn a symptom of a sexual alienation among black Americans of epidemic proportions. Drawing on the lessons of Baldwin and one of his most articulate gay cultural descendants, I conclude that one of the most urgent tasks of gay and lesbian African Americans is to demand the inclusion of black sexual freedom on the antiracist agenda.

My point of entry is a moment from *Tongues Untied,*[25] a remarkable video work by the late gay black artist and activist Marlon Riggs. In one of the most powerful segments of the video, Riggs offers an extended meditation on the vexed relation between race and sexuality in black gay experience. At one point in the narrative, a black nationalist remarks:

> They say, we're all on the same political boat. We should be brothers. But before I accept his kinship, political or otherwise, this is what I want to know. Where does his loyalty lie? . . . Priorities, that's what I want to know. Come the final throwdown, what is he first, black or gay?"[26]

Riggs responds to this set of questions with another, which are framed in terms that warrant some analysis: "How do you choose one eye over another, this half of the brain over that? Or in words this brother might understand, which does he value most, his left nut or his right?"[27]

Now, the most striking feature of this rejoinder to what Riggs calls the "absurdity" of the black nationalist demand for a statement of "priorities" lies in its metaphorical register. Riggs rightly takes this question of the politics of black identity all the way down to body. Identity is thus quite literally *refigured*. The narrative of *Tongues Untied* shifts the terms of the debate over black identity to the flesh-and-blood bodies on which racial (and other) identities are inscribed. Riggs substitutes a materialist "language of the body" which exposes the poverty of the abstract, etiolated language of black loyalty that all too many nationalist ideologues have used to mask their indifference and even contempt for real, actually existing black lives. *Tongues Untied* draws on the embodied experience of gay black men to insist that any serious discussion of the question of African American identity politics must come to grips with the ways in which "identity is fundamentally about desire and death."[28] The exchange in *Tongues Untied* may thus be read as an instance of a position to which Cornel West has recently given theoretical formulation. As West so forcefully puts it:

> How you construct your identity is predicated on how you construct desire and how you conceive of death: desire for recognition; quest for visibility (Baldwin—*No Name in the Street; Nobody Knows My Name*); the sense of being acknowledged; a deep desire for asso-

> ciation—what Edward Said would call affiliation. . . . But identity also has to do with death. We can't talk about identity without talking about death. That's what [a gay Puerto Rican] brother named Julio Rivera had to come to terms with: the fact that his identity had been constructed in such a way that xenophobes would put him to death. Or brother Youssef Hawkins in Bensonhurst. Or brother Yankel Rosenbaum in Crown Heights. Persons who construct their identities and desires often do it in such a way that they're willing to die for it—soldiers in the Middle East, for example—or under a national identity, that they're willing to kill others. And the rampant sexual violence in the lives of thousands of women who are attacked by men caught up in vicious patriarchal identities—this speaks to what we're talking about.[29]

This reworking of the terms of the identity debate from questions of ideology and consciousness to material matters of bodies, life, and death is an important one because it clears the ground for fuller consideration of issues that have been submerged by both the jargon of racial authenticity and its antiessentialist critique. As the quoted passage from the Cornel West essay suggests, chief among these is the problem of violence and the bodies of those who are its targets. As I have argued elsewhere, violence is a continuing thread of both gay/lesbian and African American experience in this country.[30] Gay and lesbian Americans of all colors and African Americans of every sexual orientation live with and under the knowledge that at any time, anywhere, we might be attacked for being gay or lesbian or bisexual, for being black, or for being both. Indeed, in the United States, the historical roots of the consistent conjunction of homophobic and racist violence are older than the nation itself. To take one only example, the 1646 Calendar of Dutch Historical Manuscripts reports the trial, conviction, and sentence on Manhattan Island, New Netherland Colony, of one Jan Creoli, "a negro, [for] sodomy; second offense; this crime being condemned of God (Gen., c. 19; Levit., c. 18:22, 29) as an abomination, the prisoner is sentenced to be conveyed to the place of public execution, and there choked to death, and then burnt to ashes."[31] On the same date the Calendar records the punishment meted out to "Manuel Congo . . . on whom the above abominable crime was committed," who was "to be carried to the place where Creoli is to be executed, tied to a stake, and faggots piled around him, for just sake, and to be flogged; sentence executed."[32]

What this common history means in political terms, I think, is that we simply cannot afford an identity politics that fails to take account of our shared, and vulnerable, embodiedness or of our shared interest in the dignity of human life. This is not to suggest that we should uncritically embrace the liberal precept that our similarities outweigh our differences and take up a mushy, ahistorical universalism. What I do want to endorse, rather, is a notion of identity politics that attends to the corporal hierarchy Iris Young has called the "scaling of bodies."[33] Black Americans and gay and lesbian Americans have historically been on the bottom of this scale, albeit for different reasons. (A comparison might be made here between the situation of black Americans in the military during World War II and that of gay and lesbian Americans today. The exclusion of the two groups from full participation in the armed forces was defended for different reasons; in both cases, it was equally effective.)

I've focused thus far on what the perspectival shift from a notion of identity based on authentic sensibility to one based on endangered embodiedness might mean for the collective self-image of African Americans generally and for their relationship to black gays and lesbians in particular. I want now to say a word about what I believe some of the concrete implications of this reworked notion of identity might be for coalitional interventions between the movements against racism and homophobia. I will take my example from the political controversy surrounding the airing of *Tongues Untied*. *Tongues*, produced for broadcast as part of the *P.O.V.* series of the Public Broadcasting System (PBS), was the subject of at least two ugly episodes. First, some twenty of the fifty PBS stations in the nation's largest markets flatly refused to air the work, and the Federal Communications Commission received a number of formal complaints filed by conservative media advocacy groups. Second, *Tongues Untied* became a flashpoint of contention when Pat Buchanan produced campaign commercials in his bid for the Republican presidential nomination that prominently featured images from the video depicting men dancing semiclothed. Shortly thereafter, legislation was introduced to abolish the National Endowment for the Arts (NEA), which had supported the production of the video. Buchanan's charge that George Bush's NEA had "glorified homosexuality" also figured in the then President's decision to fire John Frohnmayer, head of the NEA.[34]

During the ideological skirmishes for which *Tongues Untied* served as a site of intersection, the African American community remained largely silent. This silence stood in striking contrast to the charges of racism leveled by many African Americans when a series of prosecutions was initiated against the black rap group 2 Live Crew and individuals who marketed their album *As Nasty as they Want to Be* because of its graphic sexual nature.[35] In that case, the misogynistic lyrics of 2 Live Crew, which spoke of mutilating the bodies of black women, were defended in scholarly analyses as the work of "literary geniuses" whose contributions placed them squarely in the signifying traditions of black culture.

No such cultural defenses were forthcoming for Marlon Riggs, whose *Tongues Untied* had offered a trenchant critique of the violence directed against black bodies. That silence, I submit, may be laid to the fact that Riggs's critique of racist violence was pitched in the language and style of gay black male culture. Similarly, few black voices were raised during the recent campaign against a song by the reggae rapper Buju Banton, whose "Boom Bye Bye" warns "Faggots to run/Or get a bullet in the head":

> Homeboys don't condone nasty men
> They must die
> Two men necking
> Lying in a bed
> Hugging each other
> And caressing one another's legs
> Get an automatic or an Uzi instead
> Shoot them now, let us shoot them.[36]

Now, I would like to think that the perspective toward identity politics that I have offered here might well have led to a political engagement with the issues raised by these episodes, not around some notion of a pregiven, authentic black sensibility but around a common interest in black survival, or more broadly, in the dignity of black life.

To understand that antiracist and antihomophobic politics are informed by a common corporeal interest in survival is to create the possibility of coalition across difference. But that is not all. This conception of politics as the struggle for the dignity of physical existence rather than the expression of authentic, unitary sensibility permits us to see the degree to which racial identity itself must be understood as a process and product of coalition, as Kimberlé Crenshaw has recently argued.[37] The politics of racial authenticity obscure the inflection of, and antagonisms *within*, racial identity produced by differences of ethnicity, class, gender, religion, sexuality, and the like. Indeed, the politics of a pure racial identity occlude an apprehension of the extent to which race is "lived in the modality"[38] of sexuality and *vice versa*: sexuality is always "racialized" and race is always "sexuated." In this respect, the chief lesson I draw from recent work on the construction of racial and sexual identities is that the two depend on one another for their force and form. The search for independent, autonomous racial or sexual identities is fundamentally misguided because, to borrow from Nick Ashford and Valerie Simpson, "Ain't nothin' like the real thing." In their refusal to entertain the impossibility of a pure racial identity, then, the ideologists of black masculinism (not all of whom are men) demonstrate nothing so much as the depths of their own racial and sexual alienation in the signifiers of authenticity. In the retreat to a heterosexist conception of black identity, the jargon of racial authenticity does not repudiate but instead relies on the very racism from which it purports to declare its independence, which it merely transposes into a darker, homophobic key. In this respect, the heteronormative vision of racial identity that would exclude the expression of sexual difference among African Americans does not exorcise but rather incorporates the ideology of white supremacy into the very body of black America, and with it, the phobic conceptions of black sexuality *as such* that white supremacy has always insinuated.

Finally, the jargon of racial authenticity forcecloses a recognition that what Benedict Anderson has recently said of the notion of a "nation" holds true as well for the unitary conception of a "race." That is, it blinds us to the fact that membership in a race, like membership in a national community, is "imagined." Most African Americans "will never know most of their fellow-members, meet them, or even hear of them, yet in the minds of each lives the image of their communion."[39] This is most emphatically not to say that the invented racial subject comes into being in conditions of its own making. One would be remiss not to point out the institutional and ideological imperatives by which the notion of a racial community takes one form rather than another. It is to suggest that the authentically black self is in significant measure what William Connolly has called a "branded" or "entrenched" contingency.[40]

What this means, I think, is that our notions of collective racial identity must, as a political matter, be viewed historically and, what is more, strategically. In short, the racial reasoning that holds out the promise of liberation at one moment may become perilous to our survival down the road. Notions of black authenticity that once served as an indispensable tool at one historical moment in struggle have now become unwitting traps. Gay and lesbian African Americans have borne the heavy costs that the rigid adherence to outmoded notions of black identity has inflicted. The exclusion of black gay men and lesbians from full, equal participation in African American life has provided an epistemological standpoint for political analysis and intervention in what I have already called a matter of life and death. We know that the obsessive preoccupation with proof of racial authenticity deflects attention and energy away from the need to come to grips with the real, material problems in whose resolution black Americans of both genders and all sexual identifications have an immediate and urgent interest. In the spirit of James Baldwin, black gay men and lesbians must argue clearly and consistently that the burden of proof should be shifted onto those who instituted the jargon of authenticity to show its continued relevance in the "The Age of Crack"[41] and Uzis and AIDS. Baldwin wrote in *Notes of a Native Son* that because he loved America "more than any other country in the world," he insisted on the right "to criticize her perpetually."[42] Our love for black America demands no less.

Notes

1. James Baldwin, *No Name in the Street* (New York: Dell, 1972), 18.
2. James Baldwin, *Giovanni's Room* (New York: Dell, 1956), 223.
3. Richard Goldstein, "'Go the Way Your Blood Beats': An Interview with James Baldwin," reprinted in *Lesbians, Gay Men and the Law*, ed. William B. Rubenstein (New York: New Press, 1993), 41.
4. James Campbell, *Talking at the Gates: A Life of James Baldwin* (New York: Penguin, 1991).
5. Ekwueme Michael Thelwell, "A Profit Is Not Without Honor," *Transition* 58 (1992): 90. All subsequent citations will appear in the text.
6. Francette Pacteau, "The Impossible Referent: Representations of the Androgyne," in *Formations of Fantasy*, ed. Victor Burgin, James Donald, and Cora Kaplan (New York: Methuen, 1986), 62.
7. Ibid.

8. Ibid.
9. David Halperin, *One Hundred Years of Homosexuality and Other Essays on Greek Love* (New York: Routledge, 1990), 23.
10. Or, presumably, heterosexual. It bears remarking that the terms of the opposition Thelwell draws explicitly ignore this logical entailment.
11. O'Shea Jackson (Ice Cube), "Horny Lil' Devil," *Death Certificate* (Priority Records, Inc. 1991).
12. James Campbell, *Talking at the Gates*, 3.
13. Richard Goldstein, "'Go the Way Your Blood Beats'," 42.
14. James Campbell, *Talking at the Gates*, 33. Although Thelwell does not cite it, the one possible textual warrant for his insistence that Baldwin was "androgynous" is the late essay "Here Be Dragons," which originally appeared in *Playboy* under the title "Freaks and the American Ideal of Manhood." (James Baldwin, "Here Be Dragons," in *The Price of the Ticket* [New York: St. Martin's/ Marek, 1985].) Baldwin argues in this essay that "we are all androgynous, not only because we are all born of a woman impregnated by the seed of a man but because each of us, helplessly and forever, contains the other—male in female, female in male. . . ." (Ibid., 690.) Throughout the article, however, Baldwin takes care not to conflate claims regarding gender politics with those about sexual identity and practice. This much is clear from the fact that, alongside the claim that androgyny is a generalized figure of the human condition, "Here Be Dragons" is replete with quite specific references by Baldwin to his sexual experiences with other men and to "how I found myself in the gay world." (Ibid., 686.)
15. Goldstein, "'Go the Way Your Blood Beats'," 44.
16. Audre Lorde, "Scratching the Surface: Some Notes on Barriers to Women and Loving," originally published in *The Black Scholar*, 9 (7) (1978), reprinted in *Sister Outsider: Essays and Speeches* (Freedom, CA: Crossing, 1984), 52.
17. Richard Goldstein, "'Go the Way Your Blood Beats'," 44.
18. Ibid., 45.
19. Ibid., 44.
20. Ibid., 42.
21. Ibid. As these remarks suggest, Baldwin's argument has to do with the chronology of black gay and lesbian experience not the priority of black or gay lesbian identity.
22. Ibid.
23. Ibid., 41.
24. Ibid., 44.
25. *Tongues Untied,* prod. and dir. by Marlon Riggs, 55 min., color, 1985, videocassette.

26. Ibid.
27. Ibid.
28. Cornel West, "Identity: A Matter of Life and Death," in *Prophetic Reflections: Notes on Race and Power in America* (Monroe, MA: Common Courage Press, 1993), 163.
29. Ibid., 163–164.
30. See my "Beyond the Privacy Principle," *Columbia Law Review*, 92 (6) (October 1992): 1431–1516.
31. Jonathan Ned Katz, *Gay American History: Lesbians and Gay Men in the U.S.A.*, (New York: Harper & Row, 1976), 22–23.
32. Ibid., 23. What is more, for reasons that I cannot delineate in detail here, it seems fairly clear that both homophobic violence and racist violence have a distinctly erotic component. (I might note parenthetically that if you are a black gay man or lesbian, you know, too, that this eroticized violence might come from the hands of someone who looks like your father, uncle, or brother.)
33. Iris Marion Young, *Justice and the Politics of Difference* (Princeton, NJ: Princeton Univ. Press, 1990), 122.
34. A useful documentary history of the recounted episodes may be found in Richard Bolton, ed., *Culture Wars: Documents from the Recent Controversies in the Arts* (New York: New Press, 1992).
35. In June 1990, lyrics in 2 Live Crew songs about sodomy and sexual intercourse were adjudged obscene by a federal district court. *Skywalker Records, Inc.* v. *Navarro*, 739 F. Supp. 578, 596 (S.D. Fla 1990). A federal circuit court of appeals reversed this conviction in *Luke Records, Inc.* v. *Navarro*, 960 F.2d 134 (11th Cir. 1992).
36. From the album *Boom, Bye, Bye.* Produced by Clifton "Specialist" Dillon and Bobby "Digital" Dixon. Distributed by VP Records (Jamaica Queens, NY), 1992.
37. Kimberlé Williams Crenshaw, "Mapping the Margins: Intersectionality, Identity Politics, and Violence Against Women of Color," in *Stanford Law Review*, vol 43, no. 6 (1991), 1299.
38. Judith Butler, *Bodies That Matter: On the Discursive Limits of "Sex"* (New York: Routledge, 1993), 117.
39. Benedict Anderson, *Imagined Communities: Reflections on the Origin and Spread of Nationalism* (New York: Verso, 1983), 15.
40. William E. Connolly, *Identity/Difference: Democratic Negotiations of Political Paradox* (Ithaca: Cornell Univ. Press, 1991), 176.
41. Eugene Rivers, "On the Responsibility of Intellectuals in the Age of Crack," *Boston Review* 3 (Sept./Oct. 1992): 3–4.
42. James Baldwin, *Notes of a Native Son* (Boston: Beacon, 1984), 9.

NEGOTIATING “MASCULINITY”

4

VIOLENT AMBIGUITY

Martin Delany, Bourgeois Sadomasochism, and the Production of a Black National Masculinity

ROBERT REID-PHARR

> In the mythology of the modern world, the quintessential protagonist is the bourgeois, Hero for some, villain for others, the inspiration or lure for most, he has been the shaper of the present, the destroyer of the past.
>
> —Immanuel Wallerstein[1]

> Sadomasochism is fueled and motivated by a restless desire to somehow, in some way, procure recognition from the other.
>
> —Lynn Chancer[2]

Martin Delany, a man widely thought of as the father of black nationalism, was heralded by contemporary scholars as one of the most articulate and radical black intellectuals of the nineteenth century, and indeed it seems that the facts do support many of their claims. He made speeches on African civilization dressed in "traditional" African clothing, bragged about his pure African ancestry, and reveled in the blackness of his skin. Very little is made of the fact, however, that Delany often derided African Americans for *allowing* themselves to be exploited by whites. Moreover, no one seems to be able to really explain his obvious gestures toward integration in later life, namely his commission in the Union army and his support for the Democratic Party in Reconstruction South Carolina, a fact for which he was derided by the very freedpeople whom he purported to represent.[3] Most importantly, there has been almost no discussion of the fact that Delany, in the face of an economic system in which (black) human life was turned into capital, actively sought to recreate African Americans in the image of the bourgeois subjects who were arguably responsible for the construction and maintenance of the system of slavery he found so onerous.[4]

The terms of Delany's political economy are altogether different from what one might expect from a "radical" nationalist. On the one hand, his major treatise, *The Condition, Elevation, Emigration, and Destiny of the Colored People of the United States*, is an amazingly bold indictment of American slavery and racism, offering a quite compelling argument for black emigration. On the other hand, the "black" people whom Delany exhorts to leave the nation are not the totality of persons of African descent living within the United States, but a discrete minority: free blacks, particularly free blacks of the Northeast. Throughout the text Delany makes a clear distinction between "blacks" and slaves:

> the bondman is disfranchised, and for the most part so are we. He is denied all civil, religious, and social privileges . . . and so are we. They [the bondmen] have no part nor lot in the government of the country, neither have we. They are ruled and governed without representation, existing as mere nonentities among the citizens, and excrescences on the body politic—a mere dreg in community, and so are we. Where then is our political superiority to the enslaved? none, neither are we superior in any other relation to society, *except that we are defacto masters of ourselves and joint rulers of our own domestic household, while the bondman's self is claimed by another, and his relation to his family denied him.* (my emphasis)[5]

Delany's work here involves the production of a national "we" through comparison with an enslaved other that acts as the mirror of a heretofore invisible community. By focusing on "them," we (male subjects) are able to see our real relationship to the American body politic, a relationship that is formally not altogether different from that of the slaves themselves. One might argue, in fact, that Delany does such a thorough job of aligning the two communities that the one is collapsed into the other such that the black is always the slave. He introduces a caveat, however, that makes the line of demarcation between the two groups clear. "They" are property and as such are incapable of forming strong or permanent domestic ties, while "we" own ourselves and have at least nominal control over our families.

It does not take too great a conceptual leap to recognize that the condition of "The Black Family" acts in Delany's political economy as a barometer of the condition of "The Black Nation." One might argue, in fact, that as both a nationalist and a bourgeois, Delany understood the maintenance of autonomous and "respectable" households as absolutely necessary to the production of "New Africa."[6] It is important to remember that Delany wrote his critique of black domesticity, or lack thereof, within the context of an emigrationist polemic, one that dismissed the idea that blacks could ever "stand on level with the most elevated of mankind" in the midst of "white" America.[7] Moreover, upon closer examination it becomes apparent how these ideas might have worked upon northern free blacks, Delany's primary constituency. One should remember that as late as 1790 New York had more slaves than any American city, save Charleston.[8] Moreover, the experience of slavery for northern blacks usually involved living apart from one another within white domiciles.[9] It is easy to understand then how "freedom" would involve, in the northern free black imagination, the removal of the black domestic from the white home.

If we condense Delany's position, a position that I am labeling "bourgeois," to its essentials we find then that he is concerned primarily with both demonstrating and breaking the symbiotic dependence that exists between the (black) slave and the (white) master. Repeatedly Delany argues that blacks will never be fully free, fully human, until they escape white households and learn to fend for themselves. But (slaveholding) whites, as we will see below, could not function in the absence of slaves. As a consequence they were forced to deploy brute force in an effort to maintain the symbiotic process.

This symbiosis, this never-ending cycle of interdependency, of ritualistic acts of dominance and submission, is best described, I believe, as sadomasochistic. The violence inside the master/slave dyad is never completely functional. It is never designed simply to compel the slave to do more work or to produce more goods. Nor is it simply gratuitous. Masters do achieve something more than grotesque pleasure as they apply the whip. The use of violence assures the master that he is in control, that the slave will not leave him and, thereby, force him to confront his dependency; while for slaves, submitting to violence allows them to deny their autonomy, to engage in complex acts of dissimulation by which they can create (marginalized) spaces in which to express their actual independence, creativity, and humanity. As Lynn Chancer has argued in her lively and thoroughly illuminating discussion of sadomasochism,

> the sadist's best-kept secret from self and others is extreme dependency hidden behind a front of apparent independence and strength, the masochist's analogous secret is far greater relative strength and independence than she or he perceives, hidden behind a front of apparent and extreme dependency.[10]

The sadomasochistic dynamic that Chancer describes is easy enough to understand in relation to the actual masters and slaves of nineteenth-century America. The master, trapped in the myth of autonomy, had always to deny his dependence on the slave by asserting his complete control over the body *and* mind of his property. The slave as a matter of survival had, on the other hand, to deny his or her autonomy. He had to construct a self that could survive amid constant rituals of dominance and degradation. And, as I will demonstrate below, Delany gives vivid demonstrations of this phenomenon in his own work.

I would like to add to this the fact that not only the quasi-aristocratic slaver but also the bourgeois was caught up in this sadomasochistic dynamic. Delany was himself never able to escape the process of dissimulation that typifies sadomasochism. In denying the ambiguity of the bourgeois position, a position that is itself dependent upon the subordination of "other" classes, Delany was forced to engage in the very acts of ritual domination that typify the master/slave symbiosis he decries.

I would ask the reader to consider the fact that, as Doris Sommer has pointed out, the development of discourses of nationalism coincided in the West with both the development of probourgeois economic discourses *and* discourses of sexuality. Following Foucault, Sommer argues that during the early period of bourgeois consolidation, "sex was forced into a productive economy that distinguished a legitimate realm of sexuality inside a clearly demarcated conjugal relationship and 'banished' the casual pleasures of polymorphous sexuality."[11] In the work of nationalist ideologues like Delany, this phenomenon would find expression in two ways. First, some sexual and romantic activity would be marked as either nonproductive or counter-productive and, therefore, beyond the realm of the respectable. We have seen exactly this in the constant call by African American intellectuals for blacks to give up their relatively relaxed attitudes toward sexuality and to most especially sever their sexual, romantic, and familial ties to whites.[12]

Second was the pronounced tendency within African American literature for authors to encourage the practice of "productive" heterosexuality. A proper conjugal union, one that maintained gender, economic, and ideological hierarchies, was imagined as the basis on which Black America would be constructed, while sexuality and romance were imagined as precisely the glue that would bind together the conjugal union.

This is all by way of my attempting to establish sadomasochism as a category through which to read the work of Martin Delany. He regularly points to the sadomasochistic interdependency of slave and master. He alludes through the figure of "the domestic," and the dual specters of forced intimacy and miscegenation that it conjures, to the sexual underside of this same dependency. Moreover, as a bourgeois, it behooves him to delineate what is proper sexual behavior from what is improper. Productive heterosexuality is constantly reinforced in his work, and everything else is confined to the realm of the marginal and the profligate. Even so, it would be wrong to lose sight of the question of bourgeois ambiguity I alluded to in the opening of this essay by quoting Wallerstein, for in the drive to separate the good from the bad, the progressive from the retrograde, one has always to take a bit of the other to replicate at least some of the reprehensible thoughts and behaviors that one has previously condemned. In Delany's case, this means that he is never able to really explode the slave/master symbiosis but only to repress it, to force it underground, always on the brink of revival.

The conflation of Delany's gender/sexual economy with his nationalist project is made explicit in his novel, *Blake, or The Huts of America*. Delany first published twenty-six chapters of *Blake* in *The Anglo-African Magazine* from January to July 1859. The novel did not appear in its entirety, however, until its publication—again in weekly installments—in *The Weekly Anglo-African* from November 26, 1861, until May 24, 1862. It is an exemplar of "the nationalist aesthetic" in that its impetus is to demonstrate the contours, the borders, of the "national landscape." This is done, moreover, by the spacial and historical movement of what Benedict Anderson describes as a "sociological organism" through the national community.[13]

The novel's action centers on the attempt of the male protagonist, Henrico "Henry" Blacus to reunify and avenge his family. Henry, later known as Blake, is described as "a black—pure Negro—handsome, manly and intelligent," thereby referencing the dark skin and presumably unadulterated Africanity of Delany himself.[14] Blake's wife, Maggie, the "mulatta" daughter of a slave master, is "true to her womanhood."[15] In fact, she has been sold because of her refusal to succumb to the sexual advances of her master and father, Colonel Franks. As a consequence, Blake flees the plantation, taking his infant son and several others with him. The remainder of the novel is taken up with his attempt to find his wife, reunify his family, and avenge their wrongs. In the process, he travels throughout the slave South, then to Cuba and Africa, all along providing sketches of "The New African People." Throughout, Blake must not only hurdle the incredible obstacles thrown up in the runaway's path, not only discipline many disparate "African" peoples into a distinct community, but also construct his own masculinity, a masculinity that is constantly threatened, on the one hand, by the profligacy and avarice of white men and, on the other, by the weakness and culpability of blacks, both male and female. Blake's journey then is not simply a journey to liberate his people but also a journey to liberate his own "manhood" from the taint of effeminacy—and bestiality—engendered by slavery.

As one might imagine, Blake has been fully immersed in the gospel of capital accumulation. Throughout the text he admonishes the slaves with whom he comes into contact to get money at all costs, arguing that it is money that opens the door to freedom. He believes, moreover, that petty moral or philosophical concerns should not deter the nascent bourgeois from his task:

> Keep this studiously in mind and impress it as an important part of the scheme of organization, that they must have money, if they want to get free. Money will obtain them everything necessary by which to obtain their liberty. The money is within all of their reach if they only knew it was right to take it. God told the Egyptian slaves to "borrow from their neighbors"—meaning their oppressors—"all their jewels"; meaning to take their money and wealth wherever

> they could lay hands upon it and depart from Egypt. So you must teach them to take all the money they can get from their masters, to enable them to make the strike without a failure.[16]

Delany's emphasis on money might be read as a simple product of his knowledge of black people's poverty or even as an acknowledgement of the necessity of money during the runaway's attempt to break free. At the same time, however, he recognized that the bourgeois had become the central actor within the modern western imagination and that as a consequence the black needed money as a means by which to become a (bourgeois) individual. One should remember also that on one level Delany was simply rearticulating mainstream liberal thought. Not only did he give credence to the particularly American idea that the only acceptable distinctions between men were ones of individual merit, not inherited social rank, but he also expressed the notion that one's worth might not be misjudged by one's ability to accumulate capital. Bear in mind that it was not until relatively late in the nineteenth century that liberal social reformers were able to convince large portions of the middle classes that the poor did not deserve their horrible lots.[17] Moreover, the Free Labor Ideology of the era would have it that the worker extract some wage, no matter how petty, from the capitalist. In the absence of the wage, the worker could not be said to be "free."[18] He would become, it was believed, akin to the Russian serf, or worse yet the African slave, thereby undermining American democratic institutions. Blake himself defends the fact that he has "stolen" money from his master by pointing out the hypocrisy of the slave-owning aristocrat's monopolization of wealth that he has not produced. "I'm incapable of stealing from any one, but I have, from time to time, taken by littles, some of the earnings due me for the more than eighteen years service to this man Franks. . . . 'Steal' indeed! I would that when I had an opportunity, I had taken fifty thousand instead of two."[19]

The master, in Delany's social schema, becomes so isolated from the production of goods and services that he loses all knowledge of the process by which he himself is reproduced. In a conversation between a Judge Ballard, a Yankee entrepreneur who has recently traveled to the South to purchase a cotton plantation, and a Major Armsted, a Southerner well versed in the intricacies of plantation economies, we find that the Judge has a distaste for Negroes. The Major points out, however, that it is these very Negroes who produce the commodities that sustain them.

> "Did ever it occur to you that black fingers made that cigar, before it entered your white lips! . . . and very frequently in closing up the wrapper, they draw it through their lips to give it tenacity."
>
> "The deuce! Is that a fact, Major!"
>
> "Does that surprise you, Judge? I'm sure the victuals you eat is cooked by black hands, the bread kneaded and made by black hands, and the sugar and molasses you use, all pass through black hands, or rather the hands of Negroes pass through them; at least you could not refrain from thinking so, had you seen them as I have frequently, with arms full length immersed in molasses."
>
> "Well Major, truly there are some things we are obliged to swallow, and I suppose these are among them."[20]

Delany eloquently demonstrates both the ignorance of the would-be master and his vulnerability. Without the assistance of the Negro he literally cannot eat. The hypocrisy of the slaver's claims, therefore, that he has produced his wealth and that there is a pressing social need for the separation of the races is made crystal clear.

Moreover, Delany places into the slaver's mouth, as it were, the ultimate indictment of his parasitical relationship to the rest of society. The Negro has become a part of the cigars and molasses that the master consumes. He has been stripped of any identity separate from his role as producer. The life of the Negro is one with the "life" of the commodity. What the Judge is really obliged to swallow is not simply the knowledge of the always already of interracial intimacy but the very lives, one might even say the bodies, of the Negroes themselves.

Delany's intimation of the slaveholder's cannibalism is made explicit in a scene that has been placed directly at the crossroads of the narrative. It is the place at which Blake begins his transformation from slave to freeman, the place of the fugitive. In this chapter, "Solicitude and Amusement," Judge Ballard and Major Armsted are invited by their host, Colonel Franks, to "see the sights" at the nearby plantation of a Mr. Grason. The visit is designed as the initiation of Judge Ballard into Southern life. Grason fetes his guests with food and brandy, boasting "I've got a *queer* animal here; I'll show him to you after dinner." (my emphasis)

> Dinner over, the gentlemen walked into the *pleasure grounds*, in the rear of the mansion.

"Nelse, where is Rube? Call him!" said Grason to a slave lad, brother to the boy he sent for.

Shortly there came forward, a small black boy about eleven years of age, thin visage, projecting upper teeth, rather ghastly consumptive look, and emaciated condition. The child trembled with fear as he approached the group.

"Now gentlemen," said Grason, "I'm going to show you a sight!" having in his hand a long whip, the cracking of which he commenced, as a ringmaster in the circus. . . .

"Wat maus gwine do wid me now? I know wat maus gwine do," said this miserable child, "he gwine make me see sights!" when going down on his hands and feet, he commenced trotting around like an animal.

"Now gentlemen, look!" said Grason. "He'll whistle, sing songs, hymns, pray, swear like a trooper, laugh, and cry, all under the same state of feelings."

With a peculiar swing of the whip, bringing the lash down upon a certain spot on the exposed skin, the whole person being prepared for the purpose, the boy commenced to whistle almost like a thrush; another cut changed it to a song, another to a hymn, then a pitiful prayer, when he gave utterance to oaths which would make a Christian shudder, after which he laughed outright; then from the fullness of his soul he cried:

"O maussa, I's sick! Please stop little!" casting up bogs of hemorrhage.

Franks stood looking on with unmoved muscles. Armsted stood aside whittling a stick; but when Ballard saw, at every cut the flesh turn open in gashes streaming down with gore, till at last in agony he appealed for mercy, he involuntarily found his hand with a grasp on the whip, arresting its further application.

"Not quite a southerner yet Judge, if you can't stand that!" said Franks on seeing him wiping away the tears.[21] (my emphasis)

Delany makes the connection between slavery and sadomasochism crystal clear in this passage. After the men have consumed food and brandy, all presumably produced by slave hands, they proceed to ritualistically abuse the slave, in a manner that is clearly intended to express their own omnipotence in relation to the slave's absolute helplessness. But why? The answer lies, I believe, precisely in the fact that the slavers' dominance, their stoicism, their manliness is never really assured. Each of them is intimately aware of how necessary the production of slaves is to their survival. Each of them knows, moreover, that they can and do recognize the humanity of individual slaves, and that there are layers of this humanity that they can never penetrate, no matter how viciously they wield their whips. Colonel Franks could not make Maggie love him, or even submit to his desires. Judge Ballard, however, is so aware of the humanity of this most dehumanized of slaves that he cannot hold back his tears or allow the violence to proceed.

And what of the boy? His own ritualistic submission comes on cue: "'Wat maus gwine do wid me now? I know wat maus gwine do.'" "'O maussa, I's sick! Please stop little!'" And yet the boy's humanity is never absolutely squelched. Indeed, the crime for which he is punished is the fact of the indestructibility of some core self. With the swing of the lash, the masters/sadists do not reduce the boy to an animal, as they assume, but, on the contrary, crack open the mask, the studied art of dissimulation, to reveal the boy's essential humanity, his genius: "the boy commenced to whistle almost like a thrush; another cut changed it to a song, another to a hymn, then a pitiful prayer, when he gave utterance to oaths which would make a Christian shudder." It is the boy's resiliency that enables the constant repetition of the sadomasochistic ritual. He never becomes simply a lump of flesh, quivering under the shock of the men's lash, but an ever-struggling, ever-*resistant* human, determined to maintain some discrete part of himself. Indeed Grason becomes disappointed as the boy finally succumbs and begins to slip irreversibly towards death: "The little Negro don't stand it nigh so well as formerly. He used to be a trump!"[22]

But what, then, is the nature of this resistance? Following the work of Julia Kristeva, I would like to suggest that what we witness during the beating of the young slave is the revelation of the abject. The very process by which the humanity of the black subject is denied, the violence by which the distinction between the human and the animal/object gives way, leads to an awareness of the possibilities just beyond our grasp. The slave, at the point of his whipping, behaves neither as recognizable subject or object. He is a *queer* animal, existing outside of the subject/object binarism altogether. Kristeva writes,

> Owing to the ambiguous opposition I/Other, Inside/Outside—an opposition that is vigorous but pervious, violent but uncertain —there are contents, "normally" unconscious in neurotics, that become explicit if not conscious in "borderline" patients' speeches and behaviors. Such contents are often openly manifested through symbolic practices, without by the same token being integrated into the judging conscious of those particular subjects. Since they make the conscious/unconscious distinction irrelevant, borderline subjects and their speech constitute propitious ground for a sublimating discourse ("aesthetic" or "mystical," etc.) rather than a scientific or rationalist one.[23]

Kristeva's point is well taken. For not only does she argue the borderline subject brings into play "contents" that are normally absent within rational thought, that is, thought which maintains the I/Other, Inside/Outside binarism, but she also suggests that these contents represent a "sublimating discourse," one that stresses the aesthetic and the mystical over the scientific and the rational. I would argue, therefore, that as the boy whistles, sings, prays, and makes oaths, all under the same state of feelings, he creates an index of black humanity that finds its efficacy precisely in the fact that it refuses rationalist modes of thought and expression.

I am supported in this claim by the work of Henry Louis Gates, particularly his *Figures in Black: Words, Signs and the "Racial" Self.*[24] Therein he argues that from its very inception, African American literature has contested and signified upon a modernist discourse that posits the black as cultureless and subhuman, a subhumanity that is demonstrated by the black subjects' supposed lack of a tradition of letters. In the process, the black becomes the very marker of the limits of culture and humanity, the outsider who gives definition to the amorphous, European-centered community of writers and thinkers. As a consequence, the spectacle of the literate black works not only as a refutation of racist notions regarding black intellect, but of the entire project of post-Enlightenment rationality. The black writer has to create, then, a literature that both produces him as an insider, a rational subject, and that concurrently critiques and transcends this same Inside/Outside binarism that is itself produced via the *de*humanization of the black.

Ajbection works in Delany's text, then, as precisely the site at which this critique and transcendence can take place. Note the references in the boy's utterances. His singing is likened to the transcendent beauty of the bird's song. His prayers are addressed to an omnipotent God who is both pre- and postrational. Even his curses, his oaths, bear witness to a logic that stands outside of the good/evil binarism, but that nevertheless refracts the boy's innate humanity. It is almost as if the boy, trapped within a discursive universe in which his basic lack, his basic subhumanity, acts as a species of the always already, hits upon a counter discourse, aesthetic and mystical, that propels him into new ranges of meaning against which the protestations of his tormentors become altogether meaningless.

Delany anticipates the spectacle of the boy's sadistic and ritualistic whipping when he places Blake himself on the auction block. As Blake ascends the platform on which the worth of his humanity is to be judged, he occupies the space of the feminine. The eyes of the male crowd are on him, stripping him to essentials, creating him as dominated, exploited and vulnerable.

> "Come up here my lad!" continued the auctioneer, wielding a long red rawhide. "Mount this block, stand beside me, an' let's see which is the best looking man! We have met before, but I never had the pleasure of introducing you. Gentlemen one and all, I take the pleasure in introducing to you Henry—pardon me, sir—Mr. Henry Holland, I believe—am I right, sir?—Mr. Henry Holland, a good looking fellow you will admit.
>
> "I am offered one thousand dollars; one thousand dollars for the best looking Negro in all Mississippi! If all the Negro boys in the state was as good looking as him, I'd give two thousand dollars for 'em all myself!" This caused another laugh. "Who'll give me one thousand five—"
>
> Just then a shower of rain came on.[25]

The passage upon first consideration might appear to be just the simple recitation of the slavers' childish attempt to humiliate Blake by ridiculing his gentlemanly pretensions. Upon closer examination, however, we find that it is filled with double entendres that reveal the full scope of the white men's "insult." The auctioneer holds his *long red rawhide* as he invites Blake to *mount* the (emasculating) block. Several references are made to Blake's good looks, looks that increase his worth, much as good looks and fair skin suited many female slaves for the lucrative New Orleans sex markets. Just when the men have worked themselves into a frenzy, moreover, it rains, or a shower *comes*, as it were, thereby dissipating the sexual tension the passage works to build. It becomes clear, then, that for Delany slavery not only stripped away one's freedom but also one's (heterosexual, autonomous, chaste) manhood as well.

My assertion that this passage is intimately connected to the ritualistic spectacle of the boy's whipping rests on a number of formal grounds. First, these are two of only three scenes in which we see the black body closely examined within the public arena. Significantly, the gaze in these passages is directed at male bodies instead of the ubiquitous slave mother, her children clinging to her aprons as greedy man stealers vie for the opportunity to tear her away from "home" and family. In these scenes Delany dispenses with females altogether, opting instead to make explicit the homosocial and homosexual implications of the attack and commodification of black bodies. Moreover, Blake spirits away his own infant son early in the narrative, thereby shielding him from the forces that consume the young slave.

Significantly, Blake achieves his manhood immediately after the youth's death. It is within the very next chapter, "Henry At Large," that Blake with "speed unfaltering" and "spirits unflinching" makes his final break with slavery. It is only after the death of the pitiful youth that Blake is able to call out to God and be heard:

> "Arm of the Lord, awake! Renew my faith, confirm my hope, perfect me in love. Give strength, give courage, guide and protect my pathway, and direct me in my course!" Springing to his feet as if a weight had fallen from him, he stood up a new man.[26]

I submit that the death of the youth is a sacrifice, of sorts. His passing allows both Blake and the white slavers to negotiate the slippery and treacherous terrain of the crossroads. The recognition of their own vulnerability is temporarily abated as the boy stands in for all that is, on the one hand, weak, innocent, and feminine and, on the other, dirty, promiscuous, and undisciplined. Christlike, he dies for the sins of "his" people so that they might become "new men." His death is absolutely necessary for the further development of the narrative in that it allows Delany to proceed without having to directly confront the work's many contradictions.

Blake sets forth immediately after this incident on a journey in which he shuttles easily across the geographic, cultural, linguistic, political, and historical expanses that separate Africa from the Americas, the "mulatto" from the "pure," the Anglo from the Hispanic, the rich from the poor. We might say that Blake is disembodied, becoming a black everyman. His name changes from Henrico to Henry, from Blacus to Blake, depending on the particular configuration of cultures in which he finds himself. His message, his whispered appeal for the economic, political, and cultural unity of the "The Black Community" is so utterly apparent, so obviously superior to the workaday concerns of the various communities whose collective consciousness he traverses that

> the trees of the forest or an orchard illustrate it; flocks of birds or domestic cattle, fields of corn, hemp, or sugar cane; tobacco, rice, or cotton, the whistling of the wind, rustling of the leaves, flashing of lightning, roaring of thunder, and running of streams all keep it constantly before [The New African's] eyes and in their memory, so that they can't forget it if they would.[27]

I would like at this point to bring back into consideration the question of bourgeois ambiguity with which I began this essay. In both *The Condition* and *Blake,* Delany clearly demarcates the line separating the respectable bourgeois from the profligate aristocrat, ascribing to the latter the role of sadist. Yet, as I have already argued, the sadism of the masters functions in *Blake* to separate both Blake and Delany himself from those elements in the African American community, particularly the slave community, that were weak, effeminate, and (sexually) submissive. With the death of the young boy, Blake achieves his untarnished manhood and is able, thereby, to bring discipline—and definition—to African America. It is in this sense that the text's sadomasochism is functional for not only the slaveholding characters but for Blake and Delany as well. The sadomasochistic elements have not been removed but, on the contrary, inserted more deeply into the narrative. Like the masters themselves, Blake/Delany is able to deny—without seeming to—the necessity of the abused, pitiful slave in the process of community formation. As a consequence, Blake is able to act on a (false) sense of autonomy, of manhood, without ever having to admit to his own profound vulnerability and need.

Blake becomes the perfect sociological organism. His trip to the farthest reaches of "New Africa" is accomplished with the greatest of ease as he sheds and reconstructs his various identities, all the while spreading the twin gospels of Nationalism and Capitalism. His adventures, however, are ones not simply of exploration but also of conquest. Blake's work is to define the contours of the new African community, but the process of this definition necessarily involves the "domestication" of many parts of Afro-America and the out and out excision of others. The sociological organism should be understood, then, not simply as that device through which the various elements of the nation are illustrated but also and significantly as the line along which the inside is separated from the out, the national from the foreign. "His" job becomes one of banishing from vision the tensions that mitigate against the fulfillment of the nationalist project while simultaneously fashioning the "excrescences" that are the constant result of this Sisyphian task into mythology, art, history, culture. Throughout, Blake initiates thinly veiled rituals of dominance that parallel, I believe, the sadistic torture of the young boy, but that Delany is never obliged to acknowledge as sadomasochistic. He has successfully projected all profligate aggressiveness onto his debased white subjects while simultaneously ridding himself—and the narrative—of the twin specters of weakness and culpability.

In the chapter following Blake's rebirth as a "new man," he happens upon a group of handsome young slave women whose loose clothing hangs upon them in tatters but who nevertheless *instinctively* "drew their garments around and about them" when they notice Blake's approach. Their lives are full of pain and woe. They work from sunrise to sunset seven days a week, with little to eat, dressed only in frocks made of coarse tow linen. Yet when asked which they prefer, the backbreaking toil of the fields or the less demanding work of the cotton gin where Blake first encounters them, they choose the fields for in the more public space of the gin, "so many ole white plantehs come an' look at us, like we was show!"[28] Once again Delany pulls our attention back to the notion of the black as (sexual) spectacle, the word "show" having already been heavily overlain with erotic meaning.

It is at this point that suddenly we are introduced to Blake's (black) alter ego who has returned from the realm of the unthinkable. Blake asks the women upon hearing that they are threatened sexually, "Who sees that the tasks are all done in the field?" They answer that it is Jerry, the black driver, and add that he mercilessly beats them. Blake assures them that "he'll never whip another" and then moves immediately back to the issue at hand, the leering white planters and the threat to the nation's boundaries that they represent. He counsels the young women, "die before surrendering to such base purposes" and exits, telling them that his name is "Farewell."[29]

The almost gratuitous manner in which the bad black man is introduced in this passage, sandwiched between condemnations of lecherous white masculinity and complicitous or even treacherous black femininity, strikes me as significant precisely because it represents such a glaring moment of awkwardness and uncertainty in the narrative. Here we have the performance of the black obscene. The black brute himself metes out the terror that engenders these young women's vulnerability. Yet he is not depicted as some lurking, menacing threat whom the women must constantly avoid and outwit. Instead he is almost an afterthought. Following Blake's exit we are casually informed that Jerry, the driver, "was missed, and never after heard of."[30] It is almost as if the real action of this passage was Blake's call for the young women to place love of virtue above love of life. That done, their worst problems evaporate as the complicitous, tainted, animal-like elements within the black community are eradicated by the machinations of the nameless stranger or, as William Jeremiah Moses would have it, the messiah.[31]

In the process, Delany's Blake is able to force recognition of himself, that is, of the masculine, aggressive, and spotlessly moral aspects of the black community, without having to ever acknowledge his own needs and desires. Strikingly, the violence directed against the young slave women is the violence of (mis)recognition. The white planters turn them into a show, fix them in their gazes, forcing the women to see their powerlessness in the men's lecherous glances. Blake, who has himself known the degradation of the public spectacle, intercedes to alleviate these women's misery, but in the process he takes the place of the planters in the women's psyche. He takes control over the slaver's one sure method of coercion, the brute violence meted out by the (black) driver. He beomes then the "new" master. The moral (black) man has been substituted for the lecherous (white) man, reason for (un)reason, truth for (un)truth. He attaches to himself the label, "Farewell," insuring that the women will always remember but never truly know him, thereby initiating the cycle of longing and denial that is the crux of the sadomasochistic symbiosis.

I have argued in this essay that there is an intimate connection in Martin Delany's work between the production of the national and the production of the bourgeois. This is not to imply, however, that there was an easy or transparent relationship between the two. On the contrary, it was riddled with ambiguity such that it was always necessary to negotiate the tensions inherent in their juxtaposition. Specifically, Delany had to somehow displace the violence and dependency—significant aspects of (bourgeois-dominated) capitalism—that were all too similar to the sadomasochism of the slave/master dyad.[32] He accomplished this through the resurrection of the figures of the lecherous, profligate master and the helpless slave, both of whom would have to be excised from the national narrative if the bourgeois subject was ever to achieve dominance. And yet, inherent in this very act of excision was a parallel act of sadomasochistic violence. To state it bluntly, Delany literally killed off the feeble slave youth—and by inference his sadistic tormentors—in a move designed first and foremost to buy recognition for the black bourgeois protagonist, or rather to create a black masculinity strong enough and independent enough to insure the viability and autonomy of the black nation, the New Africa. Blake became fully a man only after the young boy's death. We can see him for who he "truly" is only through the suppression of another subject; that is, through a violent act of forced recognition. Strikingly, this excision, or we might say this exorcism, allowed Blake to shed even the suggestion of culpability or depravity, opening the way for him to discipline the whole of the African American community without ever having to face charges of sociocultural domination or class bias.

Inherent in the sadomasochistic symbiosis that I have just attempted to explicate is the desire, particularly on the part of the sadist, for this process of interdependency to never end. If, as Lynn Chancer has argued, sadists are compelled to engage in acts of ritualized domination and control because of the fear that they will be abandoned or misrecognized by the beloved, then it would behoove them to never push masochists beyond their limits, to never, for example, kill them, or abuse them so that they are no longer able to resist and, thereby, demonstrate awareness of the sadist's subjectivity. This explains the disappointment of the sadistic planter, Grason, as the young slave boy's resiliency begins to give way and he starts to slip toward death.

Even as the weak, profligate, and miscegenous aspects of the black community were excised, Delany, in the person of Blake, continued to thirst for recognition. Nothing was resolved with the death of the young boy. On the contrary, this act forced Blake/Delany to search for another beloved from whom he could receive recognition. He needed the slave's understanding without the slave's vulnerability, the child's talents without his perversity. He found all this in the person of Placido.

The "real" Placido was a Black Cuban revolutionary and poet who was executed in Havannah in 1844, some fifteen years before the first installment of *Blake*. Delany's Placido is described as a person of "slender form, lean and sinewy, rather morbid, orange-peel complexion, black hair hanging lively quite to the shoulders, heavy deep brow and full moustache, with great expressive black piercing eyes."[33] This description corresponds neatly with the thin, sickly slave youth. Yet there is a difference. This time we are encountering a man. The delicate poet is filled out with a deep brow and full moustache, and most especially with those great piercing eyes. He greets Blake sternly, not offering him a chair, but commanding, "Be seated sir!" Moreover, Blake is intimately connected to this man who we quickly discover is his cousin, unlike the boy whom Blake never encounters. Finally, Blake/Delany has found that other part of himself, that which is sensitive and creative but nevertheless virile. It is as if Delany set the feeble, effeminate youth free when he sacrificed him at the white slaver's altar and then sent Blake to find him, or rather the new, improved, masculine him. He erupts, "I am the lost boy of Cuba," as he rushes into Placido's arms, the two becoming one.[34]

And yet Delany never finished his novel, never demonstrated the pan-African revolt to which the work alludes, never set down in detail the contours of the government he envisioned. He did, however, accomplish his task. He created a model for how the many disparate peoples of the African diaspora might be interpellated as blacks, or more parochially as African Americans. Cubans joined hands with Africans while Henry Blake crossed continents and cultures to be reunited with Henrico Blacus. This process, as I have argued throughout, necessarily involved concurrent acts of violence and domination, with the bourgeois subject triumphing over the aristocratic master and his counterpart, the overly dependent slave. He went on, however, to adopt a system of domination similar to the one he had previously decried.

Even at the ultimate moment of bourgeois triumph, the meeting of the Grand Council in which the thorny details of African solidarity are to be worked through, the bourgeois subjects, in the persons of Blake and Placido, exercise explicit dominance over a potentially unruly other, specifically the "misses" who were admitted only through the men's courtesy.[35] Even so, the women resist, thereby providing impetus to yet another act of ritualistic domination.

The women's girlish and disruptive chatter gives way to the pointed questions of the aristocratic Madame Cordora, questions that threaten to wreak havoc on the whole endeavour. She asks, "Can we as Catholics, with any degree of propriety consistently with our faith, conform to those [nationalistic quasi-religious] observances?" Blake answers, "No religion but that which brings us liberty will we know; no god but He who owns us as his children will we serve."[36] Madame Cordora continues with an even more difficult issue: "The poet [Placido] in his prayer spoke of Ethiopia's sons; are not some of us left out in the supplication, as I am sure, although identified together, we are not all Ethiopians." Placido responds, "How are the mixed bloods ever to rise? The thing is plain; it requires no explanation. The instant that an equality of the blacks with the whites is admitted, we being the descendants of the two, must be acknowledged the equals of both."[37] It is striking that this interchange, for all its fanfare, boils down to an intellectual contest, of sorts, between Madame Cordora and the combined figures of Blake and Placido. The single and somewhat ignorant female confronts the male couple. One might argue, in fact, that if there is some confusion among the characters as to their status as Ethiopians, there can be no doubt that they are not all sons. Madame Cordora's naive questions demonstrate her lack of masculinity, her lack of clarity regarding the realities of human interaction. At the same time, the challenge allows Blake/Placido/Delany to once again demonstrate "his" virility, to squelch that which is questioning, difficult, and disruptive. The ritual of resistance and domination is reenacted, thereby, combining the nation's constituents into the never-quite-finished sadomasochistic symbiosis that has from the outset driven the narrative.

It should come as no surprise that the text comes to a close in a fit of marriages. Blake is reunited to Maggie about whom we have heard almost nothing since the beginning of the text. Gofer Gondolier, the caterer for the Cuban Captain General, marries Abyssa Soudan, formerly a successful

Sudanese trader kidnapped from her home by slavers. Juan Montego, a mulatto officer in the Cuban army, catches Madame Cordora herself, thereby giving credence to the assertion that "the consummation of conjugal union is the best security for political relations."[38] I would add that the marriages ought to be understood in the context of the very involved psychosexual drama that I have just explored. If, as I am suggesting, marriage actually helps to domesticate the differences, anxieties, and tensions of the diaspora, then we must necessarily understand it as operating beyond the realm of the interpersonal. As Blake, Gondolier, Montego, Madame Cordora, Abyssa, and Maggie marry each other, they also marry into the nation. Indeed one's marriage is as much a symbol of one's loyalty to the "race" as it is a marker of self-interest. Marriage does not, however, stop the process of resistance and domination that I explicated above. On the contrary, it simply reasserts the actors' commitment to this same process, creating them all as a species of loyal opposition. It is in this sense that the question of ambiguity with which I began this essay has not been resolved, but simply sewn more deeply into the narrative. As Delany points the accusing finger at the aristocratic master and the helpless slave, he also draws himself—and his narrative—even more deeply into the sado-masochistic symbiosis that he so loathes. The bourgeois continues then as both hero and villain, shaper of the present, destroyer of the past.

Notes

1. Immanuel Wallerstein, "The Bourgeois(ie) as Concept and Reality," in *Race, Nation, Class: Ambiguous Identities,* Etienne Balibar and Immanuel Wallerstein, eds. (New York: Verso, 1991), 135.
2. Lynn Chancer, *Sadomasochism in Everyday Life: The Dynamics of Power and Powerlessness* (New Brunswick, NJ: Rutgers Univ. Press, 1992), 69.
3. See Cyril E. Griffith, *The African Dream: Martin R. Delany and the Emergence of Pan-African Thought* (University Park: Pennsylvania State Univ. Press, 1975).
4. For more on the contemporary reception of Delany, see Nell Irvin Painter, "Martin Delany: Elitism and Black Nationalism," in *Black Leaders of the Nineteenth Century,* Leon Litwack and August Meier, eds. (Chicago: Univ. of Illinois Press, 1988), 149–171.

5. Martin R. Delany, *The Condition, Elevation, Emigration, and Destiny of the Colored People of the United States* (Salem, NH: Ayer, 1988), 14–15.

6. For more on the relationship of "respectability" to nationalism, see George L. Mosse, *Nationalism and Sexuality: Middle-Class Morality and Sexual Norms in Modern Europe* (Madison: Univ. of Wisconsin Press, 1985).

7. Delany, *The Condition*, 199.

8. Gary B. Nash, "Forging Freedom: The Emancipation Experience in the Northern Seaport Cities, 1775–1820," in *Slavery and Freedom in the Age of the American Revolution*, Ira Berlin and Ronald Hoffman, eds. (Chicago: Univ. of Illinois Press, 1983), 11.

9. Nash, "Forging Freedom," 21.

10. Chancer, *Sadomasochism,* 59.

11. Doris Sommer, *Foundational Fictions: The National Romances of Latin America* (Berkeley: Univ. of California Press, 1991), 37.

12. John Blassingame has argued that there were relatively few restrictions within the slave community itself on the sexual behavior of unmarried persons. Indeed, sex was seen as a welcome respite from the hardship and monotony of plantation life. See John Blassingame, *Slave Community: Plantation Life in the Antebellum South* (New York: Oxford Univ. Press, 1972). It was these attitudes that much of contemporary black writing was directed against. See, for example, F.J., "Speak to That Young Man," *The Colored American,* Saturday April 18, 1840, 1. One should also remember that in William Wells Brown's *Clotel, or the President's Daughter* (New York: University Books, 1969), the heroine, the mulatta daughter of Thomas Jefferson, eventually dies after being forsaken by her white lover. The tragedy in Frank J. Webb's *The Garies and Their Friends* (New York: Arno Press and the New York Times, 1969) is precipitated by (black) Mrs. Garies's naive assumption that she can live in relative comfort and freedom with her (white) husband and former master. Even the action in *Blake* itself is fueled by the sale of Blake's mulatta wife after she refuses to succumb to the lascivious desires of her master/father. Moreover, the woes of the title character in Harriet Wilson's *Our Nig, or Sketches from the Life of a Free Black* (New York: Vintage, 1983) commence when her white mother abandons her to start life anew with her black lover.

13. Benedict Anderson, *Imagined Communities: Reflections on the Origin and Spread of Nationalism* (New York: Verso, 1983), 31.

14. Martin R. Delany, *Blake, or The Huts of America* (Boston: Beacon, 1970), 16.

15. Ibid., 8.

16. Ibid., 43.

17. See Luc Sante, *Low Life: Lures and Snares of Old New York* (New York: Vintage, 1991), 12.

18. For more on Free Labor Ideology, see Eric Foner, *Politics and Ideology in the Age of the Civil War* (New York: Oxford Univ. Press, 1980).
19. Delany, *Blake*, 31.
20. Ibid., 62–63.
21. Ibid., 66–67.
22. Ibid., 68.
23. Julia Kristeva, *Powers of Horror: An Essay on Abjection* (New York: Columbia Univ. Press, 1982), 7.
24. Henry Louis Gates Jr., *Figures in Black: Words, Signs, and the "Racial" Self* (New York: Oxford Univ. Press, 1987).
25. Ibid., 26.
26. Ibid., 69.
27. Ibid., 39.
28. Ibid., 77.
29. Ibid., 77–79.
30. Ibid., 79.
31. Wilson J. Moses, *Black Messiahs and Uncle Toms: Social and Literary Manipulations of a Religious Myth* (University Park: Pennsylvania State Univ. Press, 1982).
32. Chancer had this to say about the connection between sadomasochism and capitalism: "The social psychological ramifications under capitalism of an omnipotent orientation toward exchange value is that we evaluate everything, including ourselves, with greater value with regard to meaning for *them* than for us. How can we best sell ourselves, we wonder, best package ourselves in order to obtain a particular job?" Chancer, *Sadomasochism*, 36.
33. Delany, *Blake*, 192–193.
34. Ibid., 193.
35. Ibid., 257.
36. Ibid.
37. Ibid., 260–261.
38. Ibid., 275.

5

CHAPTER ONE OF BOOKER T. WASHINGTON'S *UP FROM SLAVERY*

and the Feminization of the African American Male

DONALD GIBSON

> He [the African American] is, so to speak, the lady among the races.
>
> —Robert E. Park, Advisor to and Ghostwriter for Booker T. Washington[1]

Booker T. Washington (1856–1915) was the second nationally acknowledged African American leader of our people, following the eminent black abolitionist and political leader Frederick Douglass (ca. 1817–1895). Following his founding of Tuskegee Institute in 1881, Washington drew the attention and support of northern industrial interests, and by the turn of the century had garnered considerable political power through the support of political leaders, especially Theodore Roosevelt. Washington grew to be the most powerful and influential black leader ever to have existed before or since his advent. Although favored by the majority of black people, he was a controversial figure because some felt that, in courting the patronage of powerful whites, he did not always look after the best interests of his race. Some of his critics found his stance toward whites, both the powerful and the powerless, too conciliatory.

Washington recorded his life story in *Up from Slavery*.[2] He knew that in creating his autobiography that he, as a black male, was participating in a culture-wide project of defining black masculinity. His own representation of the black male was undertaken within a cultural matrix. He surely knew that he could not represent himself as a black male without joining the ongoing debate about race that began with eighteenth-century Quaker opposition to slavery[3] and continued to his time and beyond. He knew, for example, that his perspective on racial matters joined the national public discourse about race, specifically about (in this context) race and male gender. In conceiving *Up from Slavery,* Washington was keenly aware of the slavery debate, and of arguments pro and con defining the nature and character of the black male carried forth in lectures, sermons, novels, books, pamphlets, speeches, and all manner of public discourse. He knew of Harriet Beecher Stowe's *Uncle Tom's Cabin*; of Frederick Douglass's *Narrative of the Life of Frederick Douglass, An American Slave*; of scores of jokes and anecdotes intended to denigrate black males (he certainly included enough of them in his speeches; those anecdotes he related were almost always about black males).[4]

The importance of the first chapter of the book, "A Slave Among Slaves," lies in its author's use of it as a prefiguration of the Atlanta Exposition Address, the event that catapulted him to power in 1895 (the year of Frederick Douglass's death) and that stands at the center of Washington's narrative of his life. The description of his early life is an exemplification in the most concrete terms of the fundamental meanings of the later Atlanta address. In both cases, the African American male is feminized in that he is not defined as a man in the terms in which the time defined "man." The assertion Washington implicitly makes in the opening chapter of *Up from Slavery* is that black males neither are nor desire to be "men," in the nineteenth- and twentieth-century traditional sense of that term: to have power, to choose their own destiny, to be equal to others in the society (especially other males), to vote. He wanted to assure whites, both men and women (but especially men) that he himself neither represented nor encouraged any political, social, psychological, nor physical threat. The initial pages of *Up from Slavery* were designed to show that blacks, and here he meant black males, were not in competition with whites for political rights and that social equality was not high on our agenda at the time. If "man" is defined in terms of the freedoms and prerogatives belonging to white males politically, socially, and economically in nineteenth-century postbellum American society, then blacks who do not aspire to such power, the text tells us, are content to accept as their own the status then currently belonging to women.

Booker T. Washington's presentation of the black male as unmanned has its history. By the time of *Up from Slavery* (1901), the program to assert and establish white masculinity at the expense of black masculinity had been underway in the North American colonies since the seventeenth century, and throughout the years it had assumed many forms.

One of the earliest and most basic attempts to disempower and hence unman black male slaves was through the slave owner's power (backed by statute and court and enforced by sheriffs and the state militia) to name his slaves, to assign each of them names of his choosing.[5]

> A man's name is, of course, more than simply a way of calling him. It is the verbal sign of his whole identity, his being-in-the-world as a distinct person. It also establishes his relation with kinsmen. In a great many societies a person's name has magical qualities; new names are often received upon initiation into adulthood and into cults and secret societies, and the victim's name looms large in witchcraft and sorcery practiced against him. . . . Thus it is understandable that in every slave society one of the first acts of the master has been to change the name of his new slave.[6]

One of the first manifestations of the changed status of the African captured and put onto a slave ship bound for the new world was the change of name. Frequently the first female African to board a slave ship in Africa was called Eve, the first male, Adam, as though to recapitulate in some kind of obverse and perverse way the course of western mythology. Although eighteenth-century advertisements for runaway slaves indicated in the recording of their names that some male slaves kept their African names (Cuffey, Quash, Cudjo, Sambo), most, the evidence shows, bore other names.[7] That they were as a usual practice given other names is demonstrated by the fact that time after time the runaway slave ads said either that the slaves advertised knew little English or that they were recent arrivals, often listing their territorial origin (e.g., Angola or Ashanti, or, as they thought of it, their group or language identity, e.g., Ibo) in order to indicate their newly arrived status. Often the ad disclosed that they were newly arrived: "an African named Mungo,"[8] or "a new negro fellow."[9] Such slaves usually bore English names, names they would probably not have chosen themselves. The slaves were newly named for many reasons, but the essential impulse behind renaming slaves was to claim their souls, their essential selves.[10] As Adam claimed dominion over the animals of the earth by virtue of naming them, so the slave owner claimed dominion over his chattel. He might not have been conscious of this (his conscious motive might have been that he could not know or understand the name of the slave in the slave's language), but the effect of his act of naming was to impress upon the slave a reality and meaning felt by the namer to be far surpassing, and hence more powerful, than any sense of reality stemming from the slave's own history and culture. Naming stamped western culture, a new basic identity, upon the slave. The usurping of the capacity to name was as great an assault on the individual psyche as physical captivity—perhaps, because of its psychological nature, even greater. The conflicts and tensions underlying the relationship between namer and named are amply illustrated in the following runaway ad which appeared in the Savannah *Georgia Gazette* on 1 August 1765.

> RUN AWAY from Arthur Neil, Esq. at present in Charlestown, and supposed to have taken the road to Georgia, where he [the runaway] had formerly been in gaol by the name of ISAAC, and was then the property of Mr. Deas merchant, his name is now changed to Scipio, but commonly calls himself TOM. . .[11]

Of great import in this discussion of the attempt of the dominant culture to unman the black male and Booker T. Washington's role in that project are the gender implications of the practices surrounding the naming of slaves in eighteenth-century America. The motivations underlying the naming of male and female slaves differed. Female slaves were likely given the same names prevailing among freewomen in Colonial society: biblical names (Sarah, Rachel, Esther, Judith, Hannah); Puritan names (Grace, Patience, Faith, Charity); British names—sometimes shortened forms (Lucy, Betty, Sal, Sylvia, Amy, Peg); and classical names (Diana, Daphne, Juno, Chloe). Slave women were very rarely given names that were ironic, demeaning, whimsical, or derisive. This reflected a gendered difference in naming practices which may well point to greater underlying conflict between slave-owning males and male slaves than existed between the wives of slave owners and their female slaves.

Though most male slaves were given the same names belonging to the majority of whites—almost literally Tom, Dick, and Harry—many bore rather peculiar names. Some were whimsical or associational: Porringer, Candlemas, Christmas, Sufferer. One legless runaway was named General, surely an ironic commentary on the seeming disparity between his physical incapacity and his actual abilities (his runaway status might have proved him more "General" than might have been imagined). Others received classical names, often clearly ironic and intended to stress powerlessness by attesting to their bondage within western culture and underscoring the difference in status between the name and the namesake: Nero, Scipio, Bacchus, Aeneus. Some were given place names (almost never occurring with slave women): Shrewsbury, Windsor, Aberdeen, London, Glasgow. Still others received biblical names, such names as they or their mothers would never have bestowed upon them: Cain, Abel, Job. The slaves struck back, resisted, and in many cases clung to their African names in varying ways, a diminishing practice for many complicated reasons, as the eighteenth century wore on: Cuffy, Quash, Juber, Cudjo, Cubba. (One can imagine the history behind the name of the black, orphaned Pedro Cuffy who appeared in my third and fourth grade primary school classes in Kansas City, Missouri, in the 1940s.)

When Booker T. Washington described his self-naming in his autobiography *Up from Slavery*, he knew that he was participating in a gendered tradition. Had he not known about the gravity of naming, he would not have focused so sharply on the significance of surnames and naming.[12] He knew and understood very well the difference at twelve years old between naming himself Booker Taliaferro Washington (the name he chose) and naming himself Booker Nathaniel Turner (the name that would have allied him with the black slave insurrectionist of 1831).[13] He knew very well, because of his aims in creating his autobiography and because of the relation he wished to establish with his audience, not to tell the teacher enrolling him in his first class and prompting his self-naming, "Put me down as Booker Nathaniel Turner."

His knowledge of his time, a large part of which derived from his understanding of the relations between blacks and whites (perhaps a retrospective knowledge at the time he wrote his autobiography), informed him that he needed to say something in keeping with the dominant discourse of his time. His autobiography reveals that he knew exactly what a black male who wanted to be positively received might or might not say. He knew the competing modes of defining black masculinity. He knew that in terms of sexuality the black male might not only be feminized, he might be bestialized as well, characterized as a lascivious, sexually driven beast whose lust could only be satisfied (momentarily) by sexual intercourse with a white woman.[14] Such a sensitivity to currents of racial discourse created an awareness of the intricacies involved in the process of a black male representing himself to a white, middle-class audience composed of, as Washington would say, "the best people."

Though Washington in many respects modeled his autobiography on the slave narrative,[15] he at the same time dissociated the narrative from that of the escaped slave. The slave in Washington's narrative may "rise" but not "escape." He has no interest in attacking the institutions responsible for the near continuance of slavery through peonage after the Civil War. In keeping with his desire to diminish a view of himself as traditional black antislavery autobiographer, he minimized many of the characteristics belonging to the subject of the usual male slave narrative. Physical and psychological resistance to prevailing authority, along with the sanctioning of cunning, defiance, stealth, rebelliousness, and recalcitrance (prominent in most slave narratives), are nowhere embraced in Washington's autobiography. He rejects and denies any response that would suggest a mode of black male reaction to oppression other than compliance (however unpleasant) with slave owners' expectations. His mother may wish to be free, but she cannot, whatever the reality, do anything specifically to advance her cause, more for ideological than historical reasons. That is to say, had Washington's mother indeed been more openly rebellious, his narrative purposes would not have allowed him to say so. Specific comparison of Douglass's autobiography with Washington's illustrates the point.

Up from Slavery opens, as slave narratives often do, with the words "I was born. . . ." The first version of Douglass's autobiography, *Narrative of the Life of Frederick Douglass, An American Slave*, begins in the same manner, using on its opening page his ignorance of his age and birthdate as evidence of the inhumanity of slavery and its unwillingness to allow slaves one of the most basic elements of individual identity: knowledge of one's age.[16]

Douglass seizes the facts as he knows them of his early life and immediately employs them as weapons in his battle against slavery. Washington, on the other hand, makes it abundantly clear that he is *not* engaged in battle, converting the high seriousness and assertiveness of tone of the Douglass passage into mere frivolity, thereby subverting the whole tradition of the slave narrative insofar as that tradition is about the achievement of freedom by the enslaved black individual. At the crucial moment, Washington quips, "I am not quite sure of the exact place or exact date of my birth, but at any rate I suspect I must have been born somewhere and at some time." In terms of traditional constructions of masculine and feminine, Washington—at the beginning—feminizes himself and his text.

In the manner in which he mentions some of the horrors of slavery—the notoriously dreadful middle passage, lack of attention to the maintenance of slave family records, exposure to cold, insufficient, and inadequate food and clothing—Washington attempts to control the telling of his life in such a way as to appear consistently even tempered, reasonable, and without rancor or bitterness, to treat slavery as though it were simply an aspect of the past not unlike the ordinary past experiences of everyone. He does not describe slave existence as pleasant, but the tone of the narrative carries nothing of the caustic criticism and resentment most often characteristic of the genre. In comparison, the narratives of Douglass, William Wells Brown, and Solomon Northup virtually boil, seething with anger and barely suppressed rage. Probably because it is too unpleasant and suggests a side of slavery he chooses not to approach, Washington does not dwell on the personal cruelty and inhumanity usually so crucial to the slave narrative. In a version of his autobiography preceding *Up from Slavery*[17] he described the severe flogging of his uncle:

> The thing in connection with slavery that has left the deepest impression on me was the instance of seeing a grown man, my uncle, tied to a tree early one morning, stripped naked and someone whipping him with a cowhide. As each blow touched his back the cry, "Pray, master! Pray, master!" came from his lips, and made an impression upon my boyish heart that I shall carry with me to the grave.[18]

He may have carried it to the grave, but he did not carry it into *Up from Slavery*, because he had decided that he would not focus on such "divisive" issues as the not-uncommon existence of cruelty in slavery. The point is vividly made, however, in the parallel scene early in Douglass's *Narrative* where his Aunt Hester is also stripped and bloodily flogged.

> I have often been awakened at the dawn of day by the most heart-rending shrieks of an own aunt of mine, whom he used to tie up to a joist, and whip upon her naked back till she was literally covered with blood. No words, no tears, no prayers, from his gory victim, seemed to move his iron heart from its bloody purpose. The louder she screamed, the harder he whipped; and where the blood ran fastest, there he whipped longest. He would whip her to make her scream, and whip her to make her hush; and not until overcome by fatigue, would he cease to swing the blood-clotted cowskin.[19]

The first chapter of *Up from Slavery,* "A Slave among Slaves," seems based upon models of plantation tradition literature (literature written primarily by southerners and intended to defend or justify slavery),[20] which may be attributable to the fact that Washington was only nine years old at the end of the Civil War and perhaps had to fill in memory gaps with the constructed, proslavery vision of antebellum slave life current in his time (a portrait not unlike that current in our time). In any case, his presentation of parts of his experience as a slave through the literary lens of the plantation tradition is in keeping with his conscious intention to avoid arousing the guilt and pain of a northern and southern middle-class (mostly business oriented) public anxious to put the dissension of the Civil War and its aftermath behind. This motive is in part to avoid pointing attention to the political dimensions of sectional conflict, displacing it with descriptions of the intimate participation of slaves in the most subjective facets of their masters' lives.

> I recall the feeling of sorrow which existed among the slaves when they heard of the death of "Mars' Billy." It was no sham sorrow, but real. Some of the slaves had nursed "Mars' Billy"; others had played with him when he was a child. "Mars' Billy" had begged for mercy in the case of others when the overseer or master was thrashing them.[21]

The proslavery perspective on the relationship between slave and master is further expressed when Washington tells of the slaves' reaction when the wounded white males returned home during the war: "They [slaves, both male and female] were just as anxious to assist in the nursing as the family relatives of the wounded. Some of the slaves would even beg for the privilege of sitting up at night to nurse their wounded masters,"[22] clearly a gender-oriented "privilege." A story frequently told by narrators wanting to defend the institution of slavery was of the loyalty of the slaves while the masters were away at war practicing real men's business, fighting the North in order to keep blacks enslaved.

> In order to defend and protect the women and children who were left on the plantations when the white males went to war, the slaves would have laid down their lives. . . . Any one attempting to harm "young Mistress" or "old Mistress" during the night would have had to cross the dead body of the slave to do so.[23]

Note that Washington's commentary is general and not just about his own experience and that of the slaves on his plantation. He says that throughout the South slaves were willing to die to protect the master's family not because they were courageous or manly but because they were mainly loving and loyal. Love and loyalty, not courage or masculinity, drove these presumably male protectors of the bodies of the masters' wives and daughters (according to the plantation myth) into their roles as protectors. Familial love and loyalty also suppressed sexual desire, a point driven home by the notion that the black male slave would "lay down his life" to prevent the violation (sexual or otherwise) of the slave master's wife or children. No one would violate in any way the slave owner's mate or offspring, especially not the unmanned, emasculated slave, for he has not strong enough desire, so the myth says, neither literally nor psychosexually, to cross the threshold separating him during the nights of his vigil from the wife and daughters of his master. He is represented in Washington's text (though not in all others) as one whose sexual desire is nonexistent, suppressed by racial mythology. He has no sexuality, not even in relation to black women, for that would allow the potential of sexual threat to white women.[24] He is at one stroke both feminized and neutered.

The mythological love and loyalty of the slave for his (primarily "his" and not "her") master take other forms during the course of Washington's narrativizing of the emasculation of black men:

> I know of instances where the former masters of slaves have for years been supplied with money by their former slaves to keep them from suffering. I have known of still other cases in which the former slaves have assisted in the education of the descendants of their former owners.[25]

Along these lines is the story (related in the first chapter of the autobiography) of the slave who contracted with his master prior to the issuance of the Emancipation Proclamation to buy his own freedom. When freedom came, and despite the fact that he had no legal obligation to his former master, the former slave walked from Ohio to his former master's home in Maryland or Virginia where he "placed the last dollar, with interest, in his hands."[26] Such plantation anecdotes as these support the paternalistic vision of slavery advanced by the southern apologists for slavery and the defenders of a sentimentalized antebellum past.

This vision also supports the mythology of the orderliness of the slave's household: the male slaveholder stands as the supreme authority, the slaveholder's wife is second in command, the children third. The black male, all too often shorn of authority within his own family, is thus feminized (or neutered). Washington not only describes this feminization as truth, as the way things historically were, but also sees it as a positive good and worthwhile condition. Slavery has, in the tradition of its apologists, been in fact of the greatest benefit to slaves. *Up from Slavery* tells us so.

> The ten million Negroes inhabiting this country, who themselves or whose ancestors went through the school of American slavery, are in a stronger and more helpful condition, materially, intellectually, morally, and religiously, than is true of an equal number of black people in any other portion of the globe.[27]

In another context the point is made more vividly and pointedly. He tells, in the most obviously proslavery terms, the advantages of slavery:

> Despite all of our disadvantages and hardships, ever since our forefathers set foot upon the American soil as slaves, our pathway has been marked by progress. Think of it: We went into slavery pagans; we came out Christians. We went into slavery a piece of property; we came out American citizens. We went into slavery without a

> language; we came out speaking the proud Anglo-Saxon tongue. We went into slavery with slave chains clanking about our wrists; we came out with the American ballot in our hands.[28]

This tightly argued defense of American slavery rests upon previously plowed and manured planting grounds, for the argument only makes sense if slavery exists as a positive and humane enterprise allowing slaves a reasonably worthwhile life. Presumably Washington's observations and conclusions are based on the facts of his particular experience as a slave. We need to consider at this point, however, some other facts.

According to his biographer, Louis R. Harlan, Washington did not live on the *Gone with the Wind* plantation he allows his reader to infer in his description of his early life.[29] The careful reader will realize that while elements of the narration suggest a large, wealthy plantation, the farm buildings are in disrepair and that sometimes there is insufficient food. The census of 1860 listed ten black people as slaves of James Burroughs, Washington's owner. Four of them were adults (two men and two women) and six were children. The crowd of slaves that Washington says were present to hear the reading of the Emancipation Proclamation simply did not exist: "In company with my mother, brother, sister, and a large number of other slaves, I went to the master's house."[30] There was also no veranda, and the "big house," perhaps understandably so in the eyes of one so young as Booker, was a house of five rooms, originally a rough-hewn log cabin, three rooms downstairs and two up. The Burroughses were by no stretch of the imagination aristocrats; James Burroughs was a small farmer whose sons worked in the fields with his few slaves. There was no overseer other than James Burroughs himself. Fifty years later, Harlan tells us, "Booker would fit his early years into the plantation legend"[31] not simply, as I earlier said, to fill in gaps but because, possibly, he could not distinguish his individual experience from that delineated in the myth. At the same time, however, the myth was not inconsistent with the message he wished to convey to his audience. He wanted his white audience to feel that his voice was not threatening but calm and placid. How better to do this than to feminize that voice; to associate it, in its motherly ministrations, with the female, domestic presence, perhaps even to evoke memories of each audience member's own mother.

Slavery was, Washington insists, a condition through which Providence led us: "Ever since I have been old enough to think for myself, I have entertained the idea that notwithstanding the cruel wrongs inflicted upon us, the black man got nearly as much out of slavery as the white man did."[32] Whatever the rationalization surrounding Washington's observation, his point was that slavery was somehow mutually beneficial and mutually harmful. The middle ground lay in the familial domestic relationships claimed to prevail between slave and master. Once this is construed, all else follows. Freedom seemed in the air, although one might think that freedom, especially for slaves as far north as Virginia where Booker T. Washington was, would not have been contingent upon the formal reading of a document: the Emancipation Proclamation, which would have freed Washington, was issued January 1, 1863. Yet, despite great and joyous anticipation of freedom on the part of the enslaved, "In the fear of 'Yankee' invasions, the silverware and other valuables were taken from the 'big house,' buried in the woods and guarded by trusted slaves. Woe be to any one who would have attempted to disturb the buried treasure."[33] ("Woe be" indeed! I would suspect that there was precious little silver in Mr. Burroughs' house.) The system is defended and upheld by feminized black slaves whose vestigial power is exerted only to sustain their own enslavement. "There was more singing in the slave quarters than usual [there were two slave cabins on the Burroughs farm; one housed Booker's mother and siblings and was also the "cook house"] . . . and it was bolder, had more ring, and lasted later into the night."[34]

During the twenty-two pages of the first chapter, we are assured no less than five times that no bitterness existed in the mind of slave or master. Slavery exists in the narrative not in political terms but only in terms of personal, psychological reaction and interaction, the terms in which it exists in the southern mythology of slavery. There is some question raised, even, about whether emancipation was a good thing. The initial "wild rejoicing" during the first moments of the knowledge of freedom is soon replaced with doubts about whether the exslaves indeed want to be free, whether they can deal with the responsibility "of having charge of themselves, of having to think and plan for themselves and their children. . . . Was it any wonder that within a few hours the wild rejoicing ceased and a feeling of deep gloom seemed to pervade the slave quarters?"[35] The clear implication of the reasoning is to raise the question of whether ex-slaves *can* live outside the patriarchal system. Can male ex-slaves become men in terms of the nineteenth-century mythology surrounding gender roles; can they live without "old Marster"?

> Deep down in their hearts there was a strange and peculiar attachment to "old Marster" and "old Missus," and to their children, which they found it hard to think of breaking off. With these they had spent in some cases nearly a half century, and it was no light thing to think of parting. Gradually, one by one, stealthily at first, the oldest slaves began to wander from the slave quarters back to the "big house" to have a whispered conversation with their former owners as to the future.[36]

The question is not whether such scenes occurred (I am certain they did) but whether and why one, in representing the end of slavery for thousands of slaves, should choose to draw upon such a scenario in order to generalize about the system. Clearly the conversations alluded to were not between equals, clearly not "man to man" in the nineteenth century mode; but between (white) man, master, and feminized (whether in fact female or not) slave. This is our introduction, the first chapter, of Washington's autobiography, "A Slave among Slaves," itself feminizing because by definition a slave in the United States may be biologically male but not socially a man. To define oneself as a slave in the terms of the slaveholding culture means to define oneself as other than "man."

Washington's black male exists in conflict with a white male, a conflict represented in those elements of the narrative that force him time and again into submission to an overpowering ideology. The conflict between the black male, the unregenerated freedman, and those powers that would reform, reshape, refashion him, is reflected in the textual instances in which the narrator capitulates to an acknowledged superior force. When, for example, the narrator speaks (as above) of the slave protecting the lives of the confederate soldier's women, he is in effect dramatizing a social conflict and its resolution. The submerged conflict involves what might be a multilayered disagreement between slave and slave owner. A slave might, hypothetically, resent his enslavement; a resentful, bitter slave would not find it in his interest to act in the interest of his owner. Hence the narrative sets out to define and defuse, and thus resolve in dramatic terms, the racial conflicts that exist within the historical context in which the narrative is composed. Thus Washington does not become feminized by virtue of assuming "feminine wiles," by adopting a feminine manner. Instead he simply abandons the expression of those characteristics and prerogatives generally assumed to belong to males. He ensures that he does not threaten males either North or South with the possibility of confrontation along gender lines. He makes sure to remove, submerge, diminish the threatening element (as defined in nineteenth-century culture) of the slave's (the black man's) character, his masculinity. He thus willingly, strategically, and pragmatically feminizes himself and all black males (by implication) in order to achieve his ends.

Notes

1. Ralph Ellison refers to this quotation which appeared in his college sociology text in *Shadow and Act* (New York: Vintage, 1972), p. 308.
2. Booker T. Washington, *Up from Slavery* (New York: Penguin, 1986).
3. See Winthrop D. Jordan, *White Over Black: American Attitudes Toward the Negro 1550–1812* (Baltimore, MD: Penguin, 1969), 195–98.
4. Reported in Louis R. Harlan, *Booker T. Washington: The Making of a Black Leader, 1856–1901* (New York: Oxford Univ. Press, 1972). Washington's popular quips sometimes identified black men with animals: "There seems to be a sort of sympathy between the negro and a mule. Wherever you find a negro you are apt to find a mule somewhere about. I feel somewhat lonesome tonight." And again: "A colored man was once asked how many were in the family. He replied, 'Five of us. Myself, my brother and three mules.'" See also Houston Baker's discussion of Washington's reliance on the minstrel tradition in *Up from Slavery*. *Modernism and the Harlem Renaissance* (Chicago: Univ. of Chicago Press, 1987), 25–36. Baker's observations imply that minstrelsy dehumanizes African Americans (especially males) and thus serves to disempower.
5. I do not intend to suggest here that the laws were specifically designed to allow slave owners the right to name their slaves but rather that they were desgined to center absolute control of all slaves in the hands of slave owners. Hence the power of government stood behind the slave owner's exercise of his privileges over his chattel.

   Hundreds of eighteenth-century slave names are listed in Newbell Niles Puckett, *Black Names in America: Origins and Usage* (Boston: G.K. Hall, 1975), 1–40.
6. Orlando Patterson, *Slavery and Social Death: A Comparative Study* (Cambridge, MA: Harvard Univ. Press, 1982), 54–55. A further note on the importance of naming to Africans especially occurs in Sterling Stuckey, *Slave Culture: Nationalist Theory and the Foundations of Black America* (New York: Oxford Univ. Press, 1987), 197–98.

7. *Runaway Slave Advertisements: A Documentary History from 1730s to 1790* (Westport, CT: Greenwood, 1983), vols. 1–4. See also commentary on names in Peter H. Wood, *Black Majority: Negroes in Colonial South Carolina from 1670 through the Stono Rebellion* (New York: W.W. Norton, 1974), 181–85.
8. *Runaway Slave Advertisements,* vol. 1, 441.
9. Ibid., 419.
10. Ernst Cassirer, *Language and Myth* (New York: Dover, 1953), 3. Quoted in Patterson, *Slavery and Social Death,* 55. See also Stuckey, *Slave Culture,* 194–98.
11. *Runaway Slave Advertisements,* vol. 4, 15.
12. "In some way a feeling got among the colored people that it was far from proper for them to bear the surname of their former owners, and a great many of them took other surnames. This was one of the first signs of freedom." *Up from Slavery* (New York: Penguin, 1986), 23.
13. The insurrection of Nat Turner in 1831 in Southampton County, Virginia, was the most violent and intimidating southern slave rebellion ever to occur. Although Turner and his cohorts were eventually captured and executed, the rebellion inspired extraordinary fear and trembling in the slaveholding territory at large for years to come. As John Hope Franklin says, "The South was completely dazed by the Southampton uprising." *From Slavery to Freedom: A History of American Negroes,* 6th ed. (New York: McGraw-Hill, 1988), 134–35.
14. The most prominent example of this discourse is in Thomas Dixon's novel, *The Clansman* (New York: Doubleday, 1907) which defines black masculinity in exactly this way. It was the text on which D.W. Griffith's intensely anti-African American movie *Birth of a Nation* (1915) was based.
15. See Houston Baker's discussion of similarities between Washington's autobiography and the slave narrative, particularly Frederick Douglass's *Narrative,* in *Long Black Song: Essays in Black Literature and Culture* (Charlottesville: Univ. of Virginia Press, 1990), 87–88.
16. Frederick Douglass, *Narrative of the Life of Frederick Douglass, an American Slave* (New York: Penguin, 1982), p. 47.
17. It is not generally known that two earlier editions of Washington's autobiography preceded *Up from Slavery*, both titled *The Story of My Life and Work* (Naperville, IL: J.H. Nichols, 1900 and 1901).
18. Ibid., 36–37.
19. Douglass, *Narrative*, 51.
20. See Francis Pendleton Gaines, *The Southern Plantation* (New York: Columbia Univ. Press, 1924).
21. Washington, *Up from Slavery,* 12–13.

22. Ibid., 13.
23. Ibid.
24. I would argue that Washington's minimal references to his wives is not the result of a Victorian reticence to make public his private life so much as of his desire to minimize his self-representation as a sexual being. The relations between himself and his three wives reveal him to be a loving husband, although not always as expressive of his affection as they might have wished.
25. Washington, *Up from Slavery,* 14.
26. Ibid., 15.
27. Ibid., 16.
28. Washington, *The Story of My Life and Work*, 142–43.
29. Harlan, *Booker T. Washington,* 6–8.
30. Washington, *Up from Slavery,* 20.
31. Harlan, *Booker T. Washington,* 6.
32. Washington, *Up from Slavery,* 17.
33. Ibid., 19.
34. Ibid.
35. Ibid., 22.
36. Ibid.

6

"STAND BY YOUR MAN"

Richard Wright, Lynch Pedagogy, and Rethinking Black Male Agency

STEPHEN MICHAEL BEST

> So, in leaving, I was taking a part of the South to transplant in alien soil, to see if it could grow differently, if it could drink of new and cool rains, bend in strange winds, respond to the warmth of other suns, and, perhaps, to bloom. . . . And if that miracle ever happened, then I would know that there was yet hope in that southern swamp of despair and violence, that light could emerge even out of the blackest of the southern night.
>
> —Richard Wright[1]

As if describing a life on the lam for which his own was the prototype, Richard Wright observed, in a review of Langston Hughes's *The Big Sea*, that "out of [Hughes's] experiences as a seaman, [and] cook . . . have come his writings dealing with black gals who wore red stockings and black men who sang the blues at night and slept like rocks all day."[2] Hughes, at the *moment* when he became a seaman—and, Wright implies, a writer—made a significant and, I would argue, founding gesture. To begin his life as a writer, to prepare himself for a set of experiences that would become the longitude and latitude of his writings, Hughes tossed overboard his collection of books (save, significantly, his copy of Whitman's *Leaves of Grass*).[3] He tossed them, he claims, for they reminded him too much of his past, of a childhood spent "reading all the time . . . like life isn't."[4] The books triggered in him a sense of "always being controlled by others . . . by some outer necessity not your own" (98). In using the act of writing to escape a hated past of a controlling, omniscient, and unseen force, Hughes, Wright suggests, carried on "a manly tradition in literary expression."[5] Wright, moreover, in fingering the outlines of this tradition along the body of Hughes's writings, takes up the torch of this "manly tradition." Wright's writings address, more specifically, the controlling force of lynching. Hughes and Wright participate in a tradition that is "manly" precisely, and ironically, for its collusion of writing with flight and escape.[6] I say "ironically" for it is a tradition that stands in opposition to a position that holds writing and a tradition of letters to be "not manly enough"—in the case of black letters, writing is perceived as an inadequate site of cultural resistance.

The work that follows maps the protocols for recognizing and subjecting to resignification the discursive sign of the ostensibly "weak" black man in the interest of marking it as a site of resistance. In it, I attempt to "read" the "masculine" as it comes into view in critical writings on Richard Wright and to move beyond certain conceptions of black masculinity in America as, constitutively, masculinity denied, or the "masculine-emasculated."[7] For, from my analytical position this conception of black masculinity fits all too neatly into economies of ("black male") sexual excess and ("black male") capitalist lack, both of which, not surprisingly, need a big, black penis to emasculate in the first place, need to drive blacks beyond access to the phallus. These economies are at their core "seller's markets," "supply-side" theories in which the only stock options for the black male buyer with access to this national treasury are castration, on the one hand, and phallic investiture, on the other (Rodney King or Mike Tyson).

What concerns me most are the ideological uses of "flight"—not completely, or necessarily, as a sign of escape, but as a trope of *suspension* between poles of black and white, public and private, real and imaginary, past and present experience. In fact, flight looks just like autobiography when viewed under a poststructuralist optic, where the autobiographical "I" constitutes itself by keeping the autobiographical beginning (the position from which the text is being written) distinct from and in tension with the author's beginning (place of birth, "home") and body ("I am not the person writing the text, but the person being represented *in* the text").[8] The workings of this theoretical apparatus have been elaborated upon in other spaces.[9] For the moment, I want to focus on the efforts in Afro-American studies to maintain this binarized machinery—efforts that I think can have undesirable effects on our thinking, if only because they can be made to reproduce a natal black community untouched by the brush of theory, a community that still emits the "correct" signs of the historical oppositions between North and South, urban and rural, "us" and "the folk," the literate and the illiterate. Moreover, these oppositions are quite easily recouped by a discourse that sites the former terms as the privileged terminology of autobiography and as the locus of, or metaphors for, black elitism, alienation, and highbrow pretensions. One need only consider depictions of and Richard Wright as a figure in flight from (and afraid of) the folk to understand the links I am trying to trace.

I would reclaim Wright by arguing that the autobiographical incidents in his writings are less moments of the retroactive construction of a self prior to the writing of the text, and more moments of the suturing of theory and practice (of the potential for agency in the project of writing). Gramscian theoretical spectacles can help us to recognize the dimensions of this enterprise as they are made part of a text like *Black Boy*:

> The awareness of being part of a determined hegemonic force . . . is the first step towards a . . . self-consciousness in which theory and practice finally unite. So the unity of theory and practice is . . . not a given mechanical fact but an historical process of becoming, which has its elementary and primitive phases in the sense of "distinctiveness," of "separation," of a barely instinctive independence, and progresses up to the real and complete possession of a coherent and unitary conception of the world.[10]

With that in mind, my objective in this essay is to find what was *in* the South for Richard Wright (to see what was his "historical process of becoming") so that I might then determine if it is possible to have a revised understanding of his relation to family, community, and the South (as they are traditionally perceived). I want *too*, eventually, to figure out *how* he was in the South. (What *cognitive* experiences of the South are communicated through his writings?)

The opposition of the writing self and the lived self[11] is deeply troubling for Richard Wright and not something that is easily resolved by oppositions between autobiography and fiction or the word and history. In *Black Boy*, he locates his self between different sets of polarities—those of family (lack of community)/literacy (community), maternal nurturance/paternal deprivation, authority (subjugation)/autobiography (omnipotence), castration/phallic investiture. With each positioning he represents another aspect of an emerging impoverished social map—the troubled and troubling sites of the Great Migration. Take 1930 as a signal moment in the constitution of this new social map. As Trudier Harris points out, in that year, a few years before Wright's works began to appear and a few months after the stock market crash that triggered the Great Depression, the number of lynchings of Blacks increased almost threefold—from seven in 1929 to twenty in 1930.[12] One could read causally the relation between declining economic conditions and white terroristic violence, suggesting that the former increased idleness and irritability and led, ultimately, to the latter. These conditions mark an "emerging" social map, because it is through them that new relations between the economic, the sexual, and the racial are constituted. White *dis*enfranchisement (versus Reconstruction "protection" of civil rights) places black bodies in a new relation to the economic (antiblack advancement), the literate (antiblack literacy) and, of course, the sexual (antimiscegenation). Each relation is represented in *Black Boy*: the economic is at the center of the murder of Uncle Hoskins by jealous whites "who had long coveted his flourishing liquor business"[13]; the literate is at the center of Dick's (Wright's narrative persona) exploits in the library; and the sexual is at the center of the murder of Bob Greenly for "fooling with a white prostitute" (190). Taken together, these representations suggest that *Black Boy* is a text in which autobiographical agency—Wright's right to write—is represented in his subtle, subversive manipulation of the laws governing this emerging social map.

Lynch Law/Family Law

In their broadest schematizations, *family law* and *lynch law* condition the dynamics of place in the South broadly and in *Black Boy* narrowly. Wright depicts family law as the controlling parameters of family "normalcy," "the Southern way of life," and the code of Adventist religion—

original sin and the Fall. Family law is the perverse and ineffective order arising from an economically and juridically sanctioned condition of black placelessness. As Dick informs us: "The white South said that I had a 'place' in life. Well, I had never felt my 'place'" (283). It is a symptom of the problematic condition of people living in conflict without space.[14] From Dick's narrating perspective, family law is an heuristic tool of lynch law. That is to say, family law is the site where hegemony is made tangible, the domain where blacks *give over* their rights to agency. By the consensual definition of hegemony,[15] family law covers for a complicitous, conformist acquiescence in black communities caused by racism and segregation. Think for a moment of the linkages Dick makes upon his departure from Memphis. Excited to leave "the hated home, hunger, fear . . . days that had been as dark and lonely as death" (45), and unable to dissociate his childhood companions from his feelings of hunger and fear ("Their faces possessed the power of evoking in me a million memories that I longed to forget. . . ." [44]), Dick attempts to leave without saying good-bye. His mother orders him to return and give a proper farewell. He does as he is told, and later he reflects: "In shaking hands I was doing something that I was to do countless times in the years to come: acting in conformity with what others expected of me even though, *by the very nature and form of my life*, I did not and could not share their spirit" (my emphasis) (45). Here, Dick is responding primarily to the micro-aggression of etiquette. But we could also read the passage as a reflection on his body, in which case the struggle for bodily control would obliquely refer to the macro-aggressions of lynching.[16] This and similar passages can be read as suggestive of a grand autobiographical "plot" on Wright's part, to move swiftly and assuredly *away* from the black community. Valerie Smith stakes out this position with the greatest clarity. She argues that Wright's focus on characters he believes to be exceptional—for example, Dick (*Black Boy*), Cross Damon/Lionel Lane (*The Outsider*), and Big Boy ("Big Boy Leaves Home")—allows him to depict with contempt the larger black community, "identifying it with what he sees as an extreme tendency toward accommodation."[17]

The question of "Why accommodate," raised by Smith herself, seems inadequate to the complexities of survival under social, political, and cultural conditions of lynching. The threats to black bodies and well-being under conditions of nonaccommodation are widely known and need not be elaborated here.[18] What may be prudent for us to consider is George

Kent's contention that neither black folk culture of the 1920s nor the southern way of life "allowed a childhood to escape the compulsion toward an almost superstitious display of forms of reverence for its elders—even when 'reality' gave no justification for them" (82). How then do we read Dick's subtle and, at times, not-so-subtle gestures toward nonconformity? Are the "hard and sharp articulate terms" (81) of his selfhood, "imports from Northern urban middle-class culture" (82), as Kent argues? Is this critical position not, in part, the one that leads to the rather unsatisfying reading of *Black Boy* as fictional autobiography?[19] In other words, does this critical posture not, by perceiving Wright's assertions of selfhood as "imports" into a repressive southern geography, make all representations of resistance to Jim Crow fictional markers of his retroactive reconstruction of his subjectivity in the South? As I suggested earlier, this reading of Wright's work fits comfortably into a critical position that sees him as a figure in flight from the South.

Again, critical analyses that assume this position maintain oppositions between "the folk" and us, the South and the North, conformity (the South) and literacy (the North), the past and the present. Take as an example Henry Louis Gates, Jr.'s analysis of Wright in his study, *The Signifying Monkey* (1988). In that work, Gates argues that Wright is embroiled in the project of evolving a myth of origins of the self and race. Dick's independence of spirit reflects Wright's efforts to give "a shape and a purpose to an exceptional inherent nobility of spirit . . . [to a humanity] achieved only at the expense of his fellow blacks."[20] And Wright's overall aesthetic, based in what Gates calls an "agency of contrast,"[21] has at its center a project of foregrounding "the sensitive healthy part" against "a determined, defeated black whole."[22]

Like Gates, Abdul JanMohamed, in his article "Negating the Negation as a Form of Affirmation in Minority Discourse: The Construction of Richard Wright as Subject," grounds Wright's construction as a subject in a fundamental split between a radically autonomous author, on the one hand, and an oppressive "Southern timocracy" and defeated family, on the other. JanMohamed energizes his model with a Manichean dynamic of negation—"Manichean" in the sense that the subject's "becoming" occurs on the objective ground of good versus evil, body and soul, sacred and profane—among other binaries.[23] *Black Boy* is organized around familial plots of physical, moral, and emotional deprivation—especially those of hunger (associated with Dick's father) and suffering (associated with

Dick's mother)—and the experiences of living Jim Crow. JanMohamed suggests further that these geographies of lack and repression are maintained by Wright only to be negated by Dick's moves "into a brooding, meditative isolation" (251) and toward literature. Individuality and literacy are the currency of flight that allow Wright/Dick to escape perceiving his liminality and the social and political restrictions that surround him "not as the historical products of social relations but as natural and even metaphysical facts" (255). Dick's "spontaneous fantasies," as he calls them, are almost too effective as responses to this analytic position: "I had never in my life been abused by whites, but I had already become conditioned to their existence *as though I had been the victim of a thousand lynchings*"(my emphasis) (84). (Identity is dispersal and suturing, not coherence and contradistinction. African American autobiography is [or can be] poststructuralism by other means.) And while the above analyses—the "politics of distinction" model—can maintain watertight arguments for the position that Wright spent his entire career in flight, they leave open the question of the body *under* the law. The emphasis in African American literary theory on Wright's distinction and the autonomy resign the very calculated representations of Dick's body under conditions of lynch law into an invisibilizing critical black hole.

Wright began to develop his aesthetic of the body early in his career. In a poem published in 1935 in *The Partisan Review*, entitled "Between the World and Me," Wright constructs a scenario in which a speaker, during a walk in the woods, uncovers the charred body of a lynched man. The speaker imagines himself in turn being captured by a lynch mob and subsequently tarred and feathered, doused in gasoline, and burned alive:

> And then they had me, stripped me, battering my teeth into my
> throat till I swallowed my own blood . . .
>
> And in a blaze of red I leaped to the sky as pain rose like water,
> boiling my limbs . . .
>
> Now I am dry bones and my face a stony skull staring in yellow
> surprise at the sun . . .[24]

The poem's heightened evocations of the speaker's body at the center of a lynching ritual signal, according to Trudier Harris, aesthetic moves toward a sharper understanding of the vague fear caused by the threat of lynching: "The general human degradation becomes specific degradation of the *black* individual [of the "I"]. The 'I' becomes central for the speaker. As it becomes centralized, or specific, the 'I' reverses itself and becomes simultaneously generalized again."[25] So the historical black experience in the United States (in and around lynch violence) suggests the suffering of black individuals, which in turn suggests the suffering of the narrator. In what follows, I hope to locate aspects of this aesthetic of the body in Wright's autobiographical writings.

Unpacking "Agency"

In general, the problems I am dealing with (in criticism on Wright) concern the multiple dimensions of the law in the South and the literary-theoretical models that can recognize and perhaps contain, to some degree, the law's profound ambiguity. For this reason, I think it necessary first to outline the contours of "the Law" (and liberty) that I am applying to *Black Boy*.

Within a classical paradigm of the law, the prevailing model is an enlightenment one: one rooted historically in the bourgeois revolutions of the eighteenth century. The law is, under this rubric, all powerful, foundational, totalizing, and organized according to a center-periphery model of the social space. Under enlightenment conditions, "subjects" are always anchored to some sutured totality (e.g., democracy, the nation), and their emergence is always already determined. Following John Stuart Mill and David Hume, we might call this anchoring the "regularity determinism" of the subject, *viz.*, "that for every event x there is a set of events $y_1 \ldots y_n$ such that they are regularly conjoined under some set of descriptions [e.g., racism, the threat of lynching]."[26] Hypothetically, under historical conditions of lynching, event x might be the killing of a white man by a black man in the presence of the former's wife, event y_1 the arrest of the black man by the members of the community, event y_2 the interrogation of the white woman about the events leading up to the killing (with the presumption that the black man had a sexual interest in her), event y_n the lynching/murder of the black man.[27] So lynch law is deterministic because the final outcome is, under *all* conditions of the law, the only possible outcome—"summary justice" for threatening white masculinity, and the charge of upholding the purity of southern white womanhood make it so. A corollary to this model of the law and the constitution of subjects is, of course, that you cannot recognize the signs of agency (of a *resistant* agency) unless they are revolutionary, contrastive (Gates), or manichean (JanMohamed). A clearer sense of other possibilities for agency emerges, however, from a second model of the social space. Let us call the alternative model "poststructuralist."

The recent social theory work of Ernesto Laclau, Chantal Mouffe, and Jean-Francois Lyotard has presented a model of the social space that I think can inform our considerations of the law.[28] For these thinkers, "society" is not a founding totality—a domesticated field of differences united by necessary laws in which all subjects are anchored to organic, rational units such as "democracy," "the economy," or "the law." Rather, "society" for them is a nonessential, completely open, free-floating, and indeterminate sea of relations. Subjects emerge from this open, relational complex in and through a process of "fixing" (meaning "freezing") within the play of the *social*. However, subjects are not synonymous with "individuals" in their theory. Subjects are actually subject positions and, "as every subject position is a discursive position, it partakes of the open character of every discourse."[29] So, for example, Wright's race, class, and gender identity is not the origin of his social relations in the South—meaning, those identities do not render his experiences possible. Rather, his experiences of these positions themselves depend on precise, discursive conditions of possibility coming together at a particular moment. For Wright, as for Laclau and Mouffe, emergence of the subject is completely indeterminate: "From the discursive character of all subject positions, nothing follows concerning the type of relation that could exist among them."[30] This model of the subject under the law can be described more delicately as both Gramscian and Lacanian. Its Lacanian contours hold particular problems for me, so I shall look at it in the greatest amount of detail.

As is commonly understood, the Lacanian subject is a subject structured in language. Here, meaning is anchored at *points de capiton* (nodal points) in the midst of the free flow of signifiers: those moments of condensation whereby signifiers (e.g., "equality," "brotherhood") fall to the rank of the signified (e.g., "I am your brother!")—that is, the moment when bodies take part in political discourse. Laclau and Mouffe use this Lacanian image to describe the provisional halting of the indeterminacy of the social. It is their position that the *point de capiton* halts indeterminacy and allows the subject to partake in political choice and activity by articulating itself around the empty signifier of "rights" or "democracy." However, as Paul Smith points out, Laclau and Mouffe compromise their position on the indeterminacy of the social when they use a Lacanian model for fixity. For, the Lacanian moment of halting is, in Smith's view, the moment of the *imposition of the law of culture*. He states, "If the notion of rights or democracy or whatever is constituted at a *point de capiton,* then it is in fact not a signifier, still less an empty signifier, but a *signified*, fully implicated into the ideological and historical discourses of a particular culture."[31] In the crudest sense, Lacanian "*subject*-ion" is blurred as a Laclau/Mouffian moment of radical agency.

I spend time outlining two seemingly antithetical models of the law for two reasons. First, both models prevail in a paradigm of representation that needs a revolutionary black subject to transgress the limits of the law; and, as a consequence, both models are inadequate to the project of locating a controlling agent in the character of Dick. That is, the enlightenment model needs a hard, resistant, aggressive, essential subject to resist the empty, neutral signifiers of "citizen," "democracy," or "freedom." The Laclau/Mouffe model, however, because it cannot answer the question of why or how particular discourses are foregrounded or found appropriate at certain moments in history (all meaning is determined in the moment of articulation),[32] needs "revolution" as a discursive site in order to get outside of lynching as the prevailing discursive structure. Writ large, both analytics assume *seizure* of power as a condition of resistance and, consequently, subjectivity.

Nevertheless, I focus on enlightenment and poststructuralist models of agency because lynch/family law manifests both modes of discourse theory. That is, from one perspective, lynch/family law looks just like the law of "society," in the Laclau/Mouffian sense of a free-floating, indeterminate sea of signifiers—unencoded, unwritten, and waiting to take hold of its subjects. As an example of lynch law's indeterminacy, consider the scene in which Dick hitches a ride on the running board of a car filled with white men. When asked by one of the men, "'Wanna drink, boy?'" (199) Dick innocently responds, "'Oh, no!'" (200) At this point, he tells us, "I felt something hard and cold smash me between the eyes." (200) This was not, of course, the unrelieved rush of some soothing southern wind against Dick's body; it was the violent explosion of an empty whiskey bottle across his face. Dick falls uncontrollably from the car. The car stops and the white men file out. They hover over Dick's body and one says, in an instructive/interrogative manner, "'Ain't you learned to say *sir* to a white man?'" (200). A second adds, "'You reckon you know enough to ride now?'" (200). A third closes the lesson with, "'Nigger, you sure ought to be glad it was us you talked to that way . . . 'cause if you'd said that to some other white man, you might've been a dead nigger now'" (200). So, lynch law makes itself known, it defines itself, in the act of defining its subjects. The meaning of the altercation is not there from the start. Lynch law is, from Dick's narrative perspective, radically indeterminate.

Consider Dick's altercation with his Uncle Tom as an example of the indeterminacy of family law. The incident began, according to Dick, when Uncle Tom roused him from sleep by "calling gently and persistently. . . . 'What time have you? . . . What time have you got?'" (172) Dick responds in what he thinks is a normal, moderate respectful manner, "Eighteen past five. . . . If it's a little slow or fast, it's not far wrong." (172–3), only to be asked by Uncle Tom, "Now, is that the right time? . . . What on earth do you mean, boy?" (173) It is "time" of course, according to an oblique, cunning cultural logic, for Dick to get his behind out of bed. It is "eighteen past five" elsewhere. Taking Dick's literalness as a sign of his impudence, Uncle Tom grows progressively angrier. He swears: "I'm going to give you the whipping some man ought to have given you long ago" (173) because, in Tom's opinion, Dick needs "a lesson in how to live with people" (175). Dick reflects, while he waits to see what will happen, "now a strange uncle who felt I was impolite was going to teach me to act as I had seen the backward black boys act on the plantation, was going to teach me to grin, hang my head, and mumble apologetically when I was spoken to" (174). As in the altercation between Dick and the guys on the truck, Wright situates what Dick perceives as a pedagogy of *speech* ("'You'll swallow those words'" [175]; "'You shut that foul mouth'" [175]; "'Ain't you learned to say *sir*?'" [200]) under the sign of a pedagogy of the *body* ("grin," "hang my head," "had a nervous tic in my muscles" [174]). Both types of responses suggest "grammar books" of speech and the body; and, in predictable poststructuralist fashion, Dick fixes himself in the interstitial space between these poles, these stereotypical "folk" forms of resistance. Dick arms himself with two razor blades, while Uncle Tom prepares the switch. The altercation begins to take on deistic (not to say Oedipal) proportions: Dick threatens to cut Uncle Tom should he attempt to touch him; Uncle Tom condemns him to life as a "criminal"; Uncle Tom raises the stakes to questions of "spirit" and "baptism"; and, finally, Uncle

Tom withdraws in defeat (His "face began to twitch. Tears rolled down his cheeks. His lips trembled" [176]). In this heightened evocation of the real and necessary limits of family law, the scene clears a space for Dick to emerge as agent:

> I knew I had conquered [Uncle Tom], had rid myself of him mentally and emotionally. . . . "You are not an example to me; you could never be," I spat at him. "You're a *warning*. Your life isn't so hot that you can tell me what to do. . . . Do you think I want to grow up and weave the bottoms of chairs for people to sit in?" (176)

Dick frequently finds himself negotiating the fluid yet nomic connections between lynch/family law and the movements of black bodies and speech. This scene's fluidity, the sense that Dick ends up somewhere he never intended to be, is a symptom of the indeterminacy of family law.

From another perspective, lynch/family law is truly determinate. It conditions behaviors, emotions, and relations, among other things. It comes to control the subtlest body movements and the least conscious of thoughts and fantasies. The lesson in body control Dick receives at the hands of Griggs, an old classmate, is perhaps *Black Boy*'s clearest articulation of this aspect of lynch law. As Griggs instructs Dick, "When you're in front of white people, *think* before you act, *think* before you speak. Your way of doing things is all right among *our* people, but not for *white* people. They won't stand for it" (204). In fact, Griggs gives his lesson a bit late, for, as he informs Dick, Dick's inability to keep frustration from showing in his face has lead white people to see him as "marked already" (203). These signs are not the ones that trouble Dick, however. The gestures Griggs tells him his body *has* to manifest are the more dangerous from Dick's perspective. The signs that come bubbling to the surface when the law manifests itself in the body are what Wright calls "that-nigger-being-a-good-natured-boy-in-the-presence-of-a-white-man" (256) pattern.

In spite of the "both . . . and" nature of lynch/family law, it seems clear to me that we need to surpass both models in order to develop a clear image of agency as it manifests itself in Wright's work. Because when we insist on one of these models over another, we throw a blind eye to Dick's responses to family/lynch law that look neither like radical assertions of agency, nor like admissions of defeat—on the one hand missing their resistant elements and on the other missing their theoretical potential. We need, in other words, to reconstitute the notion of the radical agent. The "radical" is neither, as JanMohammed would have it, the revolutionary agent of absolute negation that is the subject of minority discourse, nor the pure avenging angel of marxist theory. The radical agent will emerge neither automatically nor necessarily from the most "correct" form of discourse (be it, at any one moment, marxism or Black Power or feminism or gay studies or any other social movement). Borrowing from Foucault, I would argue that identity, generally, be it radical or of any other sort, is never "there" as some primordial political object. Identity is there only as "strategy" (a concretization of an infinite set of possibilities made possible by particular episodes at particular moments in time) or "tactical productivity" (the guarantee of particular effects of power and knowledge). The agent who resists Jim Crow, economic disenfranchisement, and sexual disempowerment is not a theoretical "subject" but an active actor, "a historical entity among historically laden discourses"[33] (racism and the threat of lynching in a firmly entrenched cultural imaginary of liberalism).

Following Gramsci, I would say that to claim subjectivity is to operate philosophically. I would add that my particular objective is to locate the signs of Dick's emergence as "philosopher of blackness" and to trace the ways in which he redefines the numerous discourses that interpellate him.[34] And here Paul Smith's reading of Gramscian dynamics of power is instructive. He observes:

> If . . . the principles of hegemony are consent, negotiation, and articulation, then Gramsci is quite right when he recognizes that political power within modernity . . . could never simply be *seized*, but would rather have to be *built*—pieced together through the transformation of aspirations, values, and practices from a broadly conceived social ground.[35]

To locate the signs of this (re)constructive project, I want to close with a reading of two autobiographical moments in Wright's oeuvre.

The first example is taken from "The Ethics of Living Jim Crow," the autobiographical preface to *Uncle Tom's Children*. In this piece, Wright presents a series of nine sketches of a Jim Crow pedagogy. In the first sketch, he describes a childhood game of attacking passersby with the cinders that paved his yard: "the first woolly black head you saw pop out from behind another row of pillars was your target" (3), he tells us.[36] One day, however, Dick and his gang find themselves locked in a war with a local gang of white boys. The whites retaliate with a barrage of bottles. Dick is cut by one of the bottles, and after he turns to his mother for understanding, she teaches him a lesson by, in Dick's words, "[smacking] my rump with the stave, and . . . [imparting] . . . gems of Jim Crow wisdom" (4). He later reflects:

> From that time on, the charm of my cinder yard was gone. [White spaces] grew very meaningful, became a symbol. . . . [T]he hard, sharp outlines of white houses . . . are present somewhere in the background of my mind. Through the years they grew into an overreaching symbol of fear. (5)

So, Dick himself concludes that violent resistance (which is synecdochic for revolutionary subjectivity) does not hold the same potential later in life, yet neither (as the next example will show) is acquiescence a solution.

In the final sketch, which opens with a description of Dick's cunning strategies in the library, Wright details an incident that occurred while he worked in Memphis. He enters an elevator with his arms full of packages. In spite of his awareness that "all men must take off their hats when they enter an elevator" and that this rule applied to blacks "with rigid force" (14), Dick continues to ride with his hat on. He receives cold stares from two white men in the elevator, and one begrudgingly takes Dick's hat and places it on his bundle of packages. Dick thinks of two conditioned responses—one of which he finds distasteful, the other of which holds dangerous consequences. Either he can "look at the white man out of the corner of his eye and grin" (14), or he could say "Thank you!" The first is the somatic response conditioned by lynch/family law (and it is a distasteful marker of his submission), and the second is dangerous because the white man could think that Dick thought he was receiving "a personal service" (14)—that he could accede to the discursive terrain of "brotherhood." Dick thinks of the latter: "For such an act I have seen Negroes take a blow in the mouth" (14). In an act of bodily dissemblance, Dick charts a course that keeps him clear of these two alternatives. He pretends that the packages are about to fall and appears distressed with keeping them in his arms. This alternative "fell safely between these two poles" (14) and allows him to claim space outside of the laws of the South. He manages to "salvag[e] a slender shred of personal pride" (15).

If we see the sketches in *Uncle Tom's Children* as bracketing Wright's literary project of constructing a model for the emergence of the black male agent *in the context of the South* (from "cinders" and "clubs" to "words"), then we are almost compelled to read Wright's move toward literacy as an enabling one. Consider *Black Boy*'s (by now) infamous chapter where Dick gains access to the local library. Here, Dick pens a note ("Dear Madam: Will you please let this nigger boy . . . have some books by H.L. Mencken?"[37]) so that he might usher himself into the library as messenger (safe discursive position) and not reader/patron (undeniably dangerous position). So that he might also be able to read the books without suffering the difficult criticism of white coworkers, he wraps them in newspapers.

Dick later tells us that he engaged in this subversive play (i.e., writing degrading letters, wrapping books in newspapers) only because he believed that "outright black rebellion could never win. If I fought openly I would die and I did not want to die. News of lynchings were frequent." (276). JanMohammed, however, takes scant account of this position (and the body control it enables) and argues that Wright's privileging of the positive value of literature, "the cultural formation that provided him with the only possibility of escape from racist confinement, [leaves him] partially blind to the relation between the negative and positive components of his subjective formation."[38] He observes further that Dick's "resourceful and cunning 'triumph'" in the library "contains a profound negation of Wright."[39] Ignoring, for the moment, JanMohammed's quasi-utopic model for black resistance to racial subjugation and for the emergence of black male subjectivity, I ask: What *specific* kinds of agency are suggested by Wright's accounts of his existence in the South? Are they not very much like the kinds of resistances to subjugation we express in response to the banal, subtle, everyday microaggressions (and, on certain occasions, macroaggressions) of racism in its mercurial dimensions?

I offer this literary-critical essay as prologema to an array of critical interventions much broader in scope than the essay itself. Wright's cunning designs and his unswerving faith in the power of literacy and the subversive passivity of reading serve of course to highlight the asphyxiating sweep of the architectonics of a pre–Civil Rights southern repression. They serve as well to draw attention to the frequent incommensurability between preordained, juridical strategies of resistance and African American ways of life. From the "warmth of the other sun" of a post–Civil Rights era's "equality," Wright's association of literacy and resistance should certainly give us pause as to the consequences of recent formations of black masculinity and/as resistance. I have in mind a kid of black "new jack" posturing of the Reagan-Bush (and now Clinton) era. This posture finds itself represented in the "ghetto realness" of the recent bloom of black films, and perhaps finds its penultimate expression in the phallic hardness of a gangster rapper such as Ice Cube (a hardness which is, not surprisingly, being subtly denatured by the falsetto crooning of Snoop Doggy Dog). It can also be found in the sartorial rigidity of the Nation of Islam and the performative theatrics of its most famous son, Khalid Muhammed. And the almost simultaneous response of such political and cultural behemoths as *The New York Times*, the Anti-Defamation League of B'nai-B'rith, and the United States Congress, of all places, to the sabre-rattling rhetorics of Mr. Muhammed only goes to show how eagerly American culture *awaits* such assertions of black phallic excess, as I argued earlier. I have in mind as well the crises in black male celebrity that have accompanied the rise and fall of such figures as Arthur Ashe, Magic Johnson, Clarence Thomas, Michael Jordan, and O.J. Simpson, which, if they represent anything, represent a more deep-seated national dilemma concerning the emancipatory possibilities of a black masculinity. Suffice to say, something more than a seldom lamented black bourgeois respectability has been lost in the receeding potency of the "sly civility" that W.E.B. Du Bois championed and the emergent visibility of a particular representation of black masculine resistance we have come recently to enjoy.

Notes

1. Richard Wright, *Black Boy: A Record of Childhood and Youth* (New York: Harper & Row, 1937).
2. Richard Wright, "Forerunner and Ambassador," 28 October 1993, 600.
3. Arnold Rampersad, *The Life of Langston Hughes*, vol. 1 (New York: Oxford Univ. Press, 1986), 72.

4. Langston Hughes, *The Big Sea* (New York: Thunder's Mouth, 1986), 97. All subsequent references to this work are included parenthetically in the text.
5. Richard Wright, "Forerunner and Ambassador," 601.
6. The connection between literacy and flight is central to the genre of the slave narrative. For one of the most sustained discussions of this paradigmatic conjuncture in twentieth-century African American literature, and Richard Wright's work in particular, see "Literacy and Ascent: Richard Wright's *Black Boy*," in Robert Stepto's *From Behind the Veil: A Study of Afro-American Narrative* (Chicago: Univ. of Illinois Press, 1979), 128–162.
7. See Amiri Baraka's "American Sexual Reference: Black Male" and "Brief Reflections on Two Hot Shots," in *Home: Social Essays* (New York: William Morrow, 1966), and James Baldwin's "Everybody's Protest Novel" and "Many Thousands Gone," in *Notes of a Native Son* (Boston: Beacon, 1983).
8. For a linguist's understanding of the same problematic, see Emile Benveniste, *Problems in General Linguistics* (Miami, FL: Univ. of Miami Press, 1971).
9. See Roland Barthes, *The Rustle of Language* (Berkeley: Univ. of California Press, 1989), particularly the chapter entitled "Deliberation."
10. Antonio Gramsci, *The Modern Prince & Other Writings*, trans. Louis Marks (New York: International, 1987), 67.
11. I use an economy of language here only because mapping the distinction between these terms is not my chief objective. Houston Baker, Jr.'s discussion of the difficulties encountered in the split between the cognitive and the phenomenal are instructive of the division I cite as a problem in the project of writing (the self). He states:

    > If one begins, not with the phenomenal, but with the cognitive, then one is required to ask: How are cognitive "models" conceived, articulated, and transmitted in human cultures? Certainly one of the obvious answers here is *not* that human beings are *endowed* with a "system of signs," but rather that *models of cognition are conceived in, articulated through, and transmitted by language*. And like other systems of culture, language *is* a "social institution." Hence, if cognitive "models" of "fiction" differ from those of other spheres of human behavior, they do so not because fiction is somehow discontinuous with social institutions.

    See Baker, *Blues, Ideology, and Afro-American Literature: A Vernacular Theory* (Chicago: Univ. of Chicago Press, 1984), 100. A similar argument, and one that focuses on the split between "the word" and "history," can be found in the dialogue on apartheid between Jacques Derrida, Anne McClintock, and Rob Nixon; in *"Race," Writing, and Difference*, ed. Henry Louis Gates, Jr.

(Chicago: Univ. of Chicago Press, 1986). I thank Jason Miller for drawing these discussions to my attention.

12. See Trudier Harris, *Exorcising Blackness: Historical and Literary Lynching and Burning Rituals* (Bloomington: Indiana Univ. Press, 1984).

13. Richard Wright, *Black Boy.* All subsequent references to this work are included parenthetically in the text.

14. For a discussion of the uprooted African's impetus to *meta*, i.e., nonmaterial levels of discursive activity (e.g., conjurers, griots, spirits, among other things), in the face of this placelessness, see Houston A. Baker, Jr., *Workings of the Spirit: The Poetics of Afro-American Women's Writing* (Chicago: Univ. of Chicago Press, 1991), 39–41.

15. I take the consensual definition of hegemony to be the construction of a social bloc of forces that are the basis of consent for a certain social order, "in which the hegemony of a dominant class is created and re-created in a web of institutions, social relations, and ideas" (see Tom Bottomore, ed., *A Dictionary of Marxist Thought*, 201). Andrew Ross provides a more thorough definition of hegemony in his study of intellectuals and popular culture, *No Respect*. He contends that social formations become hegemonic when political and civil concerns are consolidated in favor of a large historic bloc (rather than a single dominant class), when that bloc succeeds in containing and articulating "in the form of a popular and seemingly unified collective will" the interests of a vast collection of subordinate groups *and* its own interests (see Ross, *No Respect: Intellectuals and Popular Culture* [New York: Routledge, 1989], 55).

16. Psychiatrist Charles Pierce divides an array of African American responses to the violence and aggression of racism into the categories of micro- and macro-agressions. See his "Offensive Mechanisms," in *The Black Seventies,* Floyd G. Barbour, ed. (Boston: Porter Sargent, 1970), 265–282.

17. Valerie Smith, *Self-Discovery and Authority in Afro-American Narrative* (Cambridge, MA: Harvard Univ. Press, 1987), 69.

18. See Ida B. Wells-Barnett, *On Lynchings: Southern Horrors, A Red Record, Mob Rule in New Orleans*, 1892; reprinted with a new introduction by August Meier, ed. William Loren Katz (Salem, NH: Ayer, 1990).

19. See W[illiam]. E[dward]. B[urghardt]. Du Bois, "Richard Wright Looks Back," *New York Herald Tribune*, 4 March 1945, sec. 5, 2. The criticism that Wright was making up stories and telling tall tales in *Black Boy* also does not leave space for family members who did not mind his exaggerating the real. His Aunt Addie defended him, arguing that if Richard had to make money to support his family that way it was all right with her; see Margaret Walker, *Daemonic Genius* (New York: Warner, 1988), 365 n. 87.

20. Henry Louis Gates, Jr., *The Signifying Monkey: A Theory of African-American Literary Criticism* (Oxford: Oxford Univ. Press, 1988), 182.
21. This is similar to a contemporary cultural phenomenon that law professor Regina Austin calls the "politics of distinction," in which "role models" and black "firsts" abound in contradistinction to the "lowlifes" and "lawbreakers" within the fantasized construct of "the black community." See Regina Austin, "'The Black Community', Its Lawbreakers and a Politics of Identification," *Southern California Law Review* 65 (1992): 1769–1817.
22. Gates, *The Signifying Monkey,* 182.
23. This contrasts with Sartrean notions of negation as freedom-constituting: the existential, analytic rupture of "saying no"; Tom Bottomore, ed., *A Dictionary of Marxist Thought*, 353.
24. Richard Wright, "Between the World and Me," *The Partisan Review* 2 (July–August 1935): 18–19.
25. Trudier Harris, *Exorcising Blackness,* 101.
26. Tom Bottomore, ed., *A Dictionary of Marxist Thought*, 117.
27. Past readers of *Uncle Tom's Children* (1940; New York: Harper & Row, 1989) will recognize this as a distillation of the narrative of Wright's short story "Down by the Riverside."
28. See Ernesto Laclau and Chantal Mouffe, *Hegemony and Socialist Strategy: Towards a Radical Democratic Politics* (New York: Verso, 1985); and Jean Francois Lyotard, *The Postmodern Condition: A Report on Knowledge*, trans. Geoff Bennington and Brian Massumi (Minneapolis: Univ. of Minnesota Press, 1984).
29. Ernesto Laclau and Chantal Mouffe, *Hegemony and Socialist Strategy*, 115.
30. Ibid.
31. See Paul Smith, "Laclau's and Mouffe's Secret Agent," in *Community at Loose Ends*, ed. Miami Theory Collective (Minneapolis: Univ. of Minnesota Press), 105. I have yet to be able fully to incorporate Smith's ideas into my own thinking on Laclau and Mouffe. However, I think his observations on the seeming contradiction(s) between their radical indeterminacy and Lacan's fixity can be helpful in mapping the ambiguities between lynch law/family law as determinate, on the one hand, and as radically indeterminate, on the other.
32. Ibid.
33. Ibid, 110.
34. According to Gramsci, to become actors in the world ("philosophers"), subjects must move from the level of language to the level of criticism and awareness. When subjects fail to achieve this move, they remain participants "in a

conception of the world 'imposed' mechanically by external environment, that is, by one of the many social groups in which everyone is automatically involved from the time he enters the conscious world"; see Antonio Gramsci, *The Modern Prince*, 58.

35. Paul Smith, "Laclau and Mouffe's Secret Agent," 109–109.

36. Richard Wright, *Uncle Tom's Children*, 3. All subsequent citations are included parenthetically in the text.

37. Richard Wright, *Black Boy*, 270.

38. Abdul JanMohammed, "Negating the Negation as a Form of Affirmation in Minority Discourse," 247.

39. Ibid., 261.

7

BODY POLITICS

Race, Gender, and the Captive Body

GEORGE P. CUNNINGHAM

> Many questions were troubling the explorer, but at the sight of the prisoner he asked only: "Does he know his sentence?" "No," said the officer, eager to go on with his exposition, but the explorer interrupted him: "He doesn't know the sentence that has been passed on him?" "No," said the officer again, pausing a moment as if to let the explorer elaborate his question, and then said: "There would be no point in telling him. He'll learn it on his body."
>
> —Franz Kafka[1]

> Every social order systematically takes advantage of the disposition of the body and language to function as depositories of deferred thoughts that can be triggered off at a distance in space and time by the simple effect of re-placing the body in an overall posture which *recalls* the associated thoughts and feelings, in one of the inductive states of the body, which as actors know, give rise to states of mind.
>
> —Pierre Bourdieu[2]

The visualness of the documentary chronicle of the Civil Rights movement, *Eyes on the Prize*, graphically preserves the ways in which that struggle was acted out and understood as dispositions and positionings of bodies. Both sides put their bodies on the line. The first episode, "Awakenings (1954–56)," begins with politics as bodily enactments: the story of Emmett Till, a fourteen-year-old who was, in the almost formulaic denouement, lynched in Mississippi for whistling at a white woman.[3] Paired with Rosa Parks's refusal to sit in the back of the bus in Montgomery, Alabama, Till's death provides one of the twin points of departure for telling and giving meaning to the Civil Rights movement. Alone, Till's dead body is emptied of its agency and can only be read as the material signifier of the position accorded blacks in southern racial discourse, but Parks's refusal to "move to the back of the bus" and to accept "her place" within that same racial discourse signals the writing of an African American embodied agency.

Although it is a woman, Rosa Parks, who symbolically acts first to create a new inscription of the body politic, the resulting narrative of Civil Rights is most often understood as authored by men. Looking backward, Michael E. Dyson said at the 1991 ceremony renaming a section of a Chicago street "Emmett Till Road":

> The unspeakable horror of Emmett's death caused shock to ripple through the entire nation. More importantly, his death galvanized a people perched on the fragile border between heroism and fear to courageously pursue meaningful and complete equality. In the curious mix of fortuity and destiny that infuse all events of epic meaning, Emmett's death gained a transcendent metaphoric value. Rosa Parks drew strength from his unintended martyrdom when she sat down with dignity so that all black people could stand up with pride. Medgar Evers cried bitter tears of frustration and pain, and he was charged to gird his loins and renew his commitment to shout justice in Mississippi's Dark Delta, leading to his own death and a rightful place at Emmett's side in the sacred pantheon of murdered martyrs. And Emmett's death gave Martin Luther King, Jr., the great social prophet and American visionary who himself answered the highest call to service and paid the greatest price of sacrifice, an irresistible symbol for the civil rights movement.[4]

In Dyson's dedication, the memory of Till is assimilated into a narrative of African American male bodily agency, the Civil Rights movement; and Till's figure of an African American death is superseded by the no less gruesome murders of the Civil Rights workers Goodman, Schwerner, and Chaney (1964); and the assassinations of Medgar Evers (1963), Malcolm X (1965), and Martin Luther King, Jr. (1968). One barely notices the displacement of Parks by the men who serve to reinscribe the figure of Till—senselessly and irrationally murdered—into a roll call of martyrs to brotherhood. Their deaths as redemptive sacrifices "written in blood" represent "racial" agency in the American body politic.

Rosa Parks's "sacrifice" provides a point from which to question the narrative beginnings of contemporary African American politics by setting in motion a discussion of gender as another dimension of body politics. Although the principle focus of this essay is on the African American male as subject, my approach is not a deferral of the project of a more equitable history but proposes an alternative notion of "beginnings" and more indirect route toward creating the possibility for a new reading of contemporary politics. The restoration of gender to the "racial" narrative is no simple gesture of addition. What is needed is an interrogation of the mutual markings that gender and race make on each other at the point of "beginnings" of a variety of subjects. Rosa Parks's displacement, however, is not a separate issue. That displacement is already a repetition that is interwoven within the persistence of figures like Till.

Many African American men are still haunted by the image of Till's death. Subtending Dyson's memorial to Till is an ever-present alternate reading of that same history:

> In the 1960s, during a crucial stage in the development of black pride and self-esteem, highly educated, deeply conscientious black men were gunned down in cold blood. This phenomenon finds paradigmatic expression in the deaths of Medgar Evers, Malcolm X, and Martin Luther King, Jr. These events of public death are structured deep in the psyches of surveying black men, and the ways in which these horrible spectacles of racial catastrophe represent and implicitly sanction lesser forms of social evil against black men.[5]

Here, the visions that Evers, Malcolm X, and King wrote with their own blood are erased and their bodies emptied by violence of the possibility of agency. Captured in another's discourse, their bodies come to speak another's message, saying: "No black man could possess an intelligent fire that would sear the fierce edges of ignorance and wither to ashes the propositions of hate without being extinguished."[6]

Dyson's first and second renderings of the same history are governed by sharply different senses of time. The first story of the Civil Rights movement is linear and progressive, while the second—"this drama of tragic demise, compressed agony, nearly impotent commiseration, and social absurdity"—is, in his own terms, "paradigmatic" and recursive.[7] Extending Homi Bhabha's argument about nationalism, the sense of self, of nation, and of peoplehood always exists in the "double time" that characterizes Dyson's reading. There is the present with its linear and progressive possibilities, "the prodigious, living principle of the people as that continual process by which the national life is redeemed."[8] Coexisting with it is a recursive moment that *tells us who we are*, "an authority that is based on the pre-given origin or event."[9] For African American men, that recursive moment is almost always figured as a violated body.

The last half of the 1980s has been marked by visible demands of the recursive, the direct and indirect "paradigmatic" enactments, not as private moments of the self but as national dramas. Although one could choose from a variety of recent public incidents, most particularly the Rodney King beating,[10] I have chosen five because of their paradigmatic affiliation with the death of Emmett Till. In November of 1987, Tawana Brawley alleged abduction and rape at the hands of white "officials." On April 21, 1989, an unnamed 28-year-old white investment banker was raped and beaten by a gang of black and Hispanic teenagers in New York's Central Park. On August 23, 1989, Yusef Hawkins was killed when some young men of Bensonhurst, New York thought he was the African American man who was attending a party given by a young Italian woman. To these, I would add two more "framing" cases. In the presidential election of 1988, George Bush appealed to white-male voters by symbolically interposing himself between the (white) woman and the black-male-as-rapist, "Willie" Horton. On October 23, 1989, in Boston, the pregnant Carol Stuart was shot and killed, allegedly by a black man, while her husband who was also almost mortally wounded looked on. In the contemporary discussions of race, these acts that intertwine power, violence, and sexuality—ultimately reduced to figures of various violated bodies—

emerged into national consciousness as public spectacles and codes for the nature and well being of the body politic.

A common structure, a triangle of desire, unites these cases on a paradigmatic level with the death of Emmett Till. Although each is a variation, the triangle positions black men and white men as adversaries in a contest over the body of women. This triangular structuring of relationships is similar, often behaves like, and can often be read as Sigmund Freud's oedipal triangle, Rene Girard's triangle of mimetic desire, and Eve Sedgwick's triangle of homosocial desire. And, much like Freud's primal scenes of the self, triangles of desire are evocations of prior paradigmatic scenes of violence and violation of the body—castration, the overthrow of the father, seduction (rape)—that have structuring capacities for the subject and that insist themselves through repetition. However, as Eve Sedgwick notes about her triangles of homosocial desire, they are not "ahistorical platonic form[s]" but are "sensitive register[s] precisely for delineating relationships of power and meaning, and for making graphically intelligible the play of desire and identification by which individuals negotiate with their societies for power."[11] Focusing on a triangulation as a configurative site of the relationship of racial and gendered bodies to each other provides a way of thinking and talking about the simultaneity of race and gender that traditional binary logics do not afford.[12] Triangles of desire chart the contours, textures, and structures that unite race and gender as an embodied and subjective experience.

Reading the triangle involves journeys. First, I return to slavery to explore a primal scene in Frederick Douglass's *Narrative* of 1845 as a moment of origins that locates the position of the African American male in the triangle of desire. Next, my discussion of Willie Horton (and me) focuses on contemporary events and the pitfalls of any specific vantage point in the triangle. At the same time, I focus on a journey from a private moment of self to the public act of contestation that involves many selves. That strategy opens up to an increasing number of reading positions within the triangle, including those of black and white feminists and white men. I am interested in examining the ways in which this paradigm of triangulation structures the often contradictory possibilities of resistance and complicity in racial and gender hierarchies. I argue that the subject positions available to black men are intimately entwined with those available to white men, black women, and white women.

"The bloodstained gate:" The Primal Triangle

> I love you Porgy, don't let him take me.
> Don't let him handle me with his hot hands.
> If you can keep me, I want to stay here
> With you forever. I've got my man.
> Some day I know he's coming back to call me.
> He's going to handle me and hold me so.
> It's going to be like dying, Porgy, when he calls me.
> But when he comes, I know, I'll have to go.[13]

> The captive body, then, brings into focus a gathering of social realities as well as a metaphor for value so thoroughly interwoven in their literal and figurative emphases that distinctions between them are virtually useless. Even though the captive flesh/body has been "liberated," and no need pretend that even the quotation marks do not matter, dominant symbolic activity, the ruling episteme that releases the dynamics of naming and valuation, remains grounded in the originating metaphors of captivity and mutilation so that it is as if neither time nor history, nor historiography and its topics, shows movement, as the human subject is "murdered" over and over again by the passions of a bloodless and anonymous archaism, showing itself in endless disguise.[14]

Any imagined moment of beginnings must, for African Americans, be located in the act of enslavement. For Hortense Spillers, the "Middle Passage" of the triangular slave trade is a place of beginnings, "where the loss of indigenous name/land provides a metaphor for the displacement of other human and cultural features and relations, including the displacement of the genitalia, the female's and the male's desire that engenders the future."[15] As the section's opening passage from Spillers suggests, the historical moment of captivity recurs, shaping and giving meaning to the present. Enslavement, the moment of captivity of the body, is marked first by material displacements and deferrals that recreate themselves as discursive sights of captivity. The African American as captive body, materially and metaphorically, is public and on the block; to be bid upon in a circuit of linguistic, discursive, and axiological exchange outside the control of its own agency.

Frederick Douglass's *Narrative* of 1845 is the classic, though not unproblematic, intervention in that circuit of displacements and deferrals. Douglass configures the dilemma of slavery and offers a paradigmatic model for reclaiming the captive body. The first chapter of Douglass's *Narrative* renders the account of the slave's origins by configuring the possibility of his own desire against the overwhelming surplus of his master's. "I was born . . ." as a statement only suggests the possibility of origins that Douglass must rescue from the master's appropriations. Douglass elaborates his problems of textual and ontological origins as a series of absences of knowledge that serve to define the nature of slavery itself: "I have no accurate knowledge of my age," "the means of knowing" his father were "withheld," he was separated from his mother "before I knew her as my mother." They are matched by the master's corresponding surplus of knowledge and power: he may have "authentic records" documenting the slave's birth, and he may remove the mother to "hinder the development of the child's affection" for her.[16]

Douglass concludes his inquiry into the nature of slavery and the problematics of origins by refiguring the absences that characterize slavery in the scene where the master whips Hester, the sister of Douglass's mother. That scene provides him, in Ned Lukacher's terms, "a step toward solving the crisis of interpretation that emerges when the question of the origin becomes unavoidable and unanswerable." His representation of the whipping of Hester provides us with a "primal scene" of the African American (male) self-gestalt interweaving slavery, racial difference, and gender difference—that continues to "figure . . . an interpretive dilemma."[17] This scene, which Douglass labels as the "blood-stained gate, the entrance to the hell of slavery" (51), is also, in Lukacher's terms, a moment "that enable[s] us to trace the emergence of new discourses."[18]

Douglass renders his own capture and disinvestment as a domestic and familial drama, a symbolic family triangle, which contains the constituent elements of the Freudian primal phantasy: the child overseeing parental intercourse.[19] Although the identity of Douglass's father is fraught with tensions never directly addressed, in the *Narrative* he reports to his readers that "the opinion was also whispered that my master was my father" (48).

If we accept as true those rumors, as many historians have, then Douglass's representation of this scene takes on new possibilities of meaning. At the point in the *Narrative* where this incident takes place, Douglass's mother has died and her sister, Hester, seems to have taken her place in his master's (father's) "favor." In this context, Douglass not only witnesses his first example of the brutality of slavery, but he is also transported to witness the mysteries associated with his own conception, his beginnings; and his domestic triangle renders in an autobiographical and subjective mode the same displacements and deferrals that Spillers's "Middle Passage" conveys.

With due regard to nineteenth-century conventions, Douglass presents the scene as sexualized, a symbolic rape. The master Aaron Anthony's jealousy of Hester's relationship with a male slave leads to this incident. Hester was "absent when my master desired her presence," and she is found with a male slave, "Ned Roberts generally called Lloyd's Ned" (51), against Anthony's express orders. Anthony whips her for disobeying him, and the whipping itself is a sexualized ritual of the master's power:

> Her arms were stretched up at their full length, so that she stood upon the ends of her toes. He then said to her, "Now, you d______d b_____h I'll you how to disobey my orders!' and after rolling up his sleeves, he commenced to lay on the heavy cowskin, and soon the war, red blood (amid heart rending shrieks from her, and horrid oaths from him) came dripping to the floor. (52)

As Houston Baker suggests, Douglass is revising a scene from earlier slave narratives. In *The Life of Olaudah Equiano*, Equiano recounts the circumstances when he and his sister were captured and transported by Africans to the Coast. One of the traders slept between Equiano and his sister. For Baker, that interposition "signals a . . . loss of familial (and by implication, conjugal) relations."[20] Douglass here tropes a scene that will recur over again in the slave narrative and in modern Afro-American texts.

The master's discourse clearly forbids the black male's presence and intervention, and only Douglass's critique of slavery allows the restoration of black men to the scene. Most gendered interpretations of that scene focus on the ambiguities of Douglass's reassertion of his own presence through an act of representation.[21] Douglass also restores another male presence to the scene who, for my purposes, provides a useful vantage point. He presents us with the doubly named "Ned Roberts generally called Lloyd's Ned." His double naming recalls exactly Spiller's notion of a "dual fatherhood . . . , comprised of the African father's *banished* name and body and the captor father's mocking presence."[22] Ned Roberts's ambiguous position is highlighted by Douglass's earlier presentation of his maternal lineage, a bloodline that he goes to some pains to show is unbroken. Douglass tells us, "My mother was named Harriet Bailey. She was the daughter of Issac and Betsey Bailey, both colored, and quite dark. My mother was of a darker complexion than either my grandmother or grandfather" (47). Douglass's certainty about his mother's appearance is one of the few emphatic claims of knowledge about her that he makes. His maternal lineage can only be guaranteed by reading the bodily rather than the cultural text, the color rather than the names. That unbroken black lineage ends, of course, with Douglass's birth.

Ned is offstage not only as the black man that Hester could not choose but also as the black man that Harriet could not choose, the black father that Douglass did not have, and possibly the black father that Douglass could never be. The whipping stands to forestall the possibility of a "Ned Roberts"—an African American manhood symbolized by a patroynm—who can claim a relationship with Hester, a man who could bestow his name, could claim wife and children and symbolically offer himself as the founder of a genealogical line that would deny the master's rights. Through his ability to represent, Douglass intervenes and belatedly answers Hester's cries; "Frederick Douglass" becomes the man that "Lloyd's Ned" could not be.

The resolution that Douglass offers perhaps is best represented in the scene of his writing and the moment when he speaks of himself as "seated by my own table, in the enjoyment of freedom, and the happiness of home, writing this Narrative" (75). However, that resolution is called into question by contemporary feminism, particularly the work of black feminist critics. Deborah McDowell's description (in a different context) of an African American male "family romance," a "story of the Black Family cum Black Community headed by the Black Male who does battle with an oppressive White world,"[23] seems to offer an instructive way of looking at Douglass's resolution of the dilemma posed by the primal triangle. McDowell's intentions, of course, are not to celebrate the reconstructed patriarchal family; she finally argues that Douglass's journey into freedom is a mimetic one that ends in the reinscription of gender hierarchy and reproduces the master's posture toward black women.

By restoring the voice of African American women, black feminist criticism provides a vantage point that reads that scene differently. Among others, they call into question any male's appropriation of rape and sexualized violence against women as a site of origins for the masculine self. As Lynn Higgins and Brenda Silver argue, sexualized violence symbolizes something completely different: "rape and rapability are central to the very construction of gender identity."[24] The restored presence of women is critical in mediating between Douglass's rendering of the primal triangle and contemporary discussions of the representation of race and gender. While McDowell questions Douglass's representation of the slave master's treatment of black women, her major concern is the repetition of that paradigm by subsequent critics who accord "widespread explanatory power and appeal" to a life and work that is "attached so solidly to the logic of beginning and origins."[25]

The multiple claims on this scene are an important indicator of its critical intertextual status among a variety of subjects.[26] To choose among claimants a "correct" vantage point is also to assume that our "gender" and "race" exists *prior* to the scene. Rather than existing in an already gendered and racial economy, the primal triangle serves as the structuring point of origins for gendered and racial differences. This scene figures not only the emergence of key aspects of the discourses of racial and gender hierarchy but also exists to represent them, to help interpellate us into gendered and racial positions. If "race" and "gender" are social constructions, this primal triangle foregrounds the impossibility and inadequacy of understanding them as separable binary oppositions, challenging us to understand that in American culture race and gender coexist in a Gordian knot.

Although this primal scene has been obsessively repeated in African American and American cultural texts, it should never be approached without some self-consciousness of the pitfalls that the structure holds for its various readers. No matter how persuasive Douglass's rendering of the primal triangle is, no matter how much it enables an explanatory point of beginning for specific racial gendered subjects, it is also a zone of discursive captivity in its own right. At least for black men and black women, the triangulated relationships that structure our sense of our gendered and racial selves are also the site of anxieties, new displacements, and new deferrals. Insofar as it is a common, though contested, point of origins, its repetition signals the continuing enactment of the dramas of "want of/for manhood" as a starting place for black men and its deferral and violation for black women. The primal scene is not only a way of representing the symbolic displacement of slavery: it is simultaneously a way of capturing, displacing, and deferring the possibilities of various subjects in its symbolic structures.

Beyond Oedipus: Willie Horton and Me

> The marchers, shouting, "Whose streets? Our streets," started at about 3:30 P.M. . . . As angry white youths and some older local residents filled the sidewalks, a bitter racial hatred permeated the atmosphere.
>
> The whites chanted, "Central Park, Central Park," referring to the rape and beating of a white investment banker in April. Six black and Hispanic youths have been charged in the attack. The black demonstrators in Bensonhurst chanted back, "Howard Beach, Howard Beach."
>
> Later the blacks' chants changed to "Yusef, Yusef." Yusef Hawkins is the 16-year-old black youth whose death sparked the protest. The whites yelled back "We want Tawana. We want Tawana," referring to Tawana Brawley, a black teen-ager from Wappingers Falls, N.Y., who told authorities that she was raped by a group of white men.[27]

In a march that Reverend Al Sharpton led through Bensonhurst shortly after the murder of Yusef Hawkins in that community, African American and progressives, on one side, and Italian American residents of the neighborhood, on the other, confronted and reduced each other to a series of race/gender epithets. Sharpton, one of the most astute players in the register of the id, led the march in order to provoke exactly the response that he received.[28] Once again, bodies were on the line, and visually that drama had to evoke, in those old enough to remember, the most brutal southern scenes of the Civil Rights movement. Yusef Hawkins, who had been killed because it was believed that he was "calling" on a white girl, evoked that collapsed temporal space contoured by Ned Roberts, a century of lynching, and Emmett Till. In their turn, each of the epithets that the participants shouted at each other opened old wounds, evoked older arguments and older sites of the individual and collective self.

Unlike Douglass's "primal scene" or McDowell's readings of it, contemporary primal triangles are public property, a common meeting ground that acts as a zone of contestation among the specific embodied positions that the triangle. Most often these cases are quickly absorbed into the electoral process. George Bush's deployment of the figure of "Willie" Horton as black male rapist helped to manufacture the majority that elected him as heir to the conservative Ronald Reagan. Yusef Hawkin's death was widely touted as one of the reasons for David Dinkins's defeat of Edward Koch in New York's Democratic primary and his subsequent election as New York City's first African American mayor.

Moira Gaten's distinction between the metaphoric and metonymic constitution of the "body politic" is useful in pointing to what is at stake here.[29] The metaphor of the body politic[30] becomes the means of figuring the common will in its most progressive sense as an assembled and orderly society that expresses itself by democratic consent. Since the Civil Rights and feminist movements, we have at least come to expect that the body politic is not racially or gender specific. Yet as Gaten suggests, there is no such thing as "an image of a *human* body. Images of human bodies are images of either men's bodies or women's bodies."[31] In the same way that any unspecified image of the universal body is always subtextually male, it is also always, at least in our culture, subtextually white. Imagining the body politic, actually giving it an image, is the process of attaching the metaphor to a specific body. Just as the marchers in Bensonhurst were contesting public space, both marchers and community were also contesting whose body could represent the broader notion of the body politic.

There would be no need for these public rituals if the gender- and race-specific alignment of the body politic functioned without question. In contemporary American society, where both the symbolic privileges of maleness and whiteness are called into question, there is a continual need—for some—to reinscribe the white male as being at the center of the metaphor. While these contemporary scenes echo the post-Reconstruction elimination of the African American male from the franchise,[32] it is clear that in contemporary renderings they speak as strongly to gender and feminism as to race and Civil Rights.

Donald Trump's response to the gang rape of a young investment banker by a group of black and Hispanic youths in Central Park reveals the dual race and gender trajectory occasioned by contemporary primal triangles.[33] In 1989, when his name was still synonymous with "real estate magnate," he took out a full-page advertisement in the *New York Times*, exhorting "Bring Back the Death Penalty, Bring Back Our Police!" Like

George Bush vis-à-vis Willie Horton, Trump positioned himself as a defender of outraged (white) womanhood. In clear pursuit of an ideological agenda, he asked, "At what point did we cross the line from the fine and noble pursuit of genuine civil liberties to the reckless and dangerously permissive atmosphere which allows criminals of every age to beat and rape a helpless woman and then laugh at her family's anguish?"[34] Liberalism of all stripes—Civil Rights, feminism, and the decisions of the Warren Court—are indicted in his query. Trump evokes the necessity of the law (of the father) to restore an oedipalized order against "helpless females" who seek a life outside of his rule and order and "criminals."

The portrayal of the rape victim in the news helped to amplify Trump's portrait of the "helpless woman." *Newsweek* depicted the unnamed woman as a jogger, or more properly a runner, and the opening paragraph of their story suggests that she is a runner already caught: "On a warm April night two weeks ago a band of young black and Hispanic teenagers chased down a young Wall Street investment banker out jogging by herself, rather daringly for the late hour, in Central Park."[35] The phrase "chased down" stands out because it takes the whole scene outside of the city and into the wild. In the wilderness—that is beyond the protection of men—the independent and capable woman becomes "helpless." That chasing can easily evoke the world of predator and prey of the wild kingdoms of many nature documentaries. The *New York Times*'s portrait of the nameless victim also deployed running as an overall metaphor for her drive and professional ambition. One of her business associates is quoted as saying, "Jogging and being extremely bright—those were the two areas she allowed to be exposed to the public." In this portrait she became the classic rape victim.

> In the course of a typical rape trial it becomes clear that women are regarded as criminals and are punished accordingly—albeit not by legal means—merely for presuming to circulate in public without men's protection, or for daring to articulate what it means for them to be in control of their bodies, in this case, by deciding where, when, with whom, and under what circumstances they will participate in a sexual act."[36]

The suggestion that she courted danger underlies the article, which cites an informant who sees her possible anorexia as evidence of her self-destructiveness: "We used to worry that she was running too much, and eating too little. She was very thin." Another friend is quoted as saying, "I think she liked the fast pace, the competitiveness. There was so much there she could do. She needed a lot of stimulation."[37]

Media criticism offers one way of understanding the way these dramas of race and gender are contained. John Fiske observes that objective and unbiased news reports frequently betray the male point of view, while other voices are excluded and marginalized. In the structure of television news reporting, the studio anchor, who is at a distance from the actual events, is seen as "speaking the objective discourse of 'the truth.'" The reporters in the field, and there may be many reporters on a given story, serve to "mediate between 'raw reality' and the final truth spoken" by the anchor. "Furthest away from the studio, both geographically and discursively, is the eyewitness, the involved spokesperson, the actuality film, the voices that appear to speak the real, and that therefore need to be brought under discursive control."[38]

In the structuring of the "objective" story of the triangle of desire, black men, black women, and white women, who may potentially have subversive or alternative views of/in the triangle, are presented as subjective points of view. When appearing in their own right, their voices are found in editorials or in alternative or "special interest" magazines, which also place them outside of the "objective." However positioned, these alternative voices are relegated to a narrower space, while the news report appears for the broader and national interests. Thus, while we are not denied alternative points of view, we perceive them as marginalized and supplementary.

It is useful to extend and transpose Fiske's spacialized understanding of the presentation of television news as a means of seeing the ways in which the primal triangle, which also spacializes subjects in different positions, works to make some subjects and their stories supplementary. Like the news report, the triangle of desire draws other stories into itself, stories of black women raped by black men, of date rape, of white women raped by white men, and of African Americans (mostly men) killed or brutalized by the police. These stories, which operate on a binary axis of race or gender, seem to belong to the triangle because they fit along one of its axes. But in only speaking to the dynamics of one axis, any binary story becomes inadequate to resolve the dilemma that the triangle poses. Even the most resistant readers, African American men, feminists black and white, are both drawn into and circumscribed by the primal triangle. The binary stories become partial, partisan views, and are structurally incapable of offering a resolution to the triangulated disturbance. Incorporated and represented, binary racial and gender struggles get subordinated and reinscribed as the triangle of desire seeks its "adequate" resolution.

Without challenging the triangulated relationship of race and gender, without reading the nuances along all axes, Oedipus always looms as an unspoken sight of restoration of order. In many ways, Donald Trump's full-page ad was an advertisement for the benefits of Oedipus. While black men, black women, and white women remember (differently) a primal triangle of violence and violation as lurking behind and defining their subjective position in contemporary triangles of desire, the white male can safely turn to Oedipus. Oedipus proposes under the conservative ideological sign of the nation as family triangle to be the only possible representation of the restored body politic. "Those who are not capable of the appropriate political forfeit are excluded from political and ethical relations. They are defined by *mere* nature, *mere* corporeality."[39] Oedipus helps to define the wild zone of Central Park as beyond its norms, and black men and women are always on the borderline between the oedipal and the unoedipalized regions.

In much the same way that Oedipus came to replace a "real" scene of seduction of daughters by their fathers in the evolution of Freud's theories, contemporary oedipal imaginaries have cast out the primal scenes of white and black women and of black men. They become fantasies, things imagined. Equally important, there is a migration in the locus and a reorientation of our inquiry into desire. Freud's early seduction theory, and Douglass's representation of the primal scene, and McDowell's critique of Douglass's resolution, focused on the excesses and aberrations of the "paternal" desire. In Oedipus, however, inappropriate desires (for the mother or father) are located in the child who must enter into the family and society by sacrificing those desires to the law of the father. In a similar movement, the oedipalized vision of contemporary triangles of desire locates aberrant desires in the white male's others, white and black women and black men. The white male becomes the innocent and offers the only possibility of reconstituting social order.[40]

Consider for a moment the way Oedipus resolution subverts the gendered reading strategies of women. In May 1989, the *Village Voice* devoted a section to the incident in Central Park. That section was one of the few places where a variety of voices, black and white, spoke in full on the subject. Andrea Kannapell, who is "like the woman beaten and gang-raped in the park, 28 years old and white," details the incidents of verbal and near physical abuse that she has experienced. Her coda is that she did not mention race, "I don't remember race or class. I remember that it's men." Near the conclusion of her essay, she says: "But women—of all races and all classes and all ages—are subject to this kind of attack from men—of all races and all classes and all ages."[41] Joan Morgan equally suggests that had she "been in the park that night my blackness certainly would not have spared me." She quickly adds, "The only relevant thing about this woman's whiteness is that it and the media prevent us from ignoring this crime."[42]

In both cases, the writers argued that "it's men" who rape, and rape is a crime of gender regardless of race. However, triangulation structures a fundamental difference between the white and implicitly oedipalized male and the black and implicitly unoedipalized male. The maleness that stands as a field of universal oppression—the "prorape culture"—is divided in such a way as to allow the white male to position himself as a representative of order and justice over and against the black male. In relation to the white male, the black male is recast as a "monstrous double," in the wild zone, "the equivocal middle ground between difference and unity that is indispensable to the process of sacrificial substitution—to polarization of violence into a single victim who substitutes for all others."[43]

African American men and their culture (which is often described as the failure of the black family/women) are made to carry the burden of the rapist, while white men are innocent and need to protect "their" women. The term "wilding" came to signify not only the characteristics of events but the characteristics of communities.[44] "Wilding" was almost always presented in quotation marks, as the words of the boys themselves; and that simple gesture made them speak their own "confession" of personal guilt. The term was characterized as "a chilling new vernacular for a recurrent urban nightmare," "a variety of bash-as-bash-can gang rampage," a sign of "mindless viciousness."[45] Their actions stood, in their own words, to mark the whole culture, the language, that many belonged to.

For African American men, defining a point of resistance is always difficult. With memory of Douglass's primal triangle, the memory of continuing material and symbolic displacement yields to the conversion of each incident into an assault on African American manhood. The Tawana Brawley case, the only one of my sample to involve a black woman as victim, most clearly recasts the scenes of Douglass's childhood.[46] The

Reverend Al Sharpton, advisor to the Brawley family, helped them to decide to withhold Tawana's testimony from the grand jury. From then on she was spoken for by men—Sharpton, Alton Maddox, and Vernon Mason. When Sharpton was asked about that decision, or when he was asked about the details of Tawana Brawley's story, his response was consistent but rarely understood. He argued—referring to himself, Maddox, and Mason—that if a white minister and white lawyers had made the same allegations about an African American man there would have been a quick trial and a conviction. In that case, Brawley's testimony was unnecessary. Sharpton's argument was often applauded by African American audiences because it seemed intuitively true. While whites sought a judicial resolution, Sharpton made the integrity of the African American male voice *the issue*.

In the absence of Tawana Brawley's testimony, the very thing that Sharpton wanted to reassure, the significance of the African American male voice, gradually collapsed. The grand jury, depending in part on the testimony of a psychiatrist, found that "there was no evidence that sexual assault occurred. The grand jury further conclude[d] there is nothing in regard to Tawana Brawley's appearance on November 28 that is inconsistent with this condition having being self-inflicted."[47] Sharpton, Maddox, and Mason were ruthlessly investigated on a number of charges. It is tempting to read, as many people did, what amounted to a judicial assault on the black men who represented Brawley as a conspiracy to protect "important" white assailants.

The case of Charles Stuart in Boston provides a coda to the others that we have discussed and, at the same time, traces the triangle of desire to the point of implosion. The Stuarts's story began with the shooting of the pregnant Carol Stuart by a black mugger in a crime-ridden district of Boston while her husband, almost mortally wounded, looked on helplessly. Shortly after their arrival at the hospital, Carol Stuart died; and her baby, delivered by Caesarean section, also died. The Carol Stuart case played itself out on our visual and aural senses as the telephone calls of the husband to police were replayed and as a video camera arrived with the EMS to record the wounded young couple's rescue from chaos. Video and audio tapes gave the sights and sounds of the death of Carol Stuart a visual and aural immediacy that has only been matched by the video tapes of the beatings of Rodney King. And, like the King case, the events themselves unfolded before our eyes.

Although Charles Stuart recovered, neither his wife nor his unborn child lived. As the narrative achieved its own momentum, first one and then a second black man became prime suspects before a third was arrested and partially identified by the surviving husband. He was William Bennett (no relation to the then-Secretary of Education) and witnesses were presented to the grand jury testifying to his discussion of his role in the event, testimony made even more certain by his knowledge of details that only the perpetrator could have known.[48]

Somewhere along the line the narrative failed and Charles Stuart committed suicide. Shortly thereafter, it became clear that he had concocted the ploy in order to kill his wife. Charles had rehearsed the events with his brother, who met the car shortly after the shooting to take away Carol's pocketbook, which also contained Charles's gun. At the end is the corpse of the white family as social construction, the feared result of violation from the "nigger rapist." After the death of Charles Stuart, all the displacements in the primal triangle became self-evident, making it increasingly clear that Stuart, himself, was the author and prime agent of every aspect of the tragedy.[49]

Everything is predictable about the Stuart case but its failure. Neither the death of Carol Stuart nor the "confession" by an African American "murderer" was unusual, nor, following the unraveling of the story, was the confusion handled in an unpredictable way. The death of Charles Stuart, however, is the most resistant event in the continually revised narrative. Despite valiant attempts by reporters, his motives are not clear. The conclusion of *Newsweek*'s article is striking. "But in the end, there is no great moral. The story will remain a mystery: the mystery of a seemingly normal man who was incapable of recognizing the humanity of his own wife and child. And if we don't understand how that kind of mind works, we can be grateful that we don't."[50] Of course, Stuart's death was convenient, for it allowed all concerned to tell his story. The term "sociopath" came easily not only to reporters, their sources, and the police, but also to social scientists—the experts called in to normalize the events. Predictably, Stuart was exiled from the body politic as all the suspicious events of all the actors were displaced onto him.

It would be easy to use the death of Charles Stuart as a fitting end to this progression. Indeed, his self-conscious use of the narrative of the primal triangle seemed to bring to an end the spate of celebrated ritual cases and to call into question the triangle of desire viability as a structuring and displacing site of origins. Charles Stuart's version of the primal triangle brings the question of desire back to its point of origin. While African Americans in Boston were vociferous about the group searches that followed Stuart's story, feminist discourse has been relatively silent. Rather than being the occasion for a combined feminist and racial analysis, the ensuing analytic silence leaves the primal triangle in waiting for its next repetition.

If Emmett Till's murder provides the opening of this discussion of race and gender, then the suicide of Charles Stuart—not the martyrdom of Goodman, Schwerner, Chaney, King, Evers, and Malcolm X—provides the possibilities of closure. For in Stuart's suicide one sees the unraveling of the bodily ties that bind black men and white men, black women and white women, to a commonly violent scene of our origins. In what must have been an extraordinarily difficult decision, Till's mother decided to let his body, considered by most too badly damaged for an open-casket funeral, to lie in state for several days in order for the nation to grasp the full nature of the horror. Likewise, if not literally then at least figuratively, Charles Stuart's body needs also to be available for public viewing in order to grasp the complexities of the primal triangle.

The Stuart case reminds us that any partial reading of the triangle is almost always complicit in the silencing of someone and condemning someone to discursive captivity. The triangle implicates us all, as it is a point of origin for constructing Afro-American men and women as well as "white" American "men" and "women." A common figure unites us all: the silent body of women; Tawana Brawley and the young girl of Bensonhurst who says nothing, and the jogger and Carol Stuart who can say nothing. And, if the women are violated and silenced in these triangles, then black men speak in languages other than their own. All black men are put in the subject position of "Willie." Like the unlucky man who was arrested for the murder of Carol Stuart, the primal scene fills in what facts do not avail, extorting the "confession" of black men to their primal guilt. In short, the inability to read the interrelations of race and gender in America's uncanny leads to more harm than mere misreading. It silences, calls out of name, and puts unspoken words in the mouth of America's others, and even makes our strategies of resistance complicitous with our captivities.

Notes

1. Franz Kafka, "In the Penal Colony," *The Complete Stories,* ed. Nahum N. Glatzer (New York: Schocken, 1971), 144–145.
2. Pierre Bourdieu, *The Logic of Practice,* trans. Richard Nice (Stanford: Stanford Univ. Press, 1990), 169.
3. The basic facts of the events leading up to the "lynching" of Emmett Till are and will remain in dispute. The gesture that transgressed the South's racial etiquette was a "wolf whistle," not the traditional gaze. Even the existence of a "wolf whistle" is in dispute. Till's mother and other relatives assert that he stuttered and used to whistle in order to clarify his diction. The story told by whites and to some degree supported by earlier versions (told by Till's cousins) suggests lewd remarks and sexual propositions. See Stephen J. Whitefield, *A Death in the Delta: The Story of Emmett Till* (New York: Free Press, 1988), 16–19.
4. Michael E. Dyson, *Reflecting Black: African-American Cultural Criticism* (Minneapolis: Univ. of Minnesota Press, 1993), 196–97.
5. Dyson, 193.
6. Dyson, 193–94.
7. Dyson, 182–83. My use of Dyson to frame my own discussion runs the risk of making him appear to say something he does not. My intention is not to use Dyson's wonderfully direct, honest, and insightful essays about African American manhood to set up a straw man for my own criticism. Although we go about the matter differently, we share the similar

    > aim of . . . present[ing] enabling forms of consciousness that may contribute to the reconstitution of the social, economic, and political relations that continually consign the lives of black men to psychic malaise, social destruction and physical death. It does not encourage or dismiss the sexism of black men, nor does it condone the patriarchal behavior that sometimes manifests itself in minority communities in the form of misdirected machismo. (185–86)

8. Homi K. Bhabha, "DissemiNation: Time, Narrative, and the Margins of the Modern Nation," in *Nation and Narration*, ed. Homi K. Bhabha (New York: Routledge, 1990), 297.
9. Bhabha, 297.
10. For a discussion of the Rodney King beating, see Robert Gooding-Williams, ed., *Reading Rodney King, Reading Urban Uprising* (New York: Routledge, 1993).

11. Eve K. Sedgwick, *Between Men: English Literature and Male Homosocial Desire* (New York: Columbia Univ. Press, 1985), 17.

12. There is a long and popular tradition that would have these triangles of desire as the intersection of sexuality and race. Calvin Hernton's *Sexism and Racism in America* (New York: Grove, 1988) is, perhaps, the best known work in that tradition. If one substitutes gender for sexuality, the following would represent much of my thesis:

> There is a sexual involvement, at once real and vicarious, connecting white and black people in America that spans the history of this country from the era of slavery to the present, an involvement so immaculate and yet so perverse, so ethereal and yet so concrete, that all race relations tend to be, however subtle, *sex* relations.(7)

13. George and Ira Gershwin, "I Loves You, Porgy," from *Billy Holiday: Live and Private Recordings,* vol. 4. New Sound Planet JUTB 3038, 1989.

14. Hortense J. Spillers, "Mama's Baby, Papa's Maybe: An American Grammar Book," *Diacritics* 17 (2) (1987): 68.

15. Spillers, "Mama's Baby," 73.

16. Frederick Douglass, *The Narrative of the Life of Frederick Douglass, An American Slave, Written by Himself*, ed. and intro. by Houston A. Baker (1845; New York: Penguin Books, 1986), 47, 48. All subsequent page references are to the 1986 edition, and are included parenthetically in the text.

17. Ned Lukacher, *Primal Scenes: Literature, Philosophy, Psychoanalysis* (Ithaca, NY: Cornell Univ. Press, 1986), 25.

18. Lukacher, *Primal Scenes,* 14.

19. Some of the material in this discussion is drawn from and revises my "Called into Existence: Desire, Gender, and Voice in Frederick Douglass's Narrative of 1845," *Differences* 1 (3) (1989): 108–136.

20. Houston A. Baker, *Blues, Ideology and Afro-American Literature: A Vernacular Theory* (Chicago: Univ. of Chicago Press, 1984), 31.

21. See, in particular, Jenny Franchot, "The Punishment of Esther: Frederick Douglass and the Construction of the Feminine," in *Frederick Douglass: New Literary and Historical Essays*, ed. Eric J. Sundquist (Cambridge: Cambridge Univ. Press, 1990), 141–61, and Deborah E. McDowell, "In the First Place: Making Frederick Douglass and the Afro-American Narrative Tradition," in *African American Autobiography*, ed. William L. Andrews (Englewood Cliffs, NJ: Prentice-Hall, 1993), 36–58.

22. Spillers, "Mama's Baby," 80.

23. Deborah E. McDowell, "Reading Family Matters," in *Changing Our Own Words: Essays on Criticism, Theory and Writing by Black Women*, ed. Cheryl A. Wall (New Brunswick, NJ: Rutgers Univ. Press, 1989), 78–79.

24. Lynn A. Higgins and Brenda R. Silver, "Introduction: Reading Rape," in *Rape and Representation*, ed. Lynn A. Higgins and Brenda R. Silver (New York: Columbia Univ. Press, 1991), 3.

25. Deborah E. McDowell, "In the First Place: Making Frederick Douglass and the Afro-American Narrative Tradition," in *African American Autobiography*, ed. William L. Andrews (Englewood Cliffs, NJ: Prentice-Hall, 1993) 36–58.

26. Although white women exist on the peripheries of this particular representation of the appropriation of desire, in the late nineteenth and through the twentieth century they, more often then not, take the place of black women in this triangle.

27. Nick Ravo, "Marchers and Brooklyn Youths Trade Racial Jeers," *New York Times,* August 27, 1989, A32.

28. While everyone else sought judicial resolution, Sharpton, who represented Brawley, consistently played out the drama in a different and archetypal register. Leading Tawana's team of advisors, he withheld her testimony from the grand jury. Sharpton, in effect, reenacted the rites of African American manhood in the public arena. Perhaps the most important way that Sharpton frustrated the general public's desire lay in his refusal to let Brawley testify; a refusal to allow her story to become an object of judicial inquiry and resolution.

29. Moira Gatens, "Corporeal Representation in/and the Body Politic," in *Cartographies: Poststructuralism and the Mapping of Bodies and Spaces,* ed. Rosalyn Diprose and Robyn Ferrell (North Sydney, Australia: Allen and Unwin, 1991), 79–87.

30. The *O.E.D.* suggests that this metaphorical use of the notion of the body may have originally had its meaning in relationship to the "headship" of the king. The term "body politic" emerged in the middle fifteenth century in a legal discourse alongside the term "corporate body," both expressing the existence of an entity that went beyond the life span of any individual(s) that constituted it. The contemporary meaning of the body politic emerges in the early seventeenth century, no doubt in association with notions of popular sovereignty, to express the independent and collective will and life of a "nation."

31. Gatens, "Corporeal Representation," 82.

32. For a useful summary of the strategies used to interpret racial lynching in America, see W. Fitzhugh Brundage's "Introduction" to his *Lynching in the New South: Georgia and Virginia, 1880–1930* (Urbana: Univ. of Illinois Press, 1993), 1–6, and Dennis B. Downey and Raymond M. Hyser's "Introduction" to their *No Crooked Death: Coatesville, Pennsylvania, and the Lynching of*

Zachariah Walker (Urbana: Univ. of Illinois Press, 1991), 1–12. Also useful is James R. McGovern's *Anatomy of a Lynching: The Killing of Claude Neal* (Baton Rouge: Louisiana State Univ. Press, 1982).

33. The details of the event and the subsequent prosecution of the perpetrators of the Central Park rape are in Timothy Sullivan's *Unequal Verdicts: The Central Park Jogger Trials* (New York: Simon and Schuster, 1992). National attention was drawn to the incident in the following articles and editorials in national news magazines: "Going 'Wilding': Terror in Central Park," *Newsweek,* May 1, 1989, 27; David Gelman with Peter McKillop, "Going 'Wilding' in the City," *Newsweek*, May 8, 1989, 65; Charles Krauthammer, "Crime and Responsibility," *Time*, May 8, 1989, 104; "*A Clockwork Orange* in Central Park," *U.S. News and World Report*, May 8, 1989, 10; Meg Greenfield, "Other Victims in the Park," *Newsweek*, May 15, 1989, 86; and Mortimer B. Zukerman, "Meltdown in Our Cities," *U.S. News and World Report*, May 29, 1989, 74.
34. Donald Trump, "Bring Back the Death Penalty, Bring Back our Police!" *New York Times,* May 1, 1989.
35. David Gelman with Peter McKillop, "Going 'Wilding' in the City," *Newsweek*, May 8, 1989, 65.
36. Winfred Woodhull, "Sexuality, Power, and the Question of Rape," in *Feminism and Foucault: Reflections On Resistance*, ed. Irene Diamond and Lee Quinby (Boston: Northeastern Univ. Press, 1988), 172.
37. Celestine Bohlen, "Hard-Working Banker Ran to Relax, Thinking Little of Park's Dangers," *New York Times*, April 28, 1989, B2.
38. John Fiske, *Television Culture* (New York: Routledge, 1987), 288.
39. Gatens, "Corporeal Representation," 82.
40. The existence of a "seduction theory" and the movement from the seduction theory to Oedipus is still a matter that is highly contested. For a useful introduction, see Charles Berhneimer and Claire Kahane, eds., *In Dora's Case: Freud—Hysteria—Feminism*, 2d ed. (New York: Columbia Univ. Press, 1990), and Dianne Hunter, ed., *Seduction and Theory: Readings of Gender, Representation, and Rhetoric* (Chicago: Univ. of Illinois Press, 1989).
41. Andrea Kannapell, "She Could Have Been Me: 28 and White," *Village Voice,* May 9, 1989, 37.
42. Joan Morgan, "The Pro-Rape Culture: Homeboys—of All Races—Stop You in the Street," *Village Voice*, May 9, 1989, 39.
43. Rene Girard, *Violence and the Sacred* (Baltimore, MD: Johns Hopkins Univ. Press, 1977), 161.
44. Barr M. Cooper, in "Cruel & the Gang: Exposing the Schomberg Posse," *Village Voice*, May 9, 1989, 27, suggests that it was a misreading of the phrase "wild thing."

45. Gelman, "Going 'Wilding,'" 27; "*A Clockwork Orange* in Central Park," 10.

46. Much of the information about the Brawley case is drawn from Robert D. McFadden, et al., *Outrage: The Story Behind the Tawana Brawley Hoax* (New York: Bantam, 1990). At least for Alton Maddox, the similarities had some personal reference. McFadden tells us of an incident in Newnan, Georgia, when the teenaged Maddox was "chased by a white mob and beaten bloody." "He never forgot the trauma. Sometimes, before an encounter with hostile whites, he would murmur to Al Sharpton or C. Vernon Mason: 'Here come the white mob at me again'" (78).

47. McFadden, *Outrage,* 367.

48. Constance L. Hays, "Officials' Handling of Suspects in Boston Killing Prompts Questions," *New York Times,* January 17, 1989, A17.

49. The details of the public representation of the Carol and Charles Stuart incident are drawn from the following: Jonathan Alter and Mark Starr, "Race and Hype in a Divided City," *Newsweek,* January 22, 1990, 21–22; Fox Butterfield, "Tribute to a Slain Daughter Helps Soothe a Shaken City," *New York Times,* January 30, 1990, A1; Fox Butterfield, "Suspicions Came Too Late in Boston," *New York Times,* January 21, 1990, A5; Fox Butterfield and Constance L. Hays, "Motive Remains a Mystery in Deaths That Haunt a City," *New York Times,* January 15, 1990, A1; Margaret Carlson, "Presumed Innocent," *New York Times,* January 22, 1990, 10–14; Walter Goodman, "The Role of Journalists in the Stuart Case," *New York Times,* January 25, 1990, C22; Constance L. Hays, "Boston Agonizes Over Street Violence," *New York Times,* October 28, 1989, A8; Constance L. Hays, "Officials' Handling of Suspects in Boston Killing Prompts Questions," *New York Times,* January 17, 1990, A17; Constance L. Hays, "Boston Murder Suspect Sought a Brother's Help, Lawyer Says," *New York Times,* January 12, 1990, A18; Alex S. Jones, "Bias and Recklessness Are Charged in Boston Reporting of Stuart Slaying," *New York Times,* January 14, 1990, 1–21; Larry Martz, Mark Starr, and Todd Barrett, "A Murderous Hoax," *Newsweek,* January 22, 1990, 16–22.

50. Larry Martz, Mark Starr, and Todd Barrett, "A Murderous Hoax," 21.

SCREENING MEN

8

"WE'RE GONNA DECONSTRUCT YOUR LIFE!"

The Making and Un-Making of the Black Bourgeois Patriarch in *Ricochet*

ELIZABETH ALEXANDER

The year 1991 was one of black men and "boyz" in and out of the 'hood in African American cinema. Movies such as Mario Van Peebles's *New Jack City*, Kevin Hooks's *Strictly Business*, Matty Rich's *Straight Outta Brooklyn*, Joseph Vasquez's *Hangin' with the Homeboys*, and, of course, John Singleton's hugely successful *Boyz in the Hood*, rewrote the black "ghetto" as "'hood" and addressed—both obliquely and at times ham-handedly—matters of urban poverty, drugs and violence, black masculinity, and African American class aspirations and immobility.

That same year saw the release of Russell Mulcahy's *Ricochet*. The director, who is white, walks a distinct and intricate path through the same terrain. I contend that *Ricochet* invents a prototypical black bourgeois family of the 1980s "buppy" generation and then dismantles it entirely, exposing the fundamental fragility of black economic progress, revealing white male antagonism to black male success, and questioning the very structure and existence of that filial unit. The role of the buppy patriarch—heterosexual by definition—is constructed and then, in the movie's own language, "deconstructed." *Ricochet* is, then, an antiaffirmative action parable for the 1990s that is propelled by unfulfilled white male homoerotic desire. As with so many white-authored texts purportedly about the so-called "other," the film is ultimately more revealing as it "deconstructs" the workings of white male anxiety over his own class prerogative—indeed, hegemony—and unrealized sexual wishes than as a direct inquiry into buppy patriarchy.

In *Ricochet*, Denzel Washington plays a black homeboy-turned-cop-turned-assistant-District Attorney-turned-political *wunderkind* named Nick Styles. John Lithgow plays a white criminal named Earl Talbot Blake who becomes obsessed with Styles after their lives intersect one night when Styles arrests him. The spectacular arrest—Styles distracts Blake with a striptease and rescues his hostage—is recorded on amateur video and broadcast on the news, and Styles becomes a media star as his career rapidly advances. Blake's mania leaves him bent on destroying Styles's successful life, a success Blake feels was won at his expense. Yet this competitive dynamic is interwoven with an erotic plot. At one point in the film, the two men arm wrestle,[1] and Blake tells his nemesis:

> There we were, both of us at the beginning of our careers, and all of a sudden one of us took off, lit up the sky like a meteor, and why? Because he met the other. I've been following your career. . . . After all that we've meant to each other, this moment here is the first time we've ever touched.[2]

The anxiety that anything a black man might have has been snatched from the rightful grasp of a more deserving white man is the engine that drives Blake's mania. But he is also, more fundamentally, propelled by sexual desire, for in the entire film Styles's appeal is theatrical, sexual, indeed pornographic, in its reproducibility and commodification. Each of his status transitions is marked by an episode in which he is center stage. These moments of theater are almost always captured on videotape, and videotape is a crucial part of his Blake-orchestrated descent and eventual "comeback" he himself designs with his homeboy/"partner," Odessa, who is played by Ice-T.

Ricochet raises some very important questions about what it means to look at black men from any number of subject positions simultaneously.

Mulcahy builds this multiplicity of perspectives into the film; Styles is the object of our ocular desire throughout, no matter who we are. Mulcahy's camera gives us the perspective of straight men (Styles's white partner), gay men (Blake), straight women (his wife, all manner of reporters, and waitresses), and women of ambiguous sexuality (the female District Attorney),[3] all looking longingly at Styles. When his videotaped escapes are televised, the entire city watches him. So the question of what it means to look directly, unabashedly, and with desire at black men from a number of subject positions is of paramount importance in considering this film. Styles participates in his own pornographizing. It is he who works the camera at any given moment.

Styles consciously manipulates his sexuality to gain success. Even if he thinks he is only being watched by women, even if he might like it to be that way, his sexuality is theatrical, and anyone can, and does, attend the theater. From the opening scene, his chosen audience may be his wife Alice, but Odessa watches him, as does his white partner, Larry. Styles is fully complicit in these seductions; even when he is caught unawares, as in the locker room, he accedes to the gaze, lets himself become a pinup, conducts himself in the mode of the coy centerfold whom the camera simply loves.

Young men on the rapid rise up the capitalist ladder is a story line that can be milked for thrills, as shown in the success of the recent film *The Firm*. In *Ricochet*'s fast opening scenes, Styles trades basketball clothes for a police uniform for a dapper suit at a dazzling pace. *Jet* magazine, in its article on *Ricochet*, summarizes the plot in a photo caption: "Everything is going great for Styles and his family, wife Alice and daughter being blessed by minister, until Blake interferes."[4] This (John) Johnsonian logic pervades the film: wives and daughters are appendages to the image of a black man's career "going great," complete with a preacher's blessing, and it is "the white man," in the person of Blake, who spoils it. This is certainly true in *Ricochet*, but the film also clearly questions (and this is largely accomplished, I think, through Washington's nuanced performance) Styles's own investment in the role, indeed in the myth, of the buppy patriarch, an ideology which *Jet* is absolutely complicit in retaining. The plot then thickens with the addition of taboo black sexuality, embodied by Denzel Washington's particular charm; his smile here is sly, but not reptilian; slick, but not quite greasy. The pun of Styles's name is inescapable in a film as rife with double entendre as this one. In one scene in which Styles is wheeling and dealing in particular glory, Shanice's pop hit "I Like Your Style" can even be heard in the background.

Heterosexual black male business-class success in this country at the time this film was made seemed so pornographic because the only viable models of black male sexuality trafficked in a mainstream economy are variations on outlaws and gladiators. But black male economic success and autonomy must be defanged for the mainstream to dilute its potential symbolic powers as desirous. The economically successful character in *Strictly Business,* for example, is a nerd in need of "street" rehabilitation; the patriarchs in *The Cosby Show* and *The Fresh Prince of Bel Air,* while wielding some authority in the family's economy, are nonetheless clownish, overweight *hausfraus* who are dwarfed by their slinky, equally workplace-successful wives. *Ricochet*'s Styles is both "gangsta'" and buppy, two personae joined in increasingly complicated ways as the film progresses.

This is a film with an unusually subtle and detailed understanding of the variegations of class status within African American communities. Across genres, most mainstream portrayals of African American life see only a crudely drawn servant class, a subgroup of that which is an entertainment class, an outlaw class, and, recently and ever so rarely, a professional class (and even within this, vestiges of the other frequently remain; how often must we see black female characters who play college students or lawyers burst into song at some point in the show's run in order to further their own recording careers?). Styles is first identified as a "P.K.," or "Preacher's Kid," and we see that while the pulpit confers class status on his father's family, it does not offer class rewards. The public-sector class success that Styles earns is different from a more privatized version. And the family's feeling about Styles's class ascent are crystallized in a shot of a framed picture of the family on the cover of the *Ebony*-wanna-be, *Upscale* magazine. On the other hand, Blake's full name is Earl Talbot Blake, and he is pale and blond. His name is an English title, but because he is in jail he is a king without a country. His entitlements actually grant him nothing at all, and this rage combusts utterly when a person like Styles—to Blake, all fortune without entitlement—comes along. *Ricochet*, then, visions a complicated class world.

What are black men in the American ocular imagination? The American theater of lynching, revisited in modern-day terms in George Holliday's videotape of motorist Rodney King being beaten by a gang of Los Angeles police officers, has made pornographic spectacle of black male bodies being violated. The inability to turn away from mostly black and Latino men beating each other insensate in the boxing ring is what Audre Lorde, in her poem "Afterimages," which addresses the murder of Emmett Till, calls "the secret relish / of a black child's mutilated body."[5]

And there is also the spectacle of black male bodies in splendor, in glory, a gladiatorial history of black male performance that has always been the grandest of American spectacles. However, the containment of the image and its means of production are necessary in order that white male desire—specifically, as I am arguing here, for black men—can be contained and have a safety valve for self-protection from the unfettered power of black male sexuality. Perhaps this sexuality is no grander or more glorious in and of itself than any other, but it is made magnificent by its sequestering and fetishization. There is the apocryphal tale of U.S. Senator Jesse Helms carrying around one of Robert Mapplethorpe's black male nudes folded up in his back pocket and obsessively unfolding and displaying it to prove his point about the necessity to ban such "obscene" images, which illustrates my point about the interrelationship of power, desire, containment, and dominion.

In his second discussion of those same Mapplethorpe nudes, Kobena Mercer has written convincingly that no matter who has agency of an image, all viewers are implicated in the racial and sexual mythology that accompany them.[6] *Ricochet* is a movie whose camera work asserts that we all want to look at black men, whether we are gay or straight, black or white, male or female. The desire to look is veiled in the trappings of bourgeois success—we "watch" Styles's ascent—but the real reason for looking, no matter who we are, is the sex of it.

The opening scene of *Ricochet* takes place on an urban basketball court, in the heat of a game between Nick Styles and his friend from the neighborhood, Odessa. The very first words of the film come from Odessa, who taunts Nick, "No competition. No comp," introducing the theme of *mano a mano* class dynamics. The homoerotics of the film are also set into motion from the opening credits, when a bullet is seen zooming from the barrel of a fired gun; from the first sweaty moments, in which the men are literally in each other's faces and the dribbled basketball beats an increasingly manic tattoo to shouted lines such as "I'm taking you right to the hole." Male couples populate the film: Nick and Odessa, Nick and his partner,

Larry; Nick and his aide; Blake and his lover Kim. Odessa and Kim are, of course, sexually ambiguous names, and these characters are in many ways the caretaking "wives" in these relationships. Certainly Odessa, when it comes down to it, is clearly more loyal to and has more faith in Nick than does Nick's wife. The script is rife with *Moby Dick* and Trojan jokes, popping balloons and blasting trumpets, and references to "kissing butt" and "assholes" overrun the dialogue. The extraordinary violence of the film is usually impaling, in a corporeal reproduction of nonconsensual sodomy.

When Odessa calls Nick "P.K." (for Preacher's Kid),[7] we learn the specifics of his class and cultural position. There is also much banter about whether or not Styles has "left the neighborhood." As this discussion takes place within their sweaty homoerotic world, sex and upward mobility are conflated. Nick's white sidekick from the police force, Larry, has been told to "stop playing like a white boy"; thus, the first white man in the film is constructed as disadvantaged from the start in terms of physical ability and "cool," which later extends to other perceived disadvantages. In the background, spatially peripheral to the world on the court, are two black women who are the first of many spectators to Nick's prowess. They watch; they smile; they clap.

After the game, the movie is temporalized in the 1980s by Ronald Reagan's voice on the radio in the background. That temporalization is crucial to the understanding of this film as an antiaffirmative-action, civil rights-backlash parable. After Nick sees and comments on Odessa's fancy car, we are meant to understand that Odessa is a drug dealer. Nick says to Odessa, through a wire fence, "I guess our playing days are over," and Odessa replies, "Just on the asphalt, homeboy." There is a heavily double-entendred flirtation between Nick and one of the women, Alice, who will become his wife and who is called by her name but once in the film, in the second half. This scene telegraphs two key pieces of information: Nick is a "homeboy" on the move who can hang in the 'hood but whose trajectory points outward to a working world of white men; and women are useful inasmuch as they remain decorative, marginal, and sexually available according to the whims of the patriarch-to-be.

The next scenes segue from the basketball courts to, by implication, the courts that comprise the legal system; this double entendre is at play throughout the film. Styles and Larry are on duty at a carnival, a world turned upside down in which the thematics of dismantling both an old world order of white male dominion as well as the film's new world order of the ascent of the buppy patriarch are inaugurated. In this scene we first see John Lithgow's character, Earl Talbot Blake, and Kim, his fawning, boy-toy sidekick and, presumably, lover. It is crucial that Kim is dark but not black. As he is Blake's lover, sexual desire for darkness is made literal but is also feminized and infantilized so that it exists well within a framework of dominion wherein the older, blonder "man" is in full control. Blake does not yield to Kim's near-constant adoration: "Tonight's gonna be the night you become a superstar all the way, and I'm gonna see it," Kim exults; the promise of glory is contingent upon its being witnessed. The two shoot up fellow criminals in a drug deal gone bad, and Blake and Styles end up in a confrontation that is one of the most startling of the film.

Blake takes a woman hostage, and the terrified crowd clears, forming a stage for the first of several showdowns between the two protagonists. Styles quickly determines how to outfox his "opponent": he strips down to his underpants, and talks fast. A fair-goer with an amateur video camera records Style's striptease. Center stage, Styles says, "I want you to trust me. I got absolutely nothing on underneath," "I'll be your hostage," and "the only weapon I got left is useless unless you're a pretty girl." The sexual double entendre of these comments is barely veiled, but what is both more interesting and elusive is the question of audience. Has Styles "read" Blake as a seduceable man susceptible to his body and charms? Is he playing to the audience? What is his stake in the seduction? Certainly, he is finding his way out of a deadly situation, but his cool never breaks, and his feline smile suggests great pleasure in the process. That sly smile is Styles's trademark through the film. It signals to us his investment and profound, sexual pleasure in his own ascent. Styles calls his penis a "weapon," which is heterosexualized in that it is intended for a "pretty girl," but Styles delivers the line with a grin that suggests he is fully aware of the homoerotic, pornographic scenario in which he plays. This is coupled with the crude misogyny of Blake's lines about his female hostage: "She's gonna need a paper bag over her head when her boyfriend fucks what's left of her." For both of them, women, though in different ways, are metaphorically useful only inasmuch as they are in some way fuckable. This introduces both themes of surrogacy and sexual rejection. Much later, Blake will lament, "Last time I held a gun in my hand a young man took off all his clothes for me." His only potency is in his weapon, and the only way he can make the man he wants come to him is through force.

Styles shoots Blake in the knee, arrests him, appears on the news, and becomes not only a hero but a hot commodity. He is summarily promoted by District Attorney Priscilla Brimleigh, played by Lindsay Wagner, who once again plays on the themes of workplace competition with the line, "I'm glad he's too young for my job." Brimleigh goes to the police locker room to offer Styles a job, and, once again, he is naked, this time, utterly, while all others around him are clothed. His relationship to Lindsay Wagner's gaze, again, is coy. He flits behind a locker but remains ever cool and collected.[8] "Where did you hide it?" Brimleigh asks, referring to the gun in the arrest. Styles holds up his jockstrap and for a split second shows its front—once again, the conflation of the penis with the gun—and then turns to a secret compartment in the back. He is always flirting and always understands that his power and his sexuality are intertwined. Brimleigh says, "From now on I don't want you wearing anything but civvies." He is the D.A.'s commodity, her hot property. The specter of unjust promotion on the basis of anything other than "merit" is present and undergirds the film's affirmative-action anxiety. Yes, he is being promoted because he has captured a dangerous criminal, but much more so it is because he is telegenic and appealing; he turns everyone on. Nick has now been explicitly constructed as an object of sexual desire in the eyes of black women, white men, white women, and, of course, the viewing audience both of the videotape and of the film itself.

For the next section of the film, the scenes emphasize, from Blake's perspective, the utterly opposite yet interdependent parallelism of his and Styles's lives. In the prison hospital, Blake is tormented by the videotape on television. An elderly man with a tray full of books tries to get him to repent. The books give him an idea, but not the one intended. "I could change a whole life," Blake says, "and it's in my hands." He asks for books, but he does not read them; instead, he tapes them to his leg and begins grueling, rehabilitative exercises. Books are useful for their heft, not for what is inside of them. To have access to books but not to read them suggests a squandered education. Blake builds up his body rather than his storehouse of knowledge with these books, and the body, both inside this film and out of it, has of course been the stereotypical domain of black men.

From this point, the scenes switch back and forth between the contrasting lives of the two men. The black man has two names and one is abbreviated; he is without a resonant etymology in his nomenclature, all "style" and no substance.[9] The white man's name cloaks him in a ritual of entitlement. Styles appears on another television show, *Busted*, and Blake, now healed, goes to jail. He replaces his cell mate's male beefcake bodybuilder pinup with a pinup of his own: Styles. Cut back to Styles, who has moved into a lovely suburban home with a wife—Alice from the basketball court—and a girl baby.

Blake writes and reorders documentary history with himself at the persecuted center. He cuts out and xeroxes pictures of Nick; and as he xeroxes them, their threat multiplies. The surrounding images of Nick represent the threat of a competitive marketplace overrun by black men at the same time that they are Blake's object of desire. "You're that dude got busted on *America's Funniest Home Videos*," he is taunted. It is the making public and visible of his "defeat" that upsets him most. In prison he puts up clippings of Nick's accomplishments; once again, a version of a life is created and constructed, cut and pasted into a newly ordered reality. Meanwhile, Nick is swiftly ascending the ladder of socioeconomic success: we see his lovely home, his wife who greets him at the door with a child on her hip, flour on her face, and a ponytail that has been fuzzed, presumably, by the kitchen heat; but when they attend community functions, she is perfectly coiffed.

In one prison scene, Blake does battle with members of the "Aryan Brotherhood." "When two white men in this prison have a grudge they settle it like Aryan warriors, one on one, hand to hand," they say, in the self-glorifying language of Reagan-era resurgents such as the Posse Comitatus. Blake armors himself, literally, with books, which he tapes into a shield: the history of the western world, perhaps, but its lessons unlearned and unread. He battles one of the "Aryans" and the fight climaxes, as it were, when Blake's eye catches a newspaper cutout of Styles on his opponent's armor. He drives his sword through the photograph and the living man beneath. Kim says, "These guys are pussies, but you, you're the true Aryan." Blake lets Kim in on his plan to "destroy" Styles's "life," to which Kim will later exult: "What's art is how you singlehandedly deconstructed Nick Styles's life. . . . That's art. . . . That's the Sistine Chapel." After this prison battle, Blake's plot to "deconstruct" the life of Nick Styles is in full swing. Styles is a nemesis who took away what Blake perceived to be his own birthright: a life of public ascent and upper-middle-class success.

Every scene with Styles highlights the theatricality of his success. He argues to prosecute a "night strangler" with seduction and flash. The white male attorney whom he beats crumples up his notes in disgust, and we are meant to be uncertain as to whether Styles won the jury by brains or theatrics. He argues with his jacket off, giving the appearance of ease and spontaneity as well as, in the antiaffirmative action mindset in the scene, a lack of professionalism and preparation. Styles goes to the crack house run by Odessa to plead for safety surrounding the community center he hopes to build, and the crack heads stop smoking the pipe to gather around and listen to him deliver a preachy speech. Innumerable scenes show him "live" and then on television, including the climactic scene in which he appears on a telethon to raise money for his center. His life, then, is as much visibly constructed as it is "real." He rejects this world of artificially constructed reality when he turns over the television set in front of his daughters, but the constructed reality of his own theater and of the theatrical bourgeois family is comfortable to him.

Styles's black aide is introduced and the film gains yet another male coupling that is more important to Styles than his nuclear family. This man is the one who will help his career ascend. After Blake has, predictably, busted loose from jail and faked his own death in order to activate his anti-Styles vendetta (and he escapes after a parole hearing in which the language of "the disadvantaged" is employed to try to free him), he kills the aide but makes it look like suicide. Blake dresses the aide in leather drag, puts child pornography is his briefcase, and makes it appear that the aide and Styles embezzled money and abused young boys. The aide's final words to Styles before he dies are, "Washington, here we come." Black men, then, are punished both for aiming too high and for believing their own hype. The movie's message is that, no matter what kind of accomplished life one has, it can be tarnished and taken apart after death, in a second. Styles receives the news of his aide's death in the middle of making love to his wife. The heterosexual family narrative is interrupted not only by the sphere of work but by the taint of scandal both present and imminent.

District Attorney Brimleigh is not amused at this turn of events. When Styles is told, "The D.A. would like to see you," she becomes the voice of legal authority that will turn against him in a moment when he is no longer a useful commodity. This story, like all the others, hits the media. Styles is no more than a commodity who has violated a contract. He is no longer a young man with a glittering career. He has outlived his usefulness.

Styles's house—the heterosexual domestic sphere—is set up as an inviolate sanctum. Alice is careful to ask, "Who is it?" even when it is her husband at the door. She opens it and he goes inside, but the camera does not follow them; the door is shut. But when Blake is on the loose and comes to the house posing as a power repairmen, the white babysitter opens the door without even asking who he is. She tells the children he is "The Powerman," thus instructing them in the ways of white male hegemony. The camera follows Blake in the house, where he drugs the babysitter, and eventually follows him up the stairs carrying the two little girls. He has full reign of the house, and when he adjusts a crooked picture on the wall—the framed *Upscale* cover—it is as though to say, your family is all image, all sham, and I even have control over that; I can right the picture just as I can deconstruct your life. When Styles and his wife return, the babysitter awakens from her drugged stupor and dreamily murmurs, "The power guy was here."

Styles is kidnapped in front of his home by Blake and Kim, drugged, and then forced into having sex with a white, blonde prostitute who gives him gonorrhea. During the kidnapping, the men arm wrestle in the scene discussed earlier. Styles uses the language of affirmative action and desire. Styles wins the first round, slamming Blake's hand to the ground; he has won fair and square, brawn to brawn, and he crows, "You lose." But Blake retorts, "No, you lose!" Kim injects Styles with drugs and Blake slams down his hand. The proverbial playing field is not level; the white man needs drugs and an accomplice to come out ahead, but he insists on behaving as though the game is fair. Styles asks, "You killed my life. Are you going to kill me?" and Blake replies, "No, I'm going to do something far worse. I'm going to let you live" (xxx). The successful black man's life is a complete construction, an entity other than the achieved life, a fiction inhabited with varying degrees of success.

Styles is dumped unceremoniously in front of City Hall, where he is pulled awake by a worker rounding up homeless people. No one believes he was set up, since Blake, after all, is thought to be dead. When Styles tells his wife, "He's trying to make me look crazy," she replies, "Well I hate to tell you, honey, it's working." To be addressed as "honey" invokes familial language, even in the face of such an utter lack of faith. The only ones who do believe are Larry and Odessa, reinforcing the way in which the heterosexual family is taken apart while the homosocial bonds remain inviolable.

He returns to the 'hood, to Odessa, to the family he can really count on when the going gets tough. The *Ebony* magazine version of the patriarchal, heterosexual black family is set up as part and parcel of what constitutes buppy success in this film. But we are continually reminded that the higher he rises, the more Styles's family life is a sham. His real family members, the ones who it turns out he can count on when the going gets toughest, are male: his white sidekick partner, Larry, and his ex-homie, Odessa. The loyalest of families in this film, and the ones that get the most time, are the unarticulated "families" of male couples. Odessa takes Alice and the children; they are safer in the crack house than they are in their own house. Styles stages his vindication against Blake and beats him at his own game; Blake ends up impaled on a spire of the very tower that will be the site of Styles's youth center, which is also the site of the crack house. When Styles thanks Odessa, he says he will see him that weekend, back on the court. He kisses his wife and is once again the buppy patriarch. At the very end of the film, after his final victory, Styles says into the camera, "Are we on the air?" When the answer is affirmative, he says, "Then you can kiss my black ass" (xxx), and the video clicks off.

It is instructive to juxtapose two definitions of the male buddy film, the genre *Ricochet* plays with and subverts. First, from Joel Silver, who produced this film as well as *Lethal Weapon* and *48 Hours,* which also featured black-white pairs:

> In most action films which revolve around the team of two men, you're introduced to two guys who hate each other and are forced to work together, and by the end of the film, learn to like each other. What fascinated me about the premise of *Ricochet* was that you started with two guys who hated each other. They get separated and when they come together again, they hate each other even more. Their hatred is as much of a bond between them as the friendship between the guys in the other movies. You might call *Ricochet* an '"anti-buddy" movie.[10]

Critic Richard Dyer sees those films another way:

> The buddy movie presented a male-male relationship that was composed of humour, tacit understanding and, usually, equality of toughness between men. This relationship was constructed by a disavowal of the very thing that would appear to bind the men together—love. The elements that compose the relationship actually effect this disavowal—badinage as a way of not expressing serious emotions, silent communication as a means for not articulating or confronting feelings, toughness as a sign that one is above tenderness. . . . A further feature of the buddy movie's representation of male-male relationships is its explicit denial of homosexuality.[11]

Dyer identifies the very thing that Silver so rigorously avoids: homosexual attraction, which the genre subsumes in "badinage" and "toughness between men." In interracial buddy movies, race, too, is disarticulated in this way. Perhaps *Ricochet* is neither "buddy" nor "anti-buddy" but rather, "I want to be your buddy," which is, in this case, a version of "I want to be you" or "I want what you have" or "I don't want to be me." For the missing scene in *Ricochet* would have Blake actually consummating his desire and sodomizing Styles. Which does he want to do more, rape him or make love to him? His extraordinary rage is part and parcel of his sexual desire.

Along with Blake, the audience has been set up as spectators to Nick's near-naked body, black and splendid. That is precisely why the heterosexual family must be destroyed: it interferes with the sexual desires of Blake, desires in which the audience has been made complicitous. He has melded desire with dominion; indeed, the history of domination walks hand-in-hand with sexual desire. Because we do not see a sex scene with Styles, Blake's character can be read as both literally and metaphorically impotent, only able to have sex through videotaped surrogacy with a drugged and kidnapped lover. He is impotent, furthermore, in the very face and presence of black male prowess, both mythical and real.

In a *Washington Post* article called "'Boyz' and the Breakthrough: The Violent Birth of Hip-Hop Cinema," conservative commentator Cal Thomas asserted that movies such as Singleton's are dangerous: "During the '70s we had *Shaft*; and all of those movies, and *Soul Train* and all the rest. . . . But it portrays an underside of the black experience that is not, in my judgement, promoting future Clarence Thomases." The interviewer asks, "Wait a minute, *Soul Train*?" and Thomas replies, "Yeah, the heavy sexual orientation of the body rhythm."[12]

Here I think about courts, about what that frame ritualizes. What is the space of the basketball court, of black male theatrics in the white male imagination? In *White Men Can't Jump*, Woody Harrelson's court pyrotechnics and bold-faced woofing are the stuff of pure fantasy. The basketball court is imagined as a classless, raceless, hypergendered space of transcendence. It is also, crucially, where white men can safely articulate and experience their desire for black men. Conversely, in the courtroom, an arena of economic competition and social justice, that desire is a threat to what the white man believes is his. He cannot be a spectator or consumer because his own livelihood and public masculinity are at stake. For white patriarchal supremacy has always worked within a conceptual framework of relativity. If there is no other to conquer, what is left of the self?

And what of the "self" of the Nick Styles's of the world who too-willingly believe the hype of buppy success, of patriarchal dominion, as a way out of the delimiting cage that is black manhood in the mainstream imaginary? Does the fact that the white director Mulcahy created this character (rather than John Johnson, or Jesse Jackson, perhaps) mean that we can dismiss what Styles represents in spite of the misdoings of "the Man"? *Ricochet*'s version of black manhood and male success is not too far from the slick, surface mythology of black bourgeois manhood that is propounded not only by the black press but also in a black public sphere, a mythology that insists on advocating a patriarchal model of leadership in which the black public is cast as the credulous wife and children of a nuclear, patriarchal family. *Ricochet* marks alternative contours of family loyalty—homosocial bonding between men—that are flagrant but silent in the nuclear model I have described.

I do not wish to veer completely from what I have described as the most pressing dynamic of the film: the linkage of desire and dominion that frequently propels white male anxiety and consequent abuses of power against black men. The historical and present force of this dynamic must never be underestimated. However, perhaps the movie can lead us to an intracommunity questioning of another order: How does a fear of the complexities of one's own desires, as well as conservative, upwardly mobile black family discourse, truncate imagining other forms of family and community? Where is a model of black male sexuality and self-pleasure that can narrate itself without a concurrent narrative of dominion that mimics the very system it abhors? And, finally, simply, how might we vision a black masculinity that resists the lure of the myth of buppy patriarchy?

Notes

1. The still photograph most frequently used to advertise the film shows the two men grasping hands in an arm wrestle, eyes locked in an intense stare. For me, it echoes the black and white hand intertwined in the advertisement for Spike Lee's *Jungle Fever*, which calls up both erotic attraction and conflict.
2. *Ricochet,* 1991, Warner Brothers Inc., HBO Video, produced by Joel Silver and Michael Levy, directed by Russell Mulcahy.
3. I say this because the white men who work with this character feel such anxiety at her success that they make comments like, "I'd like to get her tit in a wringer" and call her names like "Priscilla the Hun." This both marks her as "man" (a threat who is "worthy" of workplace competition) as well as, of course, hypergendered "woman" for whom anatomy is essence. The violent image expresses that the anxiety is very specifically integral to the fact that she is a woman. Like so many successful women in the workplace, her self-assurance brands her, by implication by the white men she works with, as "dyke."
4. "Denzel Washington stars in film *Ricochet*," *Jet* 80, vol. 26, Oct. 14 1991, 57.
5. "Afterimages," in *Chosen Poems Old and New* by Audre Lorde (New York: W.W. Norton, 1982), 103.
6. Kobena Mercer, "Skin Head Sex Thing," in *How Do I Look?*, ed. Bad Object-Choices (Seattle, WA: Bay, 1991), 169–210.
7. Haryette Mullen of Cornell University observes that this specifying of Styles as a "preacher's kid," in the context of my argument about the antiaffirmative action rhetoric of the film, comments additionally on the bankruptcy of Martin Luther King, Jr.'s "school," if you will, of civil rights. I am grateful to Professor Mullen for this insight.
8. That fleeting glimpse of Washington's penis and loin has, at least in my anecdotal observation, become legendary. Many women and men remember, indeed went to see *Ricochet* for, that moment, made all the more titillating by Washington's insistence while filming Spike Lee's *Mo' Better Blues* that he was too modest even to take off his undershirt for a love scene in which his female partner was completely naked.
9. The protagonists in John Singleton's *Boyz in the 'Hood* are called Tre and Furious Styles.
10. "Denzel Washington stars in film *Ricochet,*" *Jet*, 58.
11. Richard Dyer, "*Papillon*," in *The Matter of Images: Essays on Representations* (London: Routledge, 1993), 126–27.
12. David Mills, *The Washington Post*, July 21, 1991, C1.

9

"BUT COMPARED TO WHAT?"

Reading Realism, Representation, and Essentialism in *School Daze*, *Do the Right Thing*, and the Spike Lee Discourse

WAHNEEMA LUBIANO

Brothers and sisters, we need to talk.

—Joe Wood[1]

Underneath it all, the posse don't know. Who, in fact, are "our people"?

—Joe Wood[2]

I

One of the first things to do is to think through the limits of one's power. One must ruthlessly undermine . . . the story of the ethical universal, the hero. But the alternative is not constantly to evoke multiplicity; the alternative is to know . . . that this is a limited sample because of one's own inclinations and capacities to learn enough to take a larger sample. And this kind of work should be a collective enterprise. Other people will do some other work.

—Gayatri Spivak[3]

I am an African American feminist, with fragments of a recalcitrant cultural nationalism still in my veins, working primarily in the area of African American narrative, and I am interested in cultural studies; those four things account for the nature of my interest in Spike Lee. When I agreed to write this paper, I felt considerable frustration, because if there is one African American filmic who has gotten press, media, and academic attention to the point of saturation, Spike Lee is that one.[4] My frustration arose also from knowing that the mass media and its discourse around Spike Lee might not be accessible to a critique, for example, of that which makes him a totem. On the other hand, despite my misgivings about leftist and liberal fetishization of Lee,[5] as well as my distaste for the regressive and ultimately useless criticism from reactionary critics and commentators concerned with "negative images,"[6] I think that he and his work represent a problematic through which the political difficulties that inhere in African American cultural production in this moment can be usefully discussed. The Spike Lee discourse and his production offer a site for examining possibilities of oppositional, resistant, or subversive cultural production as well as the problems of productions that are *considered* oppositional, resistant, or subversive without accompanying analysis sustaining such evaluation.

I do not want to be misunderstood. I am not criticizing Spike Lee for his representation of what some have called "damaging" or "negative" images of African Americans, images that drove Stanley Crouch to froth at the mouth in print. I want to consider instead the tendency (and the implications of that tendency) among the majority of critical commentators to uncritically laud Lee's films—especially *Do the Right Thing*—and Lee's presence in African American filmmaking. *She's Gotta Have It* and *School Daze* do raise complicated issues despite both films' masculinized representations and the rampant homophobia of *School Daze*. I don't address *She's Gotta Have It* in this paper, because so many other feminist critics, bell hooks preeminent among them, have said everything (and some more besides!) that I would have said about that film. While I find *School Daze* a more interesting film for my own close reading and therefore address it here, I also include *Do the Right Thing* because of the importance of that to what I'm calling the "Spike Lee discourse."

The first part of my title—"But Compared to What?"—is taken from a Gene McDonald lyric (sung by Roberta Flack on her album *First Take*): "trying to make it real but compared to what?"[7] The unvoiced of my title, of course, is the "trying to make it real." Trying to make *what* real? Lee's films' cultural production? Trying to make African Americans' complicated existence in the minds of others real in their own minds? Trying to make real the possibility of a counter-hegemonic discourse on race, a critique of race? Trying to make real or concrete a set of abstractions that achieve concrete form in material practices embodied in a film, in language about a film, in the effects of a filmmaker's presence in the cultural domain? And what is race in the United States if not an attempt to make "real" a set of social assumptions about biology?

But compared to what? Compared to what is not real? Compared to other things both real and unreal? Compared to whatever else exists, has existed, or might be able to exist within the present terms of cultural production, or under terms that might be changed by our examination of what is real? Compared to who else exists, has existed, or can exist within the specific histories—past and present—of black people across the diaspora engaged in filmmaking? "But Compared to What" might just mean compared to whatever you have.

What do issues of realism, representation, and essentialism have to do with the Lee discourse and Lee's films? I am concerned with the difficulty of thinking and saying anything at all about Lee and his work without contextualizing his work's possibilities and problems as well as what Lee himself has come to mean in the current cultural/political climate. Yet much of the Lee discourse has been insufficiently contextualized. And when I say political, I mean political in the sense of discourse and cultural production concerned with issues of power. In order to talk about these things, I examine Lee's evaluation of his work (specifically *School Daze* and *Do the Right Thing*),[8] others' evaluations of his work, the problems raised by Lee's place in film production and discourse, and the films *School Daze* and *Do the Right Thing* themselves.

Gayatri Spivak, in the interview to which I refer in the epigraph above, addresses the possibilities of politically engaged criticism in the academy. I evoke her language here to consider another kind of politically engaged work: African American film production within the constraints of Euro-American film discourse. She describes an interventionist political cultural project: doing one's "sample" while others, presumably, do theirs. The problem of Spike Lee's "sample," his place in the sun, is that his presence, empowered by Hollywood studio hegemony and media consensus on his importance, can function to overshadow or make difficult other kinds of politically engaged cultural work, not because it is impossible for more than one African American filmmaker to get attention at a time, but because of the implications and manifestations of the attention given to his work.[9] Further, the availability of different strategies of representation is foreclosed by the pressure many African Americans place on any artist to "speak" for the community, a pressure against which countless African American critics have inveighed, but a pressure to which Lee himself contributes when he claims to have "told the truth."

Spivak's discussion can serve to remind us that the *context* of the "samples," their availability or unavailability, and the process of their reception, determine how centered, unitary, or authoritative Lee's work becomes. Were a variety of African American filmmakers framed with such a profile, such a salience, critics and commentators (both African American and others) might be less likely to insist that Lee's work is the "real thing" and celebrate it so uncritically. That is to say, the recognition of multiple filmic possibilities, created from variant points of view by various filmmakers, could function to preempt the unitary authority of any one of them. This is not to say that the *rhetoric* of the "real thing" would disappear under these conditions, but that a reductionist African American representational hegemony would be more difficult to maintain. In other words, the combination of the increasing financial success of Lee's films and the media's fairly general deification of him functions to marginalize other African American filmic possibilities—possibilities, for example, such as those offered by independent African American women filmmakers.[10]

II

School Daze and *Do the Right Thing* are both engaged with problems of race and racism (external and internalized) in the context of a nation where race as a construction is not much talked about outside of academic circles and where the idea of racism as an intellectual, systemic, or concrete individual practice is cause for far more anger than theory, more recrimination and defensiveness than focus. Against this background, Stuart Hall's reading of the possibilities of Antonio Gramsci's work theorizes race and racisms and enables us to focus on the ways in which race and racisms are historically specific and inconsistent, to understand that manifestations of both change across time and across the complexities of the social formation. Hall argues that, while race is consistently related to class, it is not always the *result* of class difference (nor, I want to add, is race consistently *mediated* by class difference). The political consequences of specific moments of racism differ. At one moment and geopolitical locale, racism manifests itself in colonial enclaves; at another, in slavery; at another, Bantustans; and at still another, in something referred to as an urban "underclass."[11]

This general line of theory offers a vantage point for connecting more specific arguments about constructions of "blackness" in the U.S. context, including Henry Louis Gates, Jr.'s arguments about the metaphorical nature of "blackness" in western metaphysical discourse, Anthony Appiah's work on the construction of race, and Frantz Fanon's arguments about the effects on blacks of the construction of "negroness."[12] I am not taking any of these arguments to manichean extremes and suggesting that there is no biology; for, as Spivak cogently asserts, "biology doesn't just disappear," it simply ought not to be the "ground of all explanations."[13] Hortense Spillers, for example, warns against the ideological manipulations of racialized biology.[14] In her close reading of the Moynihan Report, she remarks on that text's confirmation of "the human body as a metonymic figure for an entire repertoire of human and social arrangements."[15]

What has not changed in the history of race in the United States is its centrality within our culture, the importance of it to our socialization as produced and reinforced by schools, organizations, family, our sexual lives, churches, institutions—all of which produce a racially structured society.[16] Race is a cultural factor of overwhelming importance. I raise these issues not only because Lee's work renders visible the African American presence within the terms of Euro-American dominance, but also because he sees himself and his work in terms of racial, and hence political, engagement: he is quoted by Salim Muwakkil as saying, "Someone has to force America to come to grips with the problem of racism."[17] Additionally, Lee and his coproducer Monty Ross told an audience at the University of Texas at Austin that they wanted to make films with a message and would try to make entertaining what was also thought provoking; they insisted that they would "tell the truth."[18] Aware of the need to make changes in the film industry by bringing in African Americans, Lee has indicated that he is proud of the part that he plays. Starting with his production deal for *Do the Right Thing*, he has made his films vehicles for African American employment and entrance into film craft unions: two folks off the streets of Bedford-Stuyvesant are now part of a union because of him.[19] Being a voice for the "real," affecting "reality," then, is the way that Lee sees his cultural mission.

His confidence that he has been able to force the United States to come to grips with the problem of racism is repeated in his insistence (in response to questions at the University of Texas) that he can retain his intellectual and political independence and still be financed by the studios as long as he continues to make money. In the first instance, however, he mistakes the media noise around race, racism, and his films for evidence that this country has "come to grips" with race. In fact, he must have realized at some point that his confidence was misplaced; in an article in *Mother Jones*, he says that in viewing *do the Right Thing* white people were more upset over the destruction of Sal's property than they were over Raheem's death.[20] In the second instance, he is simply naive in his belief that profit might somehow not be tied to how much a mass-distributed film can make itself acceptable to vast numbers of U.S. citizens; he needs to consider that, if a production has to return a profit in the millions of dollars, the likelihood of that production's remaining oppositional or subversive with regard to race might well be in inverse proportion to the extent the film relies on the support of a large, multiracial, politically uncritical audience to turn a profit. I do not want to argue that studio funding always means that a compromise in form and content is inevitable—profits have been made with more politically adventurous material—nor do I want to argue that the relationship between funding and content is a simple one. In fact, in a session at the 1989 MLA convention, Ann Cvetkovich and I argued that, if one wants to engage politically with the majority of African Americans or any other marginalized group, one has to be prepared to think seriously about working in the mass-culture (and, more to the point, mass-distribution) arena.[21] But I do insist that Lee's confidence needs to be mediated by a complicated awareness of market pressure.

In that vein, James Snead has argued that "without the incessant and confining restraints of box-office considerations, studio agendas, and censoring boards, the range of artistic choice in independent films is potentially *widened*, rather than *restricted*."[22] I don't draw on Snead here in order to absolutize independent production as always politically empowered and empowering—I do not want to romanticize the coercive nature of inequitable access to the means of film production, something Sankofa Film/Video filmmaker Isaac Julien addresses in the black British context.[23] (He and the other members of black British video collectives became involved in separatist projects, opting for ethnically and/or racially based organizations, because of their exclusion from "white" institutions.[24]) Nonetheless, I think such consideration of the possible costs of studio/institutional support is especially timely when one sees critics such as Nelson George writing in the *Village Voice* about the economics of African American film production. He points out that, while some of Lee's investors have been African American, some of the most crucial have not, and therefore that it is time for African American filmmakers to learn how to sit down and talk to studio money people because the "*Black Enterprise* crowd" would still rather invest in real estate than in African American cultural production.[25]

George's thinking raises a number of other questions. Would the financing from African American capitalists necessarily be more politically adventurous than that from Euro-American capitalists? I am not so sanguine, not so sure that black nationalism breaches class walls. Black nationalist economics raise yet another issue: both Spike Lee and Keenan Ivory Wayans talk about the necessity for African Americans to be in particular positions of power in relation to African American cultural production; Lee is "appalled by the dearth of Black executives in Hollywood," and Wayans thinks that "the destiny of Black art rests on Black people and Black corporate America."[26] To that last bit, "Black corporate America," I can only reply that if our cultural production rests on anybody's *corporate* America, then may God/Goddess help us.

It is to Lee's dominant position as and his forthright claim to be a "political" filmmaker that I want to return for the next section of my essay. My impetus for thinking about Lee in this way had its genesis in my reading of Manthia Diawara's article, "Black Spectatorship: Problems of Identification and Resistance." I found his argument that Eddie Murphy's characters in *Trading Places*, *48 Hours*, and *Beverly Hills Cop I* and *II* are first allowed to appear threatening, then "deterritorialised from a black milieu and transferred to a predominantly white world" helpful in considering containment and domestication strategies for certain other kinds of characters.[27] It spurred me to consider similar phenomena within what is at least represented as African American milieux—those depicted in *Do the Right Thing* and *School Daze*. How might one account for the domesticating processes of particular kinds of representations unless one rethinks the politics of what constitutes the possible "territory" of a "black" milieu?

I find the idea of Lee as a politically radical or progressive filmmaker troubling for two reasons: (1) the politics of race, gender, class, and sexuality in *Do the Right Thing* and *School Daze* are inadequate to the weight that these films and Lee carry within the discourse of political cultural work; and (2) having Lee and his work deified by the media and critical establishment, especially (as far as my own interests are concerned) by members of the leftist and African American media and critical establishment, is bad news to other African American filmics, who remain overshadowed by the attention granted to Spike Lee, and to the larger possibility of more politically progressive and complex film production focused on African American culture and/or issues of race.

To return to the questions that I raised at the beginning of this paper, any evaluation of Lee's work as radical or counterhegemonic has to be run past the question "Compared to what?" Against the underdeveloped, stymied state of discussion about race, racism, and racialization in the United States at this moment and against the paucity of productions about African Americans that can be invoked to situate Lee's work and stylizations, evaluations of his and his films' politics require considerably more analysis than has been available.

III

School Daze and *Do the Right Thing* were films discussed by most reviewers on the grounds of realism, authenticity, and relation to the "good" of the community represented in them. Many of the arguments that addressed the issue of *reception* fell into the trap of reducing the complexities of hegemony to simple polarities—white vs. black audiences or black middle-class vs. black lower-class audiences—as though these categories are completely understood and separately distinct.[28] That is to say, the blurred lines between unstable categories of people were firmly and falsely redrawn in the Spike Lee discourse. Omitted from discussion were the ways in which aspects of U.S. culture are internalized and contributed to (in some degree) by most of us (after all, how else does hegemony function?), as well as the ways in which culture constitutes contested ground—contested by different groups even within racialized communities under different circumstances. The complex problems of realism, representation, and essentialism were as apparent in the discussions around Lee and the films as they were in Lee's presence and in the films themselves.

Most of the reviews and articles written began, were imbued with, and/or concluded with, references to how very realistic or authentic the films were; how much they captured the sounds, rhythms, sights, styles, and important concerns of African Americans.[29] Armond White tied the film's politics to its depiction of "Afro-American cultural style as triumphant opposition strategy."[30] As Michael Kamber, writing about *Do the Right Thing* in *Z Magazine* pointed out, "He's *so* authentic!" seemed to be the refrain among liberal whites.[31] That refrain, however, came from all corners—liberals, progressives/leftists, and even some conservatives and reactionaries (as troubling as such critics found the film's "reality"), as well as from the political range of African Americans. It came from organs as ideologically dissimilar as the *Guardian*, the *New York Times*, and *Ebony*. More important, whether the critic/commentator was heaping encomia on Lee for attempting to portray African American culture without the "distortions" to which we have all grown accustomed,[32] questioning whether the characters were "real,"[33] or spouting vitriolic accusations of Afro-fascism because of what one critic saw as Lee's "fantastical" (i.e., "not real") distortions,[34] "realism" (or its lack) and the effect of the films' representation of the real were the keynotes of an incredible array of commentary about them.

Realism as the bedrock of narrative is inherently problematic. Realism poses a fundamental, long-standing challenge for counter-hegemonic discourses, since realism, as a narrative form, enforces an authoritative perspective. According to Raymond Williams, *real* has denoted the actually existing as opposed to the imaginary since the fifteenth century and, at the same time, has contrasted with *apparent*; by the nineteenth century, however, the word additionally established the difference between the "true" or fundamental quality of some thing or situation and the "false" or mistaken quality, while at the same time marking the difference between concrete and abstract.[35]

Reality, as Suzette Elgin puts it, is established via the consensus of a particular group and marks the "real world, the actually existing, true and concrete world" preserved by the absence of existing alternatives.[36] Kobena Mercer argues that the "reality effect produced by realist methods depends on the operation of four characteristic values—transparency, immediacy, authority and authenticity—which are in fact aesthetic values central to the dominant film and media culture."[37] By adopting this practice as a "neutral" or "instrumental" relation for the means of representation, black filmmakers seek to "redefine referential realities of race through the same codes and forms as the prevailing film language whose discourse of racism" they seem to contest. Mercer goes on to argue that "in short, black film practices which incorporate these filmic values are committed to a mimetic conception of representation which assumes that reality has an objective existence 'out there,' that the process of representation simply aims to correspond to or reflect."[38]

Deployed as a narrative form dependent upon recognition of reality, realism suggests disclosure of the truth (and then closure of the representation); realism invites the readers/audience to accept what is offered as a slice of life because the narrative contains elements of "fact." Realism, then, temporarily allows chaos in an otherwise conventional or recognizable world, but at the end the narrative moves toward closure, the establishment of truth and order. As Michael Kamber puts it, the morning after the riot (in *Do the Right Thing*), the neighborhood is "back to normal . . . and the feeling is that, were Sal to rebuild his pizzeria"—and, I would add, slap some pictures of Malcolm X and a few others on the wall—and were the cops to avoid killing anyone in the immediate future, everyone would go on back and eat there. "Ignorant and apolitical, letting the system roll on."[39]

Realism used uncritically as a mode for African American art implies that our lives can be captured by the presentation of enough documentary evidence or by insistence on another truth. The graffiti on Sal's pizzeria asserts, "Tawana told the truth." The implication is that her story was real, was actual and concrete, was *the* story of rape. The problem presented then is further cathected: must *Tawana* be telling the truth for us to believe the larger truth about sexual abuse of African American women by Euro-American men? Is this *the* "truth" compared to the "truth" of their abuse by African American men? Compared to what other African American women say? Compared to what Alice Walker, for example, says about African American men?[40] Compared to what Jade herself is saying, or trying to say, to Mookie?[41] In the name of preserving the "truth" of Tawana and her reality, is it okay for Mookie to *insist* that he *knows* the truth?[42]

Realism establishes a claim to truth, but it also presents the ground for its own deconstruction—somebody else's truth. Telling it like it is, as John Akomfrah notes, "has to be said with a certain amount of skepticism, because ultimately one needs to challenge the assumption that you *can* tell it like it is."[43] Telling it like it is, for example, can be claimed by narratives that are politically regressive. Shelby Steele, the new African American conservative media superstar, in his numerous attacks on the victims of racism (available in a newspaper/magazine near you) claims to be "telling it like it is" from his reality.[44] "Reality" is promiscuous, at the very least.

Why the historically consistent demand for and approval of realism in African American cultural production? Fanon argues that the "natives,"[45] in the face of the colonizer's big lies about the history and culture of the colonized, make a conscious attempt to reclaim their history and aspects of their culture. Against the constant distortions of Euro-American ethnocentric dismissal and burial of the African American presence, we respond with an insistence on "setting the record straight," "telling the truth," "saying it like it is." The Harlem Renaissance intellectuals, artists, and writers went to cultural war with each other over accurate depictions of the African American community; the Black Aesthetic critics in a subsequent period built a political and intellectual movement around an assertion of a counter-truth against the distortions of cultural racism; and, because the distortions have not ended, African Americans are presently preoccupied with the need to intervene in the dominant culture's construction of African Americanness. Nonetheless (and it is here that I am most concerned with the salience of Lee and his "truth"), despite the weight of a will to counter "lies," a marginalized group needs to be wary of the seductive power of realism, of accepting all that a realistic representation implies because of its inclusion of some "facts."

The reasons for "real" as a positive evaluation are tied, of course, to scarcity, the paucity of African American presentations of *facts* and *representations*, as well as the desire for more of the first category, which in turn allows the second category to have its "selectiveness" forgotten in the rush to celebrate its mere presence. It is, however, because of the salience of Lee's representations that he and they warrant *critical* attention. In order to give them that attention, we have to first acknowledge that they are not *generally* "real" (however "factual" any part of the content might be) but *specifically* "real"—and that specific "real" might be criticizable. If Lee's strength is a certain ability to document some of the sounds and sights of African American vernacular culture—its style focus—that vernacularity cannot guarantee counter-hegemonic cultural resistance. One can be caught up in Euro-American hegemony within the vernacular, and one can repeat the masculinism and heterosexism of vernacular culture. Vernacular language and cultural productions allow the possibility of discursive power disruptions, of cultural resistance, but they do not guarantee it. The particular politics of the specifics of vernacular culture that Lee represents are problematic. The films' presentation of and the critics' acceptance of these politics without a challenge encourages audiences to consider these representations as African American essences.

Telling the "truth" demands that we consider the truth of something compared to something else. Who is speaking? Who is asking? And to what end? I don't think that the problem of addressing the construction of reality can be answered by more claims to realism without considering how and why both hegemonic realism and resistance to or subversion of the realism are constructed. Reality, after all, is merely something that resounds in minds already trained to recognize it as such. Further, what happens in the shadow behind the "real" of Spike Lee—once it becomes hegemonic for African Americans? In other words, what happens when this "representation" is accepted as "real?" What happens to the construction of "blackness" in the public discourse?

According to Roland Barthes,

> representation is not directly defined by imitation: even if we were to get rid of the notions of "reality" and "versimilitude" and "copy," there would still be "representation," so long as a subject (author, reader, spectator, observer) directed his [or her] *gaze* toward a horizon and there projected the base of a triangle of which his [or her] eye (or his [or her] mind) would be the apex.[46]

Representation refers to images that are selected from what we recognize as reality; they are tied to and have meaning within particular settings. They come "from somewhere"[47] and have meaning insofar as "there are differences of meaning."[48] Akomfrah argues that representation "is used to simply talk about questions of figuration. How one places the Black in the scene of writing, the imagination and so on. Others saw it in more juridic terms. How one is enfranchised, if you like, how one buys into the social contract."[49] In other words, we need to consider how one constructs identity through the vehicle of representation. And compared to what? If Lee is working in a small field, if too much rides on the few African American filmmakers working in this cultural domain and this pressure to variously "represent" cannot be met, how might we reconsider the possibilities of African American filmmaking?

In *Invisible Man*, Trueblood tells a white philanthropist a story explaining his incest, his daughter's pregnancy, and his wife's. The unnamed narrator is shocked by Trueblood's frankness in relating his story and wonders, "'How can he tell this to white men . . . when he knows they'll say that all Negroes do such things?'"[50] The question of representation and what anyone should say about his/her community is a constant pressure under which African American cultural workers produce. But it is a question that constantly disenfranchises even as it reinforces the notion of absolutes—absolutes such as the "African American" community, the non–African American or "Euro-American" community, or notions of the author or filmmaker as the one who does "something" that a reader or an audience then simply consumes, resists, or appropriates. Furthermore, if one is enthralled by the idea of absolute representations, then "good" or "real" cultural production is impervious to reader or audience misbehavior (misreading), and "bad" or "nonrepresentative" or "unrealistic" cultural production comforts racist Euro-Americans (or can be appropriated by them) or misleads African Americans. Believing and acting on these assumptions means deifying or demonizing African American cultural production or producers. In other words, it is as foolish to say that Lee has produced "appropriation-proof," *real* African American art as it is to say that he has produced "Afro-fascism" that distorts reality.

Lee is himself to some extent cognizant of how he is placed within the discourse of representation; however, he also produces representations that suggest particular Euro-American hegemonic politics. His *Do the Right Thing* is imbued with the Protestant work ethic: there is more language about work, responsibility, and ownership in it than in any five Euro-American Hollywood productions. The film insists that, if African Americans just work like the Koreans, like the Italians, like the Euro-American brownstone owners, problems could be averted; or, if you own the property, then you can put on the walls whatever icons you want; or, if you consume at (materially support) a locale, then you can have whatever icons you want on the walls. And its masculinized focus could be distilled into the slogan that screams at us throughout the film: "Real men work and support their families." These representations compared to what? Within the representations of *Do the Right Thing*, what are the ideologies being engaged, or critiqued, or, more to the point, not critiqued? Contrary to Salim Muwakkil's assertion that "Lee's refusal to make clear his judgments has limited his popularity among audiences weaned on formulaic narrative,"[51] I find *Do the Right Thing* relentlessly formulaic in its masculinized representations and its conventional Calvinist realism.

To paraphrase Stuart Hall, there is no law that guarantees a group's ideology is consistent with its economic—or, I would add, its racial—position, nor is there any guarantee that the ideology of a group *isn't* consistent with its economic or race position.[52] For the purposes of thinking about representation and Lee's films, we might want to consider the assumption held by his lower-class characters that work is the "right thing," that it means always what we think it means. Drug dealers (absent from this picture) work; global corporate CEOs responsible for planetary and human degradation also work. Work or nonwork, but compared to what? We (as audience) could consider this "work" emphasis to be parody, but the film uses "work" or "ownership" to justify intervention.

Or, to return again to identity politics, Hall writes "'Black' is not the exclusive property of any particular social or any single discourse . . . it has no necessary class belonging."[53] He is drawing on his experience in the Caribbean and British contexts, but it is an argument that has considerable force for race theorizing and the politics of racial representation within the U.S. context. What does "blackness" mean in *School Daze* or *Do the Right Thing*? *School Daze*, the Lee film that has received by far the least amount of national critical respect, suggests far more complicated *possibilities* around the idea of identity politics than *Do the Right Thing* (despite *School Daze's* foul gender politics and horrific homophobia, issues to which I will return). It is with regard to identity politics that unself-conscious realism and representation within the distorted discourse of Euro-American hegemony lead inevitably to a profoundly unstrategic essentialism.

Essentialism is, as Diana Fuss defines it, "commonly understood as a belief in the real, true essence of things, the invariable and fixed properties which define the 'whatness' of a given entity."[54] It assumes that certain characteristics are inherently part of the core being of a group. The idea of authenticity—a notion that implies essence—can derive from the idea that a particular group and individual entities of that group can be recognized by the ways in which they are shown with some measure of the "real" or authentic or essential qualities of that group. Fuss argues additionally, however, that, because essentialism is not in and of itself progressive or reactionary, the appropriate question is: "If this text *is* essentialist, what motivates its deployment?"[55] (my emphasis). Because I am mindful of Fuss's careful complications of essentialisms, I want to make clear my consideration of specific problem sites of essentialism—Lee, the discourse about Lee, and two of his films.

Some African American critics have shown impatience with criticisms of essentialism. Henry Louis Gates, Jr., for example, has stated his suspicions about this charge as part of his defense of African Americanist canon formation or reformation.[56] He refers to the fact that African Americanists' "attempts to define a black American canon—foregrounded on its own against a white backdrop—are often derided as racist, separatist, nationalist, or 'essentialist'—my favorite term of all."[57] He argues that "you cannot . . . critique the notion of the subject until a tradition's subjectivity (as it were) has been firmly established,"[58] but he is not clear about *who* cannot critique the African American subject at issue here, or *for whom* this subjectivity still needs to be established. I am mindful of the fact that Gates is skeptical of a *specific* charge of essentialism—that leveled against the institutionalization of an African American literary canon—and I agree with his arguments about the political usefulness at this moment of such defining. Attacks on African American "canons" are blind to certain political "realities." I am simply picking one small bone here: I think that it is possible to argue for the work of defining African American literary traditions without "saving" essentialism.

I find Gates's argument about the need to "establish" African American subjectivity a little inconsistent, given his tracing (in *Figures in Black* and *The Signifying Monkey*) of the complexity of the historical development of African American subjectivity (African Americans have been already at work developing subjectivit*ies*) and his deconstruction of the idea of a "transcendent black subject" (in "The Blackness of Blackness").[59] Part of the work of African American cultural criticism has been not only to claim, to insist on, African American subjectivity/subjectivities but also to elaborate and complicate such subjectivity/subjectivities by speculating on their varied and fragmented relations to their products—abstract and/or concrete, formalized and/or ephemeral.

Within the domain of African American cultural discourse, African Americans have been going about the business of establishing that tradition's subjectivity and have been fighting about its terms since the seventeenth century. Some African Americans, as various critics (among them Gates, Gloria Hull, Valerie Smith, Deborah McDowell, and Hazel Carby) have documented, historically resisted essences inscribed in

African American cultural commentary, even when these essences were meant to counter essences held by the dominant culture. Vernacular culture, in fact, has allowed a space and mechanism for complicating essences. And in literature and literary critical discourse, Zora Neale Hurston, Nella Larsen, Pauline Hopkins, Jessie Fauset, W.E.B. Du Bois, Sterling Brown, Jean Toomer, and Langston Hughes (to some extent) have complicated notions of African American subjectivity even against the African American male cultural and political hegemony of the Harlem Renaissance. In her interview with Spivak, Ellen Rooney states that

> to contextualize is to expose the history of what might otherwise seem outside history, natural and thus universal, that is the essence. . . . The problem of essentialism can be thought [of], in this way, as a problem of form, which is to say, a problem of reading. Context would thus emerge as a synonym for reading, in that to read is to demarcate a context. Essentialism appears as a certain resistance to reading, an emphasis on the constraints of form, the limits at which a particular form so compels us as to "stipulate" an analysis.[60]

I am moved to consider the particular situation of Lee by Spivak's warning against "antiessentialism" as yet another form of essence: "To an extent, we have to look at where the group—the person, the persons, or the movement[—]is situated when we make claims for or against essentialism. A strategy suits a situation; a strategy is not a theory."[61] Lee's films and his place in the discourse of African American and American filmmaking are situations that warrant my criticism of their essentialism; and even if what Lee does is a strategy and not an essence, it is still fair to be critical of that strategy and its power to essentialize within the context of Euro-American hegemony and African American cultural discourse. Lee's presentation of images that resonate with factual reality is glossed as the general truth. The deification of Lee as "truth sayer" and of his production as "real" means that the indexing of his selections becomes the "essence" of "black authenticity"—and thus impervious to criticism.

I understand that to be authentically "African American" or "black" has, at various times in history and in the present, meant and sometimes means to be rhythmic; or to have a predilection for playing craps, drinking, using and/or selling drugs, or raping white women; or being a jungle savage; or being uninterested in marriage; or being on welfare—the list goes on and on. The resonances of authenticity depend on who is doing the evaluating. But I want to foreground the problematic of authenticity and its relation to essentialism.

Coco Fusco has argued that "the tenet of authenticity is virtually incompatible with the strictures of narrative drama, since 'typical' experiences are presumed to stand for every black person's perception of reality."[62] To that I would add only that, when further strengthened by facticity, "typicalness" homogenizes differences. Being different within such a narrative economy, then, is read as "white" or "middle class" or whatever the current sign being used to signify "not black." In any event, dramatic "play" or manipulation (and its political possibilities) is constrained. Authenticity becomes a stranglehold for political analysis and cultural practice beyond the strictures of narrative drama. When Michele Wallace asserts that "intrinsic oppositionality c[an] not be attributed only to the so-called Other"[63]and Akomfrah argues that "Blacks are expected to be transgressive,"[64] they, along with Fusco, point to the specific problem of essentialism in the context of black film production. If, as Akomfrah, argues, we fall into the trap of Kant's categorical imperative—that categories carry with them their own imperatives, and, following that, that the category "black" carries with it an essential obligation to oppose, to transgress constantly in specific ways—then we are "saddled with the assumption that there are certain transcendental duties that Black film-making has to perform. . . . It has to work with the understanding that it's in a state of emergence . . . [and that] its means always have to be guerilla means, war means, signposts of urgency. . . . [T]he categorical imperative imprisons."[65] "Black" essence can come to be read from its activity of transgressing another, even less elaborated essence—that of "whiteness."

The categorical imperative is essentialist, whether imposed by dominance or volunteered for under the terms of Euro-American political or African American cultural hegemony. If we fail to problematize the notion that being African American *always* means *only* being embattled, that African American film is political only insofar as "someone" empowered to make the evaluation recognizes its political "reality" and calls the shots on its transgressiveness and that "authenticity" is always already known and can therefore be proven, then we have fallen into the trap of essentialism. Both the celebratory and the hostile Spike Lee discourses have been amazingly, although not entirely, uncritically essentialist.

There are "honorable" exceptions: bell hooks and Michael Kamber writing In *Z Magazine*, Herb Boyd writing in the *Guardian*, Mike Dyson writing in *Tikkun*, and some of what J. Hoberman wrote in the *Village Voice*—all regarding *Do the Right Thing*—as well as parts of the multi-voiced exchange on *School Daze* that went on in the *Village Voice*, not only moved past celebration or dismissal based on explicit language about "reality" and "authenticity" but also managed to critique assumptions of progressive or radical cultural politics based primarily on representations of African Americans on the screen in practices that too many of us have been trained to identify as "transgressive."[66]

When I ask "Compared to what?" I am asking that we consider a larger domain of possibilities than the Spike Lee discourse has made available. The end of such inquiry is not to lead simply to a fuller explication of his films or his "presence" in cultural production—although that's not a bad side effect—but to enable us to think about the terms of African American cultural production and practice generally, and African American film production and practice specifically, without falling back on an uncritical and unstrategic essentialist celebration of any representation—on screen or embodied in a particular filmmaker.

IV

Although *Do the Right Thing* received far more positive press than *School Daze*, perhaps because its working-class subjects seemed more "authentic" to critics[67] than the middle-class subjects of *School Daze*, I contend that *School Daze* is the more complicated movie. While both films are masculinist, and *School Daze* is also explicitly and viciously homophobic, *Do the Right Thing* stays, for the most part, comfortably within the boundaries of static and essentialist propositions about racial identity and about the relationship of wages and ownership to qualities of responsibility, "manhood," and freedom.[68]

Do the Right Thing makes manhood synonymous with having a job (and being able to take care of one's monetary responsibilities). When one of the block's hip-hop young men taunts Da Mayor for his drinking and other problems, Da Mayor returns (as explanation) an account of his inability (in the past) to feed his children because he had no job. The teenager sneers back that Da Mayor put himself in that position. We are given to understand that, unlike Da Mayor, the young man would make sure that he had a job and could take care of his kids; in other words, he would be a man. In this vein, Mookie's wages make him responsible enough—or man enough—that he can abjure others to "get a job," enable him to make some feeble attempts to provide for his child, and give him the standing to tell Jade what she needs to know about sexual oppression. Jade tries to make him back down by participating in the "wages = right-to-speak" discourse: "You can hardly pay the rent and you're gonna tell me what to do?" Mookie responds, "I get paid." When Jade returns with "You're getting paid peanuts," the point, I suppose, is that were Mookie to have higher wages, then it would be all right for him to tell her what to do. At the same time, Mookie is excoriated by Sal and Pino to do the work for which they are paying his wages/his peanuts.

Against, I suppose, the long-held racist charge that African Americans neither work nor want to work, this film spends much of its running time assuring its audience that African Americans in Bed-Stuy certainly do value work! (By its end, I am so overwhelmed by its omnipresent wage-labor ethos that I find myself exhausted.) I am not antilabor; however, this film makes no critique of the conditions under which labor is drawn from some members of the community nor are kinds of labor/work differentiated. Instead, without any specific contextualization, work is presented as its own absolute good, because work and ownership are what empower *men* to make decisions, to exercise freedom. The Euro-American brownstone owner need only reply to the block's hip-hoppers that he "owns" his house to have the last word in the encounter; Sal need only respond that he "owns" his pizzeria in order to maintain his freedom over decor; and Sweet Dick Willie is able to have the last word in a discussion of Korean ownership by insisting that since he has his "own" (or "owned") money, he has the freedom to ignore any form of critical analysis on the part of his buddies or Buggin' Out and patronize the grocery store and the pizzeria, respectively.

"I own," however, complicates neighborhood boundaries and identity politics. The gentrifier both "owns" his house and was born in Brooklyn and thus can be said to "belong" in the neighborhood (if not on this particular block). And, ironically, the critique of the Korean grocery store owners because they don't "belong" in the neighborhood is begun by M.L., who is himself an immigrant, as his buddies are quick to remark. Yet, while Sal "owns" his pizzeria, Pino reminds him again and again that "this" is not "their" neighborhood; they don't "belong" here. Still, no one really needs to think about what might be at stake in these contradictions; it is enough to have the money: "When you own your own pizzeria, then you can put your own pictures up."

In these contradictions, *Do the Right Thing* raises an interesting issue: What is the difference, if any, between a person "born" (and thus able to lay some kind of claim to "belonging") in a neighborhood and a gentrifier who lays claim by "buying" his belonging? Further, the gentrifier's presence—as both "born in" (and therefore "native to") Brooklyn and as "buyer" in this block—raises the larger context of the relations of racial bodies, real estate and bank practices, and class issues.

Early on, the film promises a class critique of sorts in the discussion of Sweet Dick Willie and his buddies on the corner. M.L. begins a complaint that the Koreans, like so many other immigrant groups, move into the neighborhood and seem immediately to "make it," only to lose the focus of his critique. The men make no mention of differential capital bases or accesses to bank loans—and there is no reason to think that vernacular language could not handle that analysis. M.L. concludes his discussion (simplistically): "Either them Korean motherfuckers are geniuses or you black asses are just plain dumb." The either/or proposition is reductionist: genius or dumb ass.

The discussion around, and the tensions raised by, the behavior of the Korean grocery store owners/employees as well as their economic relationship to the rest of the block degenerates completely when the film shows the rioting crowd suddenly stop seeing the Koreans as economically privileged and allows the Koreans instead to claim the common oppression of race: We are all colored (and therefore essentially equal) together. The moment's class hostility and film critique of stratification are disrupted and traded in for simplistic race unity without representing any of the complications of such a change.

Nonetheless, it is in the realm of identity politics—of place and race—that the film both raises possibilities of complicated representation and undermines them. "Stay Black" is the keystone phrase for the neighborhood, although it seems to refer to something ineffable. "Blackness" is what? Perhaps it is the roll call of musicians on the radio, the DJ's rap, the sounds and sights of vernacular culture, the claims of female genetic "tender-headedness." Yes. But "blackness" is also nailed down without specifics in the exchanges between Buggin' Out and Mookie, Mookie and Raheem, Raheem and Buggin' Out. Jade is "down for something positive" and black, and neither she nor Buggin' Out feels the need to specify exactly what the "black positive" is. "Blackness" is Malcolm X, although, as Smiley's picture and Lee's quotes after the conclusion of the film remind us, "blackness" is also Martin Luther King, Jr.; "blackness," then, is reduced to the sacredness that inheres in the proper icons.

As Joe Wood asserts, "In the ever-evolving vernacular, Malcolm X has come to mean the real (black) thing, the authentic (black) thing, as close to (black) integrity as close can be. . . . Malcolm [is] the Essential Black Man."[69] Wood goes on to argue that, if Malcolm (or, I might add, Martin Luther King, Jr.) is to be treated as a symbol of blackness, then we've backed ourselves into a religion of "essential blackness" and away from a historical analysis or exploration of its complexities, its constructedness. Iconography and fetishization is no substitute for history and critical thinking. The film offers no consistent critique of "pictures"—as icons, as fetishes—except for Jade's discussion with and aborted interruption of Buggin' Out's crude analysis. But the movie diminishes her intervention because, within its terms, after all, who is Jade but a sister who ought to but doesn't know when some white man is hitting on her and who has to be warned both by her brother and by the Tawana truth lurking behind and against her back?

Brothers and sisters, we *do* need to talk.

Blackness also seems to demand images that suggest African American males are prone to death by police violence—as bell hooks reminds us.[70] In fact, Lee dedicates this film to victims of the police, the dramatic high point of the film being Raheem's murder by the police. Lee has waxed indignant about that murder's dismissal on the part of some Euro-American viewers;[71] however, Lee has said also that if Raheem had just turned down the radio, then none of this would have happened: so much for any representation of systemic racist oppression. What are we to make of identity politics within the domain represented by this film? For a filmmaker who claims the mantle of transgression, cultural opposition, political righteousness, and truth telling, the political ambitions of this film are diffuse and, by its end, defused into nothingness.

It is *School Daze*—the film considered less politically ambitious (but equally masculinized and heterosexist)—that offers the possibilities of greater political depth; it at least raises interesting questions about identity politics "within the group." Although the film is undermined by its homophobia and sexism, it is within the terms of consideration of these areas that identity politics and essentialism are, in fact, deconstructed.

School Daze is sloppy but complicated. It shows us frat hegemony forging in action: "Q Dogs, that's what we want to be" is the refrain that bonds. "Q-Dogs are real men because it takes a real man to be a Q-dog"—tautological, yes, and therefore full of the comfort implied by unproblematized allegiances. This refrain, however, is followed by insistences that have no basis in absolutes, that could be read as critical of absolutes, having meaning only by stating differences. A "real" man is *not* a virgin, *not* a "fag." Men know themselves by virtue of their comparisons to "others"—gay men and those individuals in states of presexual being, untouched. Women, too, have their absolutes: "He's a man, he's sneakin'!" is clearly an exegesis on the nature or essence side of the argument about the ontology of male being. Nonetheless, the women also have their moments of comparison and acknowledgments of constructedness: Some sororities are not "bad," and Rachel wants to "become" a Delta even though she is *not* a wannabee.

The film offers some poststructuralist comforts. Half-Pint begins the film firmly centered: "I'm your cousin, your blood." But he ends it reconstructed and differently centered (however problematically): "I'm a Gamma man *now*" (my emphasis). That new insistence marks a historicized difference. The film offers additional critiques of identity politics. Possibilities include the town/gown split, an explicitly political one that manifests its implicit politics in aesthetics as well: The townies, who are working class and, therefore, under some rubrics "blacker" than the middle-class college kids, are also the ones with the "jeri curls" (generally recognized as evidence of aesthetic disaffection with "blackness") protected by shower caps. And a concern with international politics—South Africa and apartheid—gets read by "wannabee" Julian as evidence that the male jigs really aren't "black," because "blackness" originates in and is concerned with U.S. geopolitical sites only—like Detroit.

The film's failing, of course, is that it does not explore the ways in which its (male) politics are also tied to its own forms of aesthetization. Males are not only socialized by the behaviors of their groups, whether within fraternities or within male-oriented, internationally focused political practices such as protests, marches, or rallies, but they are also participants in the aesthetization of these practices. The film, unfortunately and myopically, presents aesthetics as formal matters of physical appearance in which women only participate.[72] Men *do*: they dance the beautifully choreographed Greek stomps, or the fellas' clever parody stomp, or make careful selections of political posters and other room decor items and arrange that decor for sexual trysts.

Women, on the other hand, *show*. They wear or don't wear make-up; they straighten or don't straighten their hair; they show off the colors of the eyes with which they were born or show different eyes through the wonders of chemical technology. *School Daze* is incapable of making the connection between what the men do and what they are showing as their aesthetics, and the film is incapable of showing that women do anything other than look like components of male aesthetics. The film is allowed its specificity, but it could have chosen to self-consciously represent male constructions of aesthetics; there is work to be done in this area. Still *School Daze*, while not recognizing its own attitude toward the gendering of its discussion of aesthetics, does make the issue available for critique.

The film's homophobia offers a similar site for examining historical identity and gender politics. In its retreat from and fear of homosexuality and the homosexual, it plays out the fear engendered during the course of African American history and concretized by Robert Park's assertion (in the 1920s) that "the Negro is the lady of the races."[73] The language around African American culture, intellectualism, and politics has been dominated by language analogous to that which has constructed and constrained women. Within a history that has used the same language to delineate the constructions of race *and* gender, that has insisted, against general Euro-American male privilege, that African American males can only share the space reserved for women, this film is a long commercial that reassures African American males that they *can* center themselves by asserting a salient difference: they are straight; all "real" men are straight; "blackness" is like real manhood—straight. So there, Robert Park.

Again, however, in defense of a critique of the specificities of this film's representations, the feeble excuse of "reality" comes into play. Lee has consistently defended his film against criticism of its homophobia by claiming and privileging its facticity, by defending realism: those (frat) guys really are that way. In so doing, he lets himself off the hook for the selection criteria at work in any representation. I respond as simply: Yes, some African Americans are like that, some are not; therefore, to what particular end is this specific "real" content being mined? If it is intended as a critique of African American homophobia, how (in form and/or content) is the critique available?

V

I would like to end where I began. The historical moment and the attention given to Spike Lee by an entire spectrum of critics, commentators, and media fora, the effects of his presence and deification on possible productions of African American presences in the cultural domain, the reductionist tendency in any U.S. discussions about race and racism all combine to make it imperative that we continue to think about the issues raised by Lee and his production. It won't hurt and might help to begin by refusing to consider Lee or his production simply within their own terms. Trying to make things "real" has been the problem. What might more contextual criticism of Lee and his production offer us?

The May 1990 issue of *Emerge* points to the recent successes of African American independent filmmakers at Sundance.[74] The news is cheering. But there were no African American women among their number and, even more troubling, the critic writing the article said nothing about their absence from Sundance or from his discussion of African American filmmaking. Instead, he described and contributed to the uncritical veneration of the work of Melvin Van Peebles, a tradition in African American film criticism that ignores both formal infelicities in Van Peebles's films and issues of sexism and homophobia.

Within the terms of simple celebration of African American male filmmakers, there is no space for the criticism that any artist needs—especially, given present political constraints, artists from marginalized and racialized communities. Yet, as critics we are responsible for the work of analysis and thoroughgoing contextualization lest we run the risk of continuing, in the name of affirming our cultural production, disabling essentialisms. Representations are not "reality"; simple, factual reproductions of selected aspects of vernacular culture are neither necessarily counterhegemonic art nor anything else. They don't even "set the record *straight*" (pun intended). Therefore, in our critical considerations we do well to heed Fanon's warnings equally against nationalist nostalgia for a precolonial past and uncritical nativist celebrations in the present. While beginning with the question of context—"Compared to what?"—does not foreclose productive discussions, it does make it harder to rest on simple resolutions. And that's the truth, Ruth.

Notes

This essay first appeared in *Black American Literature Forum,* 25, 2 (Summer, 1991), 253–282.

1. Joe Wood, , "Looking for Malcolm: The Man and the Meaning Behind the Icon," *Village Voice,* 29 May 1990, 43.

2. Joe Wood, "Self-Deconstruction," *Village Voice,* 24 April 1990, 79.

3. Gayatri Chakravorty Spivak, "In a Word: *Interview" Outside in the Teaching Machine* (New York: Routledge, 1993), 19.

4. Amazingly, the *New York Times*, not exactly famous for its in-depth analysis of African American cultural life or production, invited a group of people including academics in literature, education, and sociology; a psychiatrist; an administrative judge of the New York State Supreme Court; and a film director (among others) to "explore issues raised by the film" *Do the Right Thing*; see "*Do the Right Thing*: Issues and Images," *New York Times*, 9 July 1989, late ed., sec. 2, 1. The editors of the *Arts and Leisure* section devoted almost two full pages to excerpts from this gathering.

5. Included in this category are Pat Aufderheide, "Racial Schisms: The Daze of Our Lives," *In These Times*, 16–22 March 1988, 20; Vincent Canby, "Spike Lee Tackles Racism and Rage," *New York Times*, 30 June 1989, late ed., C16; Jeremiah Creedon, "That Cannes Can of Worms: Sex, Lies and the Right Thing," *In These Times*, 18–24 October 1989, 20–21; Thulani Davis, "We've Gotta Have It," *Village Voice*, 20 June 1989, 67–70; Barbara Day, "Spike Lee Wakes Up Movie Audiences, Confronts Questions of Black Power," *Guardian*, 5 July 1989, 24–25; Stuart Ewen, "'Do the Right Thing' Is an American Movie in the Best Sense," *New York Times*, 14 July 1989, late ed., A28; J. Hoberman, "Pass/Fail," *Village Voice*, 11 July 1989, 59, 62, 66; Stuart Klawans, rev. of *Do the Right Thing*, *Nation*, 17 July 1989, 98–100; Salim Muwakkil, "Doing the Spike Thing," *In These Times*, 5–18 July, 18, 24; and Greg Tate, "Burn Baby Burn," *Premier*, August 1989, 80–85.

6. Included in this category are Stanley Crouch, "Do the Race Thing," *Village Voice*, 20 June 1989, 73–74, 76; and Joe Klein, "Spiked," *New York*, 26 June 1989, 14–15.

7. Roberta Flack, *First Take* SC-82302 1969, CD. The subtexts of "Compared to what?" are both dominant cultural production and the possibilities for politically engaged film explored by the black British film collectives—about which I do not write at any length (or in any depth) in this paper, but against which I look at Lee.

8. Lee sees himself and his work as politically engaged; see, for example, Peggy Orenstein, "Spike's Riot," *Mother Jones*, September 1989, 32–35, 43–46. For

this reason, I take his political claims, as well as the critics who deify him, so seriously.

9. I focus only on Lee opting not to include a critique of Eddie Murphy, Robert Townsend, Keenan Wayans, or the Hudlin brothers (all African American male filmmakers getting considerable attention from the general media and African American cultural commentators) to keep this essay focused and of moderate length.

10. This is an issue raised by Ann Cvetkovich and me in a coauthored paper presented at the 1989 Modern Language Association Convention; see Cvetkovich and Lubiano, "Black Film Production as Cultural Studies Problematic," Division on Black American Literature and Culture, MLA Convention, Washington, DC, 28 December 1989.

11. Stuart Hall, "Gramsci's Relevance for the Study of Race and Ethnicity," *Journal of Communication Inquiry* 10 (2) (1986): 23–25.

12. I refer to Henry Louis Gates, Jr.'s *Figures in Black: Words, Signs, and the "Racial" Self* (New York: Oxford Univ. Press); Anthony Appiah, "The Uncompleted Argument: Du Bois and the Illusion of Race," in *"Race," Writing, and Difference*, ed. Henry Louis Gates, Jr. (Chicago: Univ. of Chicago Press, 1986); and Frantz Fanon, *Black Skin, White Masks* (1952; New York: Grove, 1967).

13. Gayatri Spivak, "In a Word. *Interview*," with Ellen Rooney, *Differences* 1 (2) (1990): 148.

14. Hortense Spillers, "Mama's Baby, Papa's Maybe: An American Grammar Book," *Diacritics* 17 (2) (1987): 65–66.

15. Ibid., 66.

16. Hall, "Gramsci's Relevance," 25.

17. Muwakkil, "Doing the Spike Thing," 18.

18. The truth of his vision was also the theme of his letter-to-the-editor response (to Joe Klein's hysterical attack) in *New York* magazine. See Spike Lee, Presentation and Discussion, University of Texas at Austin, 26 February 1989; and "Spike Lee Replies: 'Say It Ain't So Joe,'" *New York*, 17 July 1989, 6.

19. See Lee, Presentation and Discussion; and Tate, "Burn Baby Burn," 85.

20. Peggy Orenstein, "Spike's Riot," 34.

21. Cvetkovich and Lubiano, "Black Film Production," 13. I do not think, however, that all African American cultural production has to be nationally distributed for it to be a site of resistance to the dominance of Euro-American cultural hegemony.

22. James Snead, "Images of Blacks in Black Independent Films: A Brief Survey," in *BlackFrames: Critical Perspectives on Black Independent Cinema*, ed. Mbye B. Cham and Claire Andrade-Watkins (Cambridge, MA: MIT Press, 1988), 17.

23. Cvetkovich and I have argued also against seeing a simple dichotomy between politically "good" independent and politically "bad" commercial production and against the equally simple a dichotomy between avant-garde as an inherently elitist form and conventional narrative representation as an inherently popular form; see Cvetkovich and Lubiano, "Black Film Production."

24. Coco Fusco, "Fantasies of Oppositionality," *AfterImage* (December 1988): 8.

25. Nelson George, "Shady Dealin'," *Village Voice*, 27 February 1990, 37.

26. James Greenberg, "In Hollywood, Black Is In," *New York Times*, 4 March 1990, *Arts and Leisure,* 23.

27. Manthia Diawara, "Black Spectatorship: Problems of Identification and Resistance," *Screen* 29 (4) (1988): 71.

28. There were, for instance, those who thought Euro-Americans or middle-class African Americans needed to learn from *Do the Right Thing*. Consider the example of Barbara Day, who thought the movie was good because it was "as real as the nation's last urban insurrection." Middle-class people (of both races), she opened, "needed to see what the poor in New York City ghettos see too often: a Black or Latino Raheem being choked, feet dangling above the pavement." Day, "Spike Lee Wakes Up Movie Audiences." I could expend much ink and theoretical zeal on the tendency (need? pleasure?) of many Euro-American commentators to romanticize African Americans represented at the most coercive sites, sites that bestow "authenticity," but I don't feel strong enough this time around. While there are differences among segments of the African American population, some circumstances of life in the United States for African Americans are fairly general. The existence of racist police practices is one such unifying factor. I will take issue, therefore, with another aspect of Day's myopia: the argument that racist police coercion is always lower- or working-class oriented. Day connects "a Black or Latino Raheem being choked" with ghetto residents only, but one of the Miami "urban insurrections" was kicked off by the police murder of Arthur Little, a middle-class African American who worked in insurance. The violent tendencies of racist police are not unknown to middle-class African Americans: at the National Black Male Conference workshop on police abuse (Kansas City, MO, 13 July 1990), the largely academic and middle-class African American audience was unsurprised when Don Jackson, a former police officer (made famous by the videotape of an LAPD officer pushing his head through a window), said that "almost everyone in this room looks like a criminal to police officers so inclined." Class does not necessarily mediate racism. Even most middle-class African Americans understand (and many have suffered from) some form of racist police violence or hostility.

29. Salim Muwakkil ("Doing the Spike Thing"), Greg Tate ("Burn, Baby, Burn"), and Armond White ("New Dawn at Sundance, Black Filmmakers Take Top Prizes"), (*Emerge*, May 1990, 65–66) were the most enthusiastic in this cate-

gory, followed closely by Thulani Davis ("We've Gotta Have It") and Barbara Day ("Spike Lee Wakes Up Movie Audiences").

30. Armond White, "Scene on the Street: Black Cinema from Catfish Row to Stuyvesant Avenue," *MotherJones*, September 1989, 46.
31. Michael Kamber, "Do the Right Thing," *Z Magazine*, October 1989, 40.
32. Muwakkil, "Doing the Spike Thing," 24.
33. Brent Staples, "Spike Lee's Blacks: Are They Real People?," *New York Times*, 2 July 1989, late ed., sec. 2, 9.
34. Crouch, "Do the Race Thing," 74.
35. Raymond Williams, *Keywords: A Vocabulary of Culture and Society* (New York: Oxford Univ. Press), 216–17.
36. Suzette Elgin, *Native Tongue* (New York: DAW, 1984), 30–31.
37. Kobena Mercer, "Diaspora Culture and the Dialogic Imagination: The Aesthetics of Black Independent Film in Britain," in *BlackFrames*, 53.
38. Ibid.
39. Kamber, "Do the Right Thing," 40.
40. bell hooks examines the differences between critical responses to Alice Walker's representations of African American men and those of Spike Lee; "Counterhegemonic Art: The Right Thing," *Z Magazine*, October 1989, 31–36.
41. hooks also touches on this point in "Counterhegemonic Art," 35.
42. How very much Mookie's insistence on the predatoriness of Euro-American males toward African American females echoes (while countering) Euro-American males' insistence on the myth of African American male predatoriness toward Euro-American females! Of course, one might argue, such insistences are meant to be counter-mythologizing, but such countering accepts the original structure—it does not transform or subvert it. Ironically, unlike the deployments of slippery indirections—the keynote of vernacular linguistic play—counter-myths are as direct, as centered as the racist myths they mean to displace.
43. Coco Fusco, "An Interview with Black Audio Film Collective: John Akomfrah, Reece Auguiste, Lina Gopaul and Avril Johnson," in *Young, British, and Black: The Work of Sankofa and Black Audio Film Collective* (Buffalo, NY: Hallwalls/ Contemporary Arts Center, 1988), 53.
44. Peter Applebome, "Stirring a Debate on Breaking Racism's Shackles," *New York Times*, 30 May 1990, late ed., A18.
45. Fanon argues that American blacks might also be considered "natives" in the sense of being part of an internal colony. In *The Wretched of the Earth*, he

states that the "negroes who live in the United States and in Central or Latin America in fact experience the need to attach themselves to a cultural matrix. Their problem is not fundamentally different from that of the Africans." (Frantz Fanon, *Wretched of the Earth* [1961; New York: Grove, 1968], 215.)

46. Roland Barthes, "Diderot, Brecht, Eisenstein," in *The Responsibility of Forms*, trans. Richard Howard (New York: Hill, 1985), 90.

47. Ibid., 96.

48. Jonathan Culler, *Ferdinand de Saussure* (Ithaca, NY: Cornell Univ. Press, 1976), 83.

49. Coco Fusco, "An Interview with Black Audio Film Collective," 43.

50. Ralph Ellison, *Invisible Man* (New York: Random House, 1952), 57.

51. Muwakkil, "Doing the Spike Thing," 24.

52. Hall, "Gramsci's Relevance for the Study of Race and Ethnicity," 15–16.

53. Stuart Hall, "Signification, Representation, Ideology: Althusser and the Post-Structuralist Debates," *Critical Studies in Mass Communication* 2 (2) (1985): 112.

54. Diana Fuss, *Essentially Speaking: Feminism, Nature & Difference* (New York: Routledge, 1989), xi.

55. Ibid.

56. Henry Louis Gates, Jr., "On the Rhetoric of Racism in the Profession," *African Literature Association Bulletin* 15 (1) (1989): 11–21. This defense might or might not be superseded—time will tell—by his more recent calls for a liberal humanist pluralism and attacks on social theory and critiques of race, class, and gender.

57. Gates is right to take issue with some pejorative descriptions of his work as essentialist. To this end, I disagree with Diana Fuss's argument, for example, that Gates's and Houston Baker's analyses inherently romanticize the vernacular (although some of their specific uses of vernacular analysis have done so—see Gates's media pieces on 2 Live Crew, for example) and that they speak *about* the vernacular and not *in* it. Such an argument is itself a romanticization, because it is not necessary to write in the vernacular to theorize about it. Most metacommentary systems employ their own jargon: theoretical discussions about fictional texts, for example, do not necessarily go on in the language of the texts themselves. More importantly, African American vernacular is *not* necessarily synonymous with "black English" or any form of black dialect (rural or urban), although the vernacular and vernacular users often employ black English and/or black dialects. African American vernacular is an attitude toward language, a language dynamic, and a technique of language use. See Houston A. Baker, Jr., *Blues, Ideology, and Afro-American Literature: A Vernacular Theory* (Chicago: Univ. of Chicago Press, 1984);

Henry Louis Gates, Jr., *The Signifying Monkey: A Theory of Afro-American Literary Criticism* (New York: Oxford Univ. Press, 1988); and Claudia Mitchell-Kernan, "Signifying," in *Mother Wit from the Laughing Barrel: Readings in the Interpretation of Afro-American Folklore*, ed. Alan Dundes (Englewood Cliffs, NJ: Prentice-Hall, 1973), 310–28. African American fiction writers such as Toni Morrison frequently "signify" in standard English. And both Baker and Gates have also used vernacular signifying practices from time to time in their oral and written presentations. Vernacularity is not simply a marker for African American working-class or "street" verbal practices. To attach it only to such sites is to be caught in a search for false authenticity.

Fuss further argues that "the quest to recover, reinscribe, and revalorize the black vernacular" is inherently essentialist. See Fuss, *Essentially Speaking*, 90. The vernacular is not in need of recovery or reinscription; it is alive and well—and multiclass amongst African-Americans. To graph the specificities of African American cultural production, its textual theoretical possibilities, is not to go on a ghost hunt.

58. Gates, *Signifying Monkey*, 15.

59. Henry Louis Gates, Jr., "The Blackness of Blackness: A Critique of the Sign and the Signifying Monkey," *Black Literature and Literary Theory* (New York: Methuen, 1984), 297. See also Gates, *Figures in Black* and *The Signifying Monkey*.

60. Spivak, "In a Word," 124.

61. I refer to Gayatri Spivak's interview in *Differences*, 127. While I am aware that the exigencies of specific political moments and their attendant strategies have historically demanded essentialism on the large scale—nationalism—I, nonetheless, want to think about unreflective essentialism as a problematic generally and specifically in regard to the Spike Lee discourse. I try to be very careful about the way that I use Spivak here because her interview is long and complex; I pick and choose parts of it because, while I think that her warnings about essentialism and antiessentialism are very much to the point, working through the implications of all of her (and Rooney's) discussion would demand more time and space than I have here. I use, therefore, what seems to me to be most to the point. Spivak argues, among other things, that antiessentialism risks being another form of essence, that antiessentialism's insistence (in some quarters) on the primacy of "overdeterminations" leads to paralyzing strategic anarchy. Further, she asserts, "essences . . . are just a kind of content. All content is not essence. Why be so nervous about it?" (145). I am nervous, however, because within the terms of Euro-American dominance, as far as African American cultural production and its reception are concerned, there is no such thing as "just a kind of content."

62. Fusco, "Fantasies of Oppositionality," 8.

63. Quoted in Ibid., 9.

64. Fusco, "An Interview with Black Audio Film Collective," 55.

65. Ibid., 53.

66. hooks, "Counterhegemonic Art," 21–36; Kamber, "Do the Right Thing," 37–40; Herb Boyd, "Does Lee 'Do the Right Thing'?", *Guardian*, 5 July 1989, 8, 24; Michael Dyson, "Film Noir," *Tikkun* 4 (5) (1989): 75–78; Hoberman, "Pass/Fail," 59, 62, 66.

67. Sarah Shulman is an exception to this generality, although I find problematic her article's insistence that Lee usurped "authentic" working-class voices and substituted his middle-class voice; see Sarah Shulman, "I Don't Like Spike," *Outweek*, 7 August 1989, 48–49. I am not interested in taking sides on whether or not he does so,. However, while I find much useful in Shulman's reading of the film, this issue of African American middle-class lack of authenticity vs. African American working-class authenticity simply reinscribes another debate contained in terms of essentialism: Who is the "real" black person? The insistence that only the working-class African American carries African American culture is one side of a pointless debate that has gone on for more than a century. All African Americans, in their complexity—of which class difference is a part—make up African culture. One need only watch Cornel West and Hortense Spillers (to name just two) make academic presentations in order to see variations of African American academic, middle-class, vernacular culture at work.

68. bell hooks, Michael Kamber, and Michael Dyson have all provided excellent extended readings of *Do the Right Thing*. My work here contributes to discussions they have begun. See hooks, "Counterhegemonic Art," 31–36; Kamber, "Do the Right Thing," 98–100; Dyson, "Film Noir," 75–78.

69. Joe Wood, "Looking for Malcolm: The Man and the Meaning Behind the Icon," *Village Voice*, 29 May 1990, 43.

70. See hooks, "Counterhegemonic Art," 31, 40. The death of an African American male by police is a television and cinematic cliché and hooks argues that Lee's representation of Raheem's death does not explode or remap that cliché. Further, as Kamber also notes ("Do the Right Thing," 40), despite the tragedy of the disproportionately high numbers of African American males killed by police, such murders are still fairly atypical—less than one percent of African American homicides (40). The vast majority of African American male and female homicides are committed by African American males, and the relationship of that fact to the representation of African American male homicide in *Do the Right Thing* is a fair enough question, since representation is the "practice" of the filmmaker's selection. Is the simplicity of the murder by cops somehow more "real" than the complexities of murder by African American males? I am not ranking factual horrors, but I am interested in the representation "selection" at work in this film. Does the spectrum of male socialization within African American communities and its

participation in hegemonic violence and masculinism seem too "inauthentic" to be represented?

71. Orenstein, "Spike's Riot," 34.

72. Vernon Reid touches on Lee's depiction of African American color line internalization as played out by women only; see Thulani Davis, et al., "Daze of Our Lives," *Village Voice*, 22 March 1988, 35–39.

73. Robert Park, *Race and Culture: Essays in the Sociology of Contemporary Man* (Glencoe: Free Press, 1950), 280.

74. White, "New Dawn at Sundance," 65–66.

10

THE ABSENT ONE

The Avant-Garde and the Black Imaginary in *Looking For Langston*

MANTHIA DIAWARA

One way to read Isaac Julien's 1989 film *Looking For Langston* against the Harlem Renaissance and the cultural significance of Langston Hughes is to see the film solely as a gay film, and to question its modes of existence. The central issue of such an investigation is to discover whether or not Langston Hughes was gay. The critic proceeds by linking the role of one the characters, Alex for example, to Hughes's own experience and by asking whether the film is "true to life" or not. In other words this critic approaches the film as a biography of Hughes and questions whether it is morally correct and relevant to represent certain aspects of the poet's life on film. While it is necessary to read *Looking For Langston* as a gay film, it is also necessary to see the film as a contribution to the discourse of blackness. Already in *The Passion of Remembrance* (1986), Sankofa Film and Video Collective has reminded us that it is unproductive and homophobic to refuse to acknowledge homosexuality in black cultural and political organizations or to dismiss it as "a white informed issue." To see *Looking For Langston* solely as a gay film may also be, for the gay viewer, an attempt to create a utopian space outside the relationship between race and sexuality and class. In fact, the plastic beauty of the images in *Looking For Langston*, and the expressed desire of some of the characters to "love outside the race, the class and the attitude," tends to support the notion of a raceless homosexual ethnicity. The fact that the film fast became a cult classic at gay and lesbian film festivals, and that it has been rarely seen at mainstream ones, also indicates that there is a gay essentialism at play.

For me, a comprehensive reading of the film begins with its use of Langston Hughes and the black tradition as enabling texts for black gays to tell their stories. The opening credits state that the film is a "meditation" on Langston Hughes and the Harlem Renaissance. In other words, the film looks back at a discourse of Blackness that marked the second and third decades of the twentieth century in order to empower its own discourse in the present. The word "meditation" implies the invocation of an idea or a force in order to draw energy from it. And indeed, *Looking For Langston* empowers itself by conjuring up Hughes and other figures of the Renaissance. Other names outside of the Renaissance lend support to the film as well: it is dedicated to the memory of James Baldwin, and the closing credits list Toni Morrison and Stuart Hall as readers on the soundtrack. The film also strategically thanks several famous people in the credits, thereby rooting itself in the black tradition.

To read *Looking For Langston* as a meditation on the black tradition, a signifyin' on black aesthetics, we must first look at ways in which the young generation of gay men articulate their relation to what Jean-Pierre Oudart calls the Absent Ones—i.e., to Hughes, his colleagues of the Renaissance, and James Baldwin. The film opens with a character, played by director Isaac Julien himself, literally taking the place of Langston Hughes: he is lying in a casket amid flowers, surrounded by friends who have come to see him for the last time. A Riverside radio program taped in memorium to Hughes in 1967 plays on the soundtrack. This, along with the 1920s costumes and the black-and-white film stock, creates a mood that is simultaneously that of the Harlem Renaissance, of 1967 (when Hughes died), and of the present, denoted by the presence of contemporary black British actors around the casket.

The cinematic illusion is ruptured by putting Isaac Julien in Langston Hughes's place in the casket, and the spectator becomes conscious of the presence of the camera behind the fourth wall of the frame. The desire for Hughes's place in the casket is prolonged by its uncanny echo of another mourning beyond the fourth wall: a mourning associated with young black men killed by AIDS. The film makes several references to the threat of the virus to black gays, and indeed it is as if Hughes is being sought in death to protect the young people from it.

But I am jumping ahead of myself. I propose, first, to look at the mise-en-scène and editing in *Looking For Langston* in order to illustrate its formal affinity with experimental cinema and then to examine the ways in which the presence of black gays at the center of this formal device subverts and redefines the genre itself. Judith Williamson has argued that it is

> particularly striking that the black British work that's been taken up most widely in the world of theory, been most written about and also picked up at festivals, on tours, and so on, is the work that fits most obviously into that category avant garde. . . . [T]he reception in somewhere like New York of Black Audio's and Sankofa's work has as much to do with it being formally inventive and for lack of a better term avant-garde, as to do with its being black, it's to do with the combination of the two.[1]

I want to look at this issue in more detail, for it seems to me that Williamson drops the black half of the equation when she later argues that there is no such thing as a homogeneous black aesthetic.[2] Williamson seems to forget that there is no such thing as a homogeneous western aesthetic, either, and that this fact does not stop people from defining things as "western art." Her essay denies the notion of a black aesthetics which is engaged or debunked by films such as *Passion of Remembrance* or *Looking For Langston*; on the contrary, Williamson is mainly concerned "with the place of avant-garde cinema, or rather these films within that place." She is more interested in revealing the way in which black British filmmakers use the avant-garde style to pitch their work: "If there isn't such an aesthetic, then black filmmakers are faced with precisely the problem which confronts all filmmakers, . . . which is how to pitch your work."[3]

The Content of the Form

In *Looking For Langston*, Isaac Julien defamiliarizes avant-garde cinema in much the same way that other black artists speak for themselves in the West. Houston Baker, Jr., explains this most eloquently in *Modernism and the Harlem Renaissance*, where he locates Booker T. Washington's modernity in Washington's ability to master a form and thereby become uncolonizable by it. Pointing to Washington's canny appropriation of the minstrel style in his autobiography, Baker points out that the author of *Up From Slavery* "demonstrates in his manipulations of form that there are rhetorical possibilities for crafting a voice out of tight places."[4] What Baker calls "mastery of form" is therefore a recovery of one's own voice, which sounds in the text as a constant embarrassment to the semantic order of the established canon.

Similarly, a close look at the "mastery" of the avant-garde form in *Looking for Langston* reveals what Baker calls the "Black sounding" on the avant-garde genre. The newness of the text depends less on its deployment of the latest avant-garde devices and more on black artists performing in the established territory of the avant-garde, sounding its formal elements for black inclusion. Julien's brilliant direction of *Looking For Langston* recreates the Harlem Renaissance effect, but this time the center of the mise-en-scène and editing is occupied by black homosexuality: black men looking at black men as objects of desire. Julien's style is thus doubly scandalous: on the one hand, it brings to the surface that which was repressed in the Renaissance, i.e., homosexuality. On the other, insofar as the avant-garde constructs itself outside of linearization and extratextual reference, the film confronts the avant-garde with its Other, i.e., race.

Looking For Langston is about a memorium to Langston Hughes and the Harlem Renaissance as reconstructed from a black gay perspective. The film opens with a statement that it is a meditation on the life of Hughes and its dedication to James Baldwin. It segues to the prelude, which shows images of Harlem in the Renaissance period while a voiceover narrator situates Hughes in an international context. The prelude also includes the fictional recreation of Hughes's memorium mentioned above, in which Julien himself takes the place of the poet in the casket and Toni Morrison reads a eulogy to him.

Formally, the function of every prelude is to establish an aesthetic contract between the film and the spectator. It delimits the subject and the narrative conventions to be put into play. Admittedly, Julien's subject matter—black homosexuality linked to Hughes and the Renaissance—is radical for a spectator who is black, heterosexual, and middle class. The experimental style that Julien employs is difficult to negotiate as well, because it violates the temporal and spatial conventions of continuity editing. Julien's prelude includes, therefore, disclaimers that describe the film as only a meditation, a subjective statement about the Renaissance. Julien, whom I consider *l'enfant terrible* of our time, also seduces the spectator with nostalgic black-and-white reconstructions of images of the Harlem Renaissance, the Cotton Club, the art and music of the period. Clearly, the filmmaker is using the aesthetic contract of the prelude to ask the spectator to avoid a one-to-one comparison of events in the film with the lived experience of Langston Hughes.

By the time the title letters of the film take shape out of the melted screen, the narrative has positioned the spectator to imagine the Harlem of the Renaissance period. The "Looking" in *Looking For Langston* is an invitation to the spectator to visualize a time when Harlem was the capital of the black world, an invitation to see oneself in a dream about the Renaissance. The canvas of *Looking For Langston* becomes a space where the spectator is free to fantasize about the figures of the Renaissance and have his or her identity changed by it.

The transition from the prelude to the film proper is important for other reasons as well. The Riverside Radio station, WRBR, announces the death of Hughes in 1967 and broadcasts a memorium to him. The film thus draws us further into an imagined Harlem through a montage of scenes of Hughes reading to the accompaniment of a piano, Bessie Smith singing, and a neon sign showing that we are at the Cotton Club. There is also newsreel footage of events involving figures of the Renaissance, still photographs from the period, and clips from Oscar Micheaux films. These historical elements are mixed and strung together with fictional reconstructions of the memorium to Hughes and the nightlife at the Cotton Club.

The defamiliarization effect of *Looking For Langston* derives mainly from the avant-garde mise-en-scène and editing, which force the historical documents and fictional events to share the time and space of the same narrative. *Looking For Langston* surprises the spectator through its substitution of the libertine heterosexual desire that the Cotton Club was known for with the inscription of captivating homosexual desires. The avant-garde style of the film can also be seen in its use of repetition and subjective shots that may be attributed to several different characters at the same time. I want to designate as *content of the form* these elements of the mise-en-scène and montage. Later on I will look at the *form of the content*, which is related to the black imaginary in the film. For the time being, it is important to discuss in some detail the mise-en-scène and editing in order to show the film's subversive relation to the avant-garde.

Mise-en-scène, or the formal disposition of objects in front of the camera, is a pleasure to look at in *Looking For Langston*. The plastic beauty of the images in classic black-and-white film and the construction of male body parts in the same way that Hollywood fetishizes its goddesses of the screen, position the spectator to identify with the camera. The dominant space in the film is the Cotton Club, which is fictionally constructed as a building with two stories, the top floor for the memorial service and the bottom story for the bar. The top floor also serves as a heaven-like place where there are angels holding posters of Hughes and Baldwin. The camera goes back and forth between the Cotton Club and other spaces, such as a field of lilies, a bedroom, and streets in Harlem—all subjective spaces constructed by characters at the bar or the memorial. The actors are dressed in black suits and bow ties, except for those in the subjective scenes (when some of the characters are completely naked) and for the angels (who wear wings). The lighting follows the classic Hollywood style in black-and-white cinema, with typical back lights and frontal lights to emphasize shadows and facial emotions. The sound is mostly nondiegetic music and voiceover narration, with some prolonged moments of silence. The action emphasizes men dancing with men, kissing and looking. The classical Hollywood love triangle is recast here between three men, two black and one white, and the camera positions are determined by the exchanges of looks among them.

The film uses sound to link the spaces of the archival footage with the spaces in the fictional narrative. The voiceover readings and the songs that describe different scenes are usually in the first person, implying that they may be either narrational commentaries or memories of the characters involved in the scenes. Some of the lines are in fact excerpts from commentaries made by actual members of the Renaissance movement. But when they are read over the scenes of specific events, they seem attributable to the characters in the fictional construction. Similarly, the film uses songs and poems by contemporary black gay writers, which can be interpreted as the desires of the men of the Renaissance. The editing of *Looking For Langston* is also remarkable for the way in which it incorporates still photographs in the animate world of the moving images. The rare archival photographs and clips from Micheaux films are edited together with the fictional narrative in such a way that they become part of the same space, i.e., the Cotton Club, and the same time, i.e., the Renaissance period. From the montage, it is not always easy to attribute a subjective shot to a specific character in the film. But there are two or three scenes that are clearly constructed as the fantasies of a character named Alex. We see a close-up of Alex at the beginning of these fantasies, and we see him again at the end. The first scene involves Alex, a character the voiceover calls "Beauty," and Beauty's white lover. The three of them are naked in a bedroom. The second fantasy shows Alex dressed in a black suit, walking in a lily field, and running into Beauty, who is naked.

On the Threshold of the Avant-Garde

It is obvious from my brief summary that the content of the form of *Looking For Langston* is the discourse of the avant-garde. I use the term avant-garde here in the broad sense to include not only the surrealist and impressionist films of the 1920s and 1930s, but also the post–New Wave films of Godard and the experimental films of Michael Snow. By avant-garde form, I mean the way in which these films make departures from the norms of conventional cimenatography, departures from what Noel Burch calls "technological image norms."[5] Avant-garde form is typically self-reflexive, intransitive and concerned solely with "the process of filmic production itself."[6] Certainly, *Looking For Langston* also plays with conventional narrative forms by staging historical footage and contemporary fictional events in the same space and time, by blurring the distinction between fiction and documentary, between black gayness in the Renaissance period and black gayness in the present.

The dreamlike quality of Alex's fantasies recalls *Sang d'un Poete* (Cocteau, 1930) and *Un Chien Andalou* (Bunuel, 1928). Like these films, *Looking For Langston* narrativizes the profound desires of the characters and gives center stage to their repressed feelings. In a sense, *Looking For Langston* is a silent film: apart from the statement "I'll wait!" uttered by Beauty in Alex's fantasy and the laughter and sound of glasses breaking at the end, there are no profilmic sounds in the fictional part of the film. The voiceover readings and songs, even though they are first-person narratives, are not diegetic. They are commentaries, facts that took place before the fictional reconstruction.

Looking For Langston is remarkable for its construction of dialogues—statements including "you" and "I"—while remaining a "silent" film. Hughes's reading of poems from *Montage of a Dream Deferred* sets the blues mood in the first half of the film. Bessie Smith's singing also helps to establish the Cotton Club effect. It is possible, therefore, to see these as profilmic elements. Like a collage painting, they share the same space on the screen with the fictional characters, and they enter into a relation with these characters that changes the identities of both for the spectator. But I would argue that this is a narrative effect, just as sound effects and nondiegetic music on the soundtrack are narrative effects and therefore parts of what Burch calls the "outer limits" of the diegetic effect.[7] The treatment of sound in *Looking For Langston* recalls that of *Moi un noir* (Jean Rouch), a film that was shot without sound, after which the actors were asked to comment on their performances. Julien's experimentation with film form also relates *Looking For Langston* to films such as *Wavelength* (Michael Snow, 1967) that call into question conventional expectations of spectator identification. I have already mentioned the defamiliarizing effect of the love triangle between Alex, Beauty, and Beauty's white lover and how the Cotton Club becomes a homosexual club; conventional narratives like *The Cotton Club* (Francis Ford Coppola, 1984) depict the place as a libertine haven for heterosexual patrons. The prolonged silences of some scenes in *Looking For Langston* disrupt the spectator's identification with the camera, leaving him or her wondering whether there is something wrong with the sound. At the beginning of Alex's fantasy in the lily field, for example, the silence reigns for more than one minute before the voiceover reading takes its place.

However, *Looking For Langston* is not just about metafilmic references. I would argue that films like *My Beautiful Laundrette* (Stephen Frears/Hanif Kureishi, 1985), *Desperately Seeking Susan* (Susan Seidelman, 1985), and *Looking For Langston* make recourse to the avant-garde form because it provides the directors with an opportunity to express their lifestyles on film. The classical narrative, with its strong reliance on continuity editing, reproduces normative expectations and the sovereignty of white subjecthood that ban contradictions, discontinuities and excesses from the text.[8] Directors such as Julien—whose subjects of deployment involve the construction of relativistic aesthetics, the empowerment of black gays, the positioning of ambivalent identities and the undermining of white privilege over language, law, and economics—often repudiate the classical narrative as oppressive and find solace in the alternative discourse of the avant-garde.

However, the avant-garde is a discourse that is anchored in an order that gives it its foundation and explanation. In other words, the avant-garde style is a form that is trapped within the classical narrative in the sense that it is always already a film about classical films that it tries to rewrite, and, like them, it does not question the stereotypical images of blacks in western discourse. Thus, while it is possible to discuss *Looking for Langston* and other black British films within the avant-garde genre, it is also possible to argue that these films construct their originality on the outer limits of the avant-garde. Black British films render audible and visible black voices and black desires within what is supposed to be the avant-garde form.

In the avant-garde, the idea of the *game* dominates the structure of the film. Games are based on repetitions, departures, and eternal returns to an original place. Thus games can be said to be intransitive in the way in which they refer us, through the perfectibility of the structures they deploy, to the original game. The avant-garde's intransitivity derives also from a playful attitude—childlike, silly, clumsy, that which is not serious—toward the form, which makes any idea of extratextual reference seem a breaking of the complicity between the text and the spectator.

The rearticulation of the avant-garde in *Looking For Langston* affects the intransitiveness of the form by detaching it from its original roots and making it signify the condition of black gayness. With *Looking for Langston*, race and sexuality become the modalities of the avant-garde. I realize that this contradicts Williamson's thesis, which assumes that the passage of Black British cinema to the avant-garde form enables us "to stop asking 'what is Black cinema' and start addressing some of the more complex questions raised by actual films and their audiences."[9] This old thesis of assimilation posits that film spectatorship is only about a class phenomenon, not race. Thus there is nothing relevant to a black aesthetic about the black British avant-garde, which Williamson suggests belongs to a cultural capital specific to an elite class of film viewers.[10] The assimilationist argument wishes to render invisible the blackness of the texts with their passage to the avant-garde. For example, the original avant-garde movement of the 1920s thrived on a primitivism that forced African art and the Harlem Renaissance to signify the same as primitive art. But films such as *Looking For Langston* parody the avant-garde in order to reveal its racism, which empties black art of its content and appropriates it as form. To quote Baker, I will put *Looking For Langston* where he puts Chesnutt's *The Conjure Woman* and put the avant-garde where he puts Harris's Uncle Remus stories, and say that the real force of *Looking for Langston,* "however, does not reside in the febrile replay of an old [avant-garde] tune. Rather, the [film's] strength lies in the deep and intensive recoding of form that marks it stories. The work is best characterized as a drama of transformation."[11]

To illustrate the transitiveness of *Looking For Langston* toward the recoding of black gayness on the surface of avant-garde cinema, I now turn to Alex's fantasy about Beauty in the field of lilies and poppies. The scene portrays Alex walking somewhere under the open sky when he runs into a beautiful naked man. It seems that specific signs lead him to Beauty, because the road is mapped by ponds and posts carrying white flags. At one level, the scene is metafilmic because it thematizes the cinematic reconstruction of a dream. Like the characters in such surrealistic films as *Un Chien Andalou* and *Sang d'un Poete*, Alex is led, without resistance, to a destination and confronted with the object of his most profound desire. The notion that the scene is purely about the replay of cinematic reconstruction of dreams is also reinforced by the long moment of heavy silence in the beginning of the scene and by Alex walking in slow motion past the ponds and posts carrying the flags. At another level, *Looking For Langston* inscribes its avant-gardeness by constructing the scene as if it were only about spectator identification with the camera. The camera lingers on the body curves of the man whom the voiceover commentator redundantly calls Beauty. His lips and eyes are shown in close-ups as the voiceover comments on their plastic beauty. The narrative of Alex's discovery of Beauty is itself about a defamiliarization of the classical heterosexual theme of the boy meeting the most beautiful girl in the wilderness.

However, the racial and sexual identities of the director posit excesses in this and other scenes of the film that cause an embarrassment to the formal disposition of the avant-garde. The most important element of the excess is voice. By assuming responsibility for the construction of a film like *Looking for Langston* and occupying the center of narrative agency, the black and gay director transforms the perception of the formal elements of the avant-garde genre. Because the history of film production is unevenly developed from white directors to black directors, the most innocent black-directed film calls attention to race. When we turn to black experimental films, we find that they are preoccupied not only with the reconstruction of form but also with the history of film and the avant-garde's tradition of excluding black voices. The positioning of a black voice in the avant-garde cinema is therefore a new way of constructing the genre. This may be seen as a burden of representation, but it is linked to the uneven development in film production, and it should be a thing of history when more black people gain access to film production. The complexity of being gay in the black tradition constitutes another level of abstraction to be discussed later in this essay.

In *Looking for Langston*, Alex's attraction to Beauty inaugurates a homoerotic relation between Black men that both the avant-garde and white gayness have repressed. For example, in a scene at the Cotton Club, Alex and Beauty exchange looks and Beauty's white lover censors their desire by banging a champagne bottle on the table. The film also criticizes the dehumanization of black gays in the art of white gays such as Mapplethorpe, whose deconstruction of classical forms does not extend to the questioning of the monstrous and exotic images of black gays in the minds of white gays. The scene that depicts black gays as prostitutes serving the desires of white gays demonstrates that black gays are to white gays what black people in general are to white people in general: i.e., monstrous, bodies without heads, primitive and exotic. The relation between black gays and white gays is taken up by another film, *Tongues Untied* (Marlon Riggs, 1990), which shows its structure to be one of slavery and freedom. White gays are relatively free on Christopher Street and Castro Street, and they have a visible cultural style that they use not only to challenge the definition of the law, the body, and the economics of gay issues, but also to exclude black gays. The black gays, on the other hand, are not free: they are silent and invisible; they can only express their gayness through the camouflage of other expressive forms such as music, dance, and transvestite attires, which are more reassuring to heterosexuals.

In *Looking for Langston*, the construction of one black man as beautiful in the eyes of another black man humanizes black gayness and removes it from the pathological space reserved for it by heterosexuals and white gays. Even though a first viewing of *Looking for Langston* and other black British films may assimilate them to the avant-garde cinema and the experimental films of the 1970s and deny them any part of originality, I submit that such films appropriate the forms of the avant-garde not for mere inclusion in the genre but in order to redefine it by changing its content and reordering its formal disposition. The recuperation of the avant-garde elements becomes Julien's way of speaking for himself in *Looking for Langston*. In other words, Julien performs the avant-garde technique to reveal that which the genre itself represses.

The Form of the Content

When we turn to the suturing process in *Looking For Langston*, which puts the spectator in relation with the formal elements on the screen, it is crucial to examine the characters' articulation of their identities with blackness on the one hand and with Britishness on the other. The suturing of the spectator involves the articulation of his/her identity with the images on the screen and the Absent One, which seems to determine the images and to be determined by them. In *Looking for Langston*, the Absent One seems to be constituted by the images on the screen that stand for the black imaginary. Because the images represent a hiding place for an originary discourse, textual interpretation can speak of a certain availability of the Absent One on the screen. There is here, for example, the temptation to reduce the identity of the Absent One to that of the historical Langston Hughes. While this pseudo-identification is necessary, it is important to know that the characters on the screen are *not* the Absent One. The screen performs an image of black living conditions in the West in such a way that *Looking for Langston* becomes part of the black imaginary at the same time that it transforms that imaginary.

Each of Sankofa's films deploys a discourse about an Absent One. In *Territories* (1989/1985), the discourse of the BBC is what the film identifies as the Absent One.[12] In *Passion of Remembrance*, the Absent One is the rhetoric of Black Power which is rethematized with a new content, i.e., black feminist discourse, a politics of positionality against the rise of a police state in England in the 1980s. In *Dreaming Rivers* (1988), the Absent One is symbolized by the mother who wants to return to the Caribbean. Her departure is necessary for the children to experience her as part of their blackness, their memory of the Caribbean.[13] In *Looking for Langston*, as I have pointed out, the discourse of blackness, symbolized by Langston Hughes and other figures of the Harlem Renaissance as well as by James Baldwin, constitutes the Absent One. The younger generation's attempt to identify with them in the film, to fill in the void left by their absence, to stand in their place, is a way of shifting the issues away from those debated during the Harlem Renaissance, to using these figures to confront new themes of the discourse of blackness, i.e. homosexuality. I call *form of the content* the substance of the black imaginary which the film puts into play here.

Hughes and Julien

Two important theorists of the black expressive tradition have already pinpointed the place of Julien and his film in that canon. bell hooks has argued that "The poetic voice in the film passionately states, 'I long for my past.' A longing that is reiterated when we are told 'it's not wrong for the boy to be looking for his gay black fathers.' Such testimony speaks about the connection between the recognition and self-actualization."[14] Henry Louis Gates, Jr., also states that "there is a relation, even a typology, established between Black British cinema of the 80's and the cultural movement of the 1920's that we call the Harlem Renaissance. By its choice of subject, it brings out, in a very self-conscious way, the analogy between this contemporary ambit of Black creativity and a historical precursor. We look for Langston, but we discover Isaac."[15]

The comparison between Julien and Hughes, while risky because of the regression into pseudo-identification—a certain form of closure—is necessary in order to shed light on their use of the black imaginary to participate in and advance the arts of their respective epochs. For Alain Locke, champion theorist of the Harlem Renaissance, the break with the traditional view of blacks as "an American problem" toward a view of blacks as "participants in American civilization" constitutes the key to understanding Hughes and his colleagues. For Locke, the *new* in the Harlem Renaissance "has been their [blacks'] achievement [in bringing] the artistic advance of the Negro sharply into stepping alignment with contemporary artistic thought, mood and style. They are thoroughly modern, some of them ultra-modern, and Negro thoughts now wear the uniform of the age."[16] Of course, Arnold Rampersad, in his monumental two-volume work on Langston Hughes, addresses more thoroughly the issue of modernism in the work of Alain Locke and Langston Hughes. And it was W.E.B. Du Bois who claimed most decisively that race is the modality in which modernity is lived. Similarly, Locke shows that "the radical idioms" of blacks contribute something distinctive to the general arts. For Locke, when black artists perform on the canvas of modernity, they create a transfusion of modernistic styles with racial idioms that are brought to the center of expressive preoccupations.

What impressed Locke about the Harlem Renaissance was the movement's embracing of the tenets of modernism and its using them as tools of self-procuration. Locke writes: "Our poets have now stopped speaking for the Negro—they speak as negroes. Where formerly they spoke to others and tried to interpret, they now speak to their own and try to express."[17] Crucial to this statement is the notion of speaking for oneself, or expressing oneself. Locke traces black self-expression in modernism by valorizing what he calls in Hughes's poetry "a distinctive fervency of color and rhythm, and a Biblical simplicity of speech that is colloquial in derivation, but full of artistry."[18]

One of the achievements of Locke, in defining the art of Hughes and his colleagues of the Renaissance, is his insistence first on the specificity of their works, which announce their modernity through recourse to local experiences. Locke then posits this local experience—called the Harlem Renaissance—as universal artistic experiences that enter in the definition of both modernism and the creativity of black peoples: to put it in Locke's words, "the tendency to evolve from the racial substance something technically distinctive, something that as an idiom of style may become a contribution to the general resources of art."[19]

Houston A. Baker, Jr., also sees the creation of a universalist style in the way in which the Renaissance members seized upon the tools of modernism to speak for themselves, to express the black self as American. Baker is well known for his rearticulation of conventional definitions of such concepts as form, the folk, and the vernacular in order to provide a theory for the appreciation of the contribution of blacks to modernity. Without such theorization to remove blackness from the pathological space that whiteness reserves for it, critics of modernity push the burden of authenticity onto the black artists, expecting to see something completely new in the works of these artists or relegating them to the status of minor imitators of white artists. As Baker puts it, the *new* in the Harlem Renaissance "cannot be perceived (much less evaluated) by the person who begins with the notion that recognizably standard form automatically disqualifies a work as an authentic and valuable Afro-American national production."[20]

One of the ways in which Baker defines the specificity of a black modernism is through a theorization of his concept of black *sounds*. Baker uses the word interchangeably as a verb, a noun, and an adjectival verb to conjure up Locke's notions of "expressing yourself" and "speaking as Negroes" and to show how the rearranging of voice alters the meaning of familiar forms. First, Baker posits the concept of Afro-American sounding as a "writing/righting" of modernism. For him, the "deformation of Mastery" takes place when turn-of-the-century blacks sound modernism for the possibilities it can offer Afro-Americans. Sounding here takes the form of a critical modernism whereby the movement is confronted with its exclusion of blacks, or with what Locke calls the movement's participation in the "conventional blindness of the Caucasian eye with respect to the racial material at their immediate disposal."[21] For Baker, the writing of the black Renaissance is the righting of the white Renaissance, a willful deformation of mastery that "shares the task of Sycorax's son in so far as he or she must transform an obscene situation, a cursed and tripled metastatus, into a signal self/cultural expression."[22]

Second, Baker conceives of sounding as a black cultural performance that takes place in a black "spirit house" conjoined to "centuries of moral heroism, dedicated to sacrifice, and earnest inquiry into the riddle of life."[23] For Baker, the structure of feeling entailed by the sounding of the tutelary spirits and the African American masks does not refer to a fixed version of a song. Every sounding is the occasion to occupy the space of black habitation and simultaneously to deform it. As Baker puts it, a performance of Sterling Brown's poem "Ma Rainey" leaves us wondering whether Zora Neale Hurston and Richard Wright, thought to be opposed to each other, do not "move to the same rhythm witnessed in Brown's ritual."[24]

The comparison between Hughes and Julien helps us to understand that the black British film collectives are to postmodernism what the Harlem Renaissance was to modernism. Furthermore, it enables us to talk about critical postmodernism in the way that Locke and Baker refer to the Renaissance as a critical modernism. In *Looking for Langston*, too, the important issues include "speaking for the subject" and "self-expression." Julien seizes the tools of experimental cinema to speak black gayness. Such self-expression stands as a critique of discourses in both black and white communities that silence black gayness.

On the one hand, the film criticizes the black community through the ironic language of the blues, which narrativizes suffering, deferral of freedom for black gays, abandonment, and deception: "history as the smiler with the knife." It is crucial to notice here that the blues occupies most of the soundtrack. The blues effect is created by clips of Hughes reading poetry selections from *Montage of a Dream Deferred,* Bessie Smith singing "St. Louis Blues," and the lyrics of contemporary poet Essex Hemphill, which describe beautiful black men, desire denied, and the threat of AIDS. The use of the blues to narrativize the condition of black gay suffering in the black community is even more interesting in light of the fact that black women writers such as Alice Walker and Ntozake Shange also employ the same paradigm to denounce the abuse of black women.

On the other hand, self-expression in the film leads to a critique of the white gay community. In the scene that depicts a white male looking at still photographs of black bodies, the narrator comments on the way in which white gays render black gays invisible. Hemphill's poem, "If His Name Were Mandingo," insists on the difficulties of eliding the cultural and economic differences between black and white gays: "You don't notice many things about him. He doesn't always wear a red skicap, eat fried chicken and fuck like a jungle. He doesn't always live with his mother, or off the street, or off some bitches as you assume. . . . He doesn't dance well but you don't notice. To you he's only visible in the dark."[25] These lines echo, with all the irony of the blues, a poem by Hughes entitled "Minstrel Man," where he pulls the reader in past his exterior to see the pain inside.

> Because my mouth
> Is wide with laughter,
> You do not hear
> My inner cry,
> Because my feet
> Are Gay with dancing,
> You do not know
> I die.[26]

Julien appropriates for black gayness the discourse of freedom and equality inherent in the paradigm of blackness. In other words, for new identities to be engendered, black and white Gays must meet on equal terms. White identities, too, must be modified in their encounters with blacks; to put it in the words of the poem, "You want cross-over music. You want his pleasure without guilt or capture."[27]

The last sequence of *Looking for Langston* makes a movement away from singing the blues to performing jazz. As the tunes change from the period songs of the Renaissance era to contemporary free jazz, the young generation affirms its own identities through a transformation of blackness. Julien's revisiting of the place of the Renaissance, his dances with the ancestor figures, are sounding steps of the black imaginary that transfer the power and the knowledge of the ancestors to the young generation. The celebratory steps in the last sequence bring into the open the black homosexuality that the blues of Hughes and his colleagues of the Renaissance disguised. The carnivalesque mood that is created by the youths dancing on broken champagne glasses, exchanging loud laughter, and admiring their doubles in mirrors, denotes their defiance to the intolerant mob that is advancing with clubs in their hands. The film calls into question the notion that homosexuality is a "sin against the race," and that "it had to be kept secret, even if it was a widely shared one."[28] This transgressive performance, not unlike the last performance in *Territories*, is the black gay youths' way of defining their space in the urban areas, heavily guarded by the police and the black middle class.

Conclusion: The Black Imaginary as Artistic Paradigm

The comparison between Julien and Hughes is important as well in revealing the artistic ambiguities shared by the black British Renaissance in the 1980s and the Harlem Renaissance. Julien's envy of Hughes, denoted by the filmmaker taking the place of the deceased poet in the casket, subjects both the Harlem Renaissance and the British Renaissance to criticism about exoticizing blackness. The dependency of the artists and writers of the Renaissance upon their white patrons and the links between the movement and modernist primitivism are betrayed in *Looking for Langston* as moments of ambiguity and ambivalence: "They [white patrons] didn't want modernism; they wanted black art to keep art and artists in their place."[29] Furthermore, it is possible to criticize *Looking for Langston* itself for stereotyping black gayness through its glamorization of their clothes and its linking of their culture to night-clubs, song, and dance. As bell hooks puts it, "There is so much elegance and beauty in the film that it has both the quality of spectacle and masquerade."[30]

The comparison between Julien and Hughes is also important to show the discourse of blackness as an enabling paradigm for other repressed discourses such as feminism, gay and lesbian rights, and minority discourses in totalitarian system. Thus, the black imaginary, far from being a fixed place guaranteed in nature, is a transforming and transformative space to be filled by freedom-seeking people. In *Looking for Langston*, black gays seek the space of blackness against the oppression from the black middle class and white gays. Crucially, the linking of blackness to the categories of freedom and equality prevents it from ever reaching closure and fixity. The discourse of blackness is always moving toward the zones of oppression. It is for this reason that it has been used as a model by feminism, Chicano studies, and gay and lesbian liberation movements.

In *Looking For Langston*, the young generation stands in Hughes's place and seeks his protection, empowering itself with his energy. Every sequence in the film is juxtaposed to the scene of mourning. Thus, the young generation uses Hughes as a text to comment on their present condition of life. The posters of Hughes and Baldwin are held by the angels in some scenes as a way to declare a political position or to shield themselves from prejudice and intolerance. As a consumable sign, a writerly text, the black imaginary posits itself as a lack; to be black in the West does not only link one to the search for freedom but also creates the conditions for one to be opposed to all types of oppression. *Looking for Langston* invites the spectator to enter this black imaginary, to perform a new identity for him/herself by stepping into the void left by his/her predecessors in blackness and thereby to carry on the eternal search for freedom. In this essay, I posit the black imaginary as a critical modernist and postmodernist invention by focusing on the newness of the cinematic language in *Looking for Langston*. I also analyzed the conditions of possibility for entering this imaginary by linking the Absent One to the categories of freedom and liberty.

Notes

This article first appeared in *Wide Angle* 13, 3–4 (July–October 1991): 96–109.

1. Judith Williamson, "Two Kinds of Otherness," *ICA Documents* 7 (special issue, *Black Film, British Cinema*) (1988): 35.

2. Williamson's argument is derived from a statement by Stuart Hall, which is not so much a denial of black aesthetics as it is an attempt to problematize such notions as homogeneity, essentialism, strong thought, binary oppositions, etc. Hall's argument goes as follows:

   > Films are not necessarily good because black people make them. They are not necessarily "right-on" by virtue of the fact that they deal with the black experience. Once you enter the politics of the end of the essential black subject you are plunged headlong into the maelstrom of a continuously contingent, unguaranteed, political argument and debate: a critical politics, a politics of criticism.

   See Hall, "New Ethnicities," *ICA Documents* 28. Please notice that my reading of *Looking for Langston* here tries to bring out some of the discontinuities that Hall is talking about. I do not, however, intend to use the notion of discontinuity as a sign of the absence of black aesthetics. Such a denial will plunge us into the kind of nihilism that Gianni Vattimo proposes in order to launch his theory of "West Thought" in *Les Aventures de la Difference*, translated from the Italian by Pascal Gebellone, et al. (Paris: Les Editions de Minuit, 1985).

3. Judith Williamson, "Two Kinds of Otherness," 34.

4. Houston A. Baker, Jr., *Modernism and the Harlem Renaissance* (Chicago: Univ. of Chicago Press, 1987), 33.

5. Noel Burch, *Life to Those Shadows* (Berkeley: Univ. of California Press, 1990), 257.

6. Ibid., 256.

7. Ibid., 255.

8. Manthia Diawara, "Englishness and Blackness: Cricket as a Discourse on Colonialism," *Callaloo* 13 (1990), 830–844.

9. Judith Williamson, "Two Kinds of Otherness," 36.

10. See a variant of this position in Salman Rushdie, "Songs Doesn't Know the Score," *ICA Documents* 7 (1988): 16–17. For Rushdie, a black British film like *Handsworth Song* "is not good, and the trouble does seem to be one of language" (16). By language, Rushdie means the experimental style.

11. Houston A. Baker, Jr., *Modernism and the Harlem Renaissance* (Chicago: Univ. of Chicago Press, 1987), 41.

12. See Manthia Diawara, "Black British Cinema: Spectatorship and Identity Formation in *Territories*," *Public Culture* 3 (1) (1990).
13. See Manthia Diawara, "The Nature of Mother in *Dreaming Rivers*," *Third Text* 13 (Winter 1991).
14. bell hooks, "*Looking for Langston*," *Z Magazine* (May 1990): 17.
15. Henry Louis Gates, Jr., "Looking for Modernism," in *Black American Cinema*, ed. Manthia Diawara (New York: Routledge, 1993).
16. Alain Locke, ed., *The New Negro* (New York: Atheneum, 1968), 50. For more on modernism, the Harlem Renaissance, and Langston Hughes, see Arnold Rampersad's two-volume *The Life of Langston Hughes* (New York: Oxford Univ. Press, 1986 and 1988).
17. Alain Locke, ed., *The New Negro*, 48.
18. Ibid., 52.
19. Ibid., 51.
20. Houston A. Baker, Jr., *Modernism and the Harlem Renaissance*, 86.
21. Alain Locke, *The New Negro*, 264.
22. Houston A. Baker, Jr., *Modernism and the Harlem Renaissance*, 56.
23. Ibid., 67.
24. Ibid., 95.
25. Essex Hemphill, "If His Name Were Mandingo," *Earth Life* (Washington, D.C. 1985), 13–14.
26. Langston Hughes, "Minstrel Man," in *The New Negro*, 144.
27. Hemphill, "If His Name Were Mandingo," 13.
28. Isaac Julien, *Looking for Langston,* 1989.
29. Ibid., xx.
30. bell hooks, "*Looking for Langston*," 77.

SELECTED BIBLIOGRAPHY

Appiah, K. Anthony. *In My Father's House: Africa in Philosophy and Culture*. New York: Oxford University Press, 1992.

Baker, Houston, Jr. *Blues, Ideology, and Afro-American Literature: A Vernacular Theory*. Chicago: University of Chicago Press, 1984.

———, *Workings of the Spirit: The Poetics of Afro-American Women's Writing*. Chicago: University of Chicago Press, 1984.

Cham, Mbye B. and Claire Andrade-Watkins, eds. *BlackFrames: Critical Perspectives on Black Independent Cinema*. Cambridge: MIT Press, 1988.

Crouch, Stanley. *Notes of a Hanging Judge: Essays and Reviews, 1979–1989*. New York: Oxford University Press, 1990.

Diawara, Manthia, ed. *Black American Cinema*. New York: Routledge, 1993.

Dudley, David L. *My Father's Shadow: Intergenerational Conflict in African American Men's Autobiography*. Philadelphia: University of Pennsylvania Press, 1991.

Duneier, Mitchell. *Slim's Table: Race, Respectablity, and Masculinity*. Chicago: University of Chicago Press, 1992.

Dyson, Michael E. *Reflecting Black: African-American Cultural Criticism*. Minneapolis: University of Minnesota Press, 1993.

Evans, Brenda J. and James R. Whitfield, eds. *Black Males in the United States: An Annotated Bibliography from 1967 to 1987*. Washington, DC: American Psychological Association, 1988.

Fanon, Frantz. *Black Skin, White Masks*. 1952. New York: Grove, 1967.

———. *The Wretched of the Earth*. 1961. New York: Grove, 1968.

Fuss, Diana. *Essentially Speaking: Feminism, Nature & Difference*. New York: Routledge, 1989.

Gates, Henry Louis, Jr. *Figures in Black: Words, Signs, and the "Racial" Self*. New York: Oxford University Press, 1987.

Gary, Lawrence E., ed. *Black Men*. Beverly Hills, CA: Sage Publications, 1981.

Glasgow, Douglas. *The Black Underclass*. San Francisco, CA: Jossey-Bass, Inc.: 1980.

Golden, Thelma. *Black Male: Representations of Masculinity in Contemporary American Art*. New York: Whitney Museum of American Art, 1994.

Hare, Nathan and Julia Hare. *The Endangered Black Family: Coping with the Unisexualization and Coming Extinction of the Black Race*. San Francisco: Black Think Tank, 1984.

Harris, Trudier. *Exorcising Blackness: Historical and Literary Lynching and Burning Rituals*. Bloomington, ID: Indiana University Press, 1984.

Hemphill, Essex, ed. *Brother to Brother: New Writings by Black Gay Men*. Boston: Alyson Publications, 1991.

Hernton, Calvin. *Sex and Racism in America*. New York: Grove Press, 1965.

hooks, bell. *Black Looks: Race and Representation*. Boston: South End Press, 1992.

hooks, bell and Cornell West. *Breaking Bread: Insurgent Black Intellectual Life*. Boston: South End Press, 1991.

Johnson, Cary A., Colin Robinson, and Terence Taylor, eds. *Other Countries: Black Gay Voices*. New York: Other Countries, 1988.

Liebow, Elliot. *Tally's Corner: A Study of Negro Streetcorner Men*. Boston: Little, Brown and Co., 1967.

Majors, Richard and Janet M. Bilson. *Cool Pose: The Dilemmas of Black Manhood in America*. New York: Lexington Books, 1992.

Majors, Richard G. and Jacob U. Gordon, eds. *The American Black Male: His Present Status and His Future*. Chicago: Nelson-Hall Publishers, 1994.

McDowell, Deborah E. "Reading Family Matters." In *Changing Our Own Words: Essays on Criticism, Theory and Writing by Black Women*, ed. Cheryl A. Wall. 75–97. New Brunswick: Rutgers University Press, 1989.

McGhee, James D. *Running the Gauntlet: Black Men in America*. Washington, D.C.: National Urban League, Research Department, 1984.

Madhubuti, Haki R. *Black Men: Obsolete, Single, Dangerous? The African Family in Transition: Essays in Discovery, Solution and Hope*. Chicago: Third World Press, 1990.

Mercer, Kobena. *Welcome to the Jungle: New Positions in Black Cultural Studies*. New York: Routledge, 1994.

Monroe, Sylvester and Peter Goldman. *Brothers: Black and Poor—A True Story of Courage and Survival*. New York: William Morrow and Company, Inc., 1988.

Spillers, Hortense. "Mama's Baby, Papa's Maybe: An American Grammar Book." *Diacritics* 17.2 (1987): 65–81.

Staples, Robert. *Black Masculinity: The Black Male's Role in American Society*. San Francisco, CA: Black Scholar Press, 1982.

Wilkinson, Doris Y. and Ronald L. Taylor, eds. *The Black Man in America: Perspectives on His Status in Contemporary Society*. Chicago: Nelson-Hall, 1977.

LIST OF CONTRIBUTORS

Elizabeth Alexander teaches in the English Department at the University of Chicago. Her poetry has been widely anthologized and she is the author of a collection of poetry, *The Venus Hottentot.* She has recently completed a second collection, "Bodies of Light," and is currently working on a book, *Feminist Readings of Black Masculinity.*

Michael Awkward teaches Afro-American literature at the University of Michigan, where he directs the Center for Afroamerican and African Studies. He is the author of *Negotiating Difference: Race, Gender, and the Politics of Positionality* and *Inspiriting Influences: Tradition, Revision, and Afro-American Women's Novels*, and editor of *New Essays on* Their Eyes Were Watching God.

Stephen Michael Best is completing his dissertation on lynching, spectacle, and early American cinema in the Department of English at the University of Pennsylvania.

Marcellus Blount teaches in the English and Comparative Literature Department at Columbia University. He is the author of *In A Broken Tongue: Rediscovering African American Poetry* (forthcoming). He is currently working on a study of black gay men and the crisis of representation.

George P. Cunningham teaches in the Africana Studies Department of Brooklyn College (CUNY). He is the author of *Langston Hughes and the Discourse of the Harlem Renaissance* (forthcoming). He is currently working on a study of the relationship between gender and subjectivity, "Frederick Douglass, Subjectivity and Slavery".

Manthia Diawara teaches film and comparative literature at New York University. He is the author of *African Cinema: Politics and Culture* and editor of *Black American Cinema.*

Donald Gibson is Professor of English at Rutgers University, has edited *Five Black Writers: Essays on Wright, Ellison, Baldwin, Hughes and LeRoi Jones*; *Modern Black Poets*; and is the author of *The Politics of Literary Expression: A Study of Major Black Writers*. He is currently working on a monograph titled "Hidden Name and Complex Fate": The Designs of Booker T. Washington.

Cora Kaplan is Professor of English and Director of the Institute for Research on Women at Rutgers University. She is the author of *Sea Changes; Essays on Culture and Feminism* (1986) and is at work on a study of gender and the rise of racial thinking in nineteenth century Britain.

Wahneema Lubiano teaches English and Afro-American Studies at Princeton University. She is the author of *Messing with the Machine: Modernism, Post Modernism and Black American Fiction* (forthcoming, Verso)

Robert Reid-Pharr teaches in the English Department of Johns Hopkins University. He has recently been a Phorzheimer Fellow in the English Department of City College (CUNY), and has completed a dissertation on gender and sexuality in antebellum African American literature.

Kendall Thomas teaches in the Law School of Columbia University. He is a coeditor of the forthcoming volume, *Critical Race Theory*.

INDEX

DATE DUE